Data Management on Distributed Databases

Computer Science:
Distributed Database Systems, No. 7

Harold S. Stone, Series Editor

Professor of Electrical and Computer Engineering
University of Massachusetts, Amherst

Other Titles in This Series

Data Management on Distributed Databases

by
Benjamin W. Wah

UMI RESEARCH PRESS
Ann Arbor, Michigan

Produced and distributed by
UMI Research Press
an imprint of
University Microfilms International
Ann Arbor, Michigan 48106

Library of Congress Cataloging in Publication Data

Wah, Benjamin W.
Data management on distributed databases.

(Computer science. Distributed database systems ; no. 7)
"Revision of the author's thesis, University of California,
Berkeley, 1979"–
   Bibliography: p.
   Includes index.
   1. Electronic data processing–Distributed processing.
2. Data base management.   I. Title. II. Series.

QA76.9.D3W32 1981   001.64   81-12982
ISBN 0-8357-1222-2   AACR2

Contents

Figures

Tables

Acknowledgments

The author would like to express his sincere gratitude to a number of individuals for their help in the research and preparation of this research. Special thanks is due to Professor C. V. Ramamoorthy: throughout the years, Professor Ramamoorthy has been a constant source of advice, guidance, support and encouragement. Without his support, none of this would have been possible.

The author would like to thank Professors D. Ferrari and I. Adler for reading the manuscript, and for providing much helpful and valuable advice and encouragement. Special thanks are also due to Miss Y. W. Ma, for her comments and suggestions on part of the draft. In addition, his colleagues, Messrs F. Bastani, F. Ho, G. Ho, J. Favaro, C. Jen, T. Krishnarao, F. Leung, R. Mok, C. Nam, H. H. So, and K. Wu are thanked for providing many helpful comments and a friendly environment for research.

The author would also like to thank Professor S. Bing Yao, his coauthor on the paper "DIALOG—A Distributed Processor Organization for Database Machine" (Proc. NCC, Vol. 49. 1980) and the AFIPS Press for permission to use part of the material in this paper.

He also wants to acknowledge the Ballistic Missile Defense, the Army Research Office, and the National Science Foundation for its support through contracts DASG-60-77-C-0138, DAAG29-78-G-0189 and grants MCS-77-27293, MCS-77-28361. Messrs C. R. Vick and J. E. Scalf are also thanked for their many helpful discussions.

Finally and most importantly, the author wishes to thank his parents for their unselfish and devoted support, both spiritually and financially.

This manuscript was originally typed on a DEC VAX 11/780 computer supported by NSF grant MCS78-07291.

1

Introduction

The recent advances in large scale integrated logic and communication technology, coupled with the explosion in size and complexity of the application areas, have led to the design of distributed architectures. Basically, a *Distributed Computer System* (*DCS*) is considered as an interconnection of digital systems called *Processing Elements* (*PEs*), each having certain processing capabilities and communicating with each other. This definition encompasses a wide range of configurations from a uni-processor system with different functional units to a multiplicity of general purpose computers such as ARPANET. In general, the notion of "dis-tributed systems" varies in character and scope with different people [RAM76]. So far, there is no accepted definition and basis for classifying these systems. In this work, we limit our discussion to a class of DCSs with an interconnection of dedicated/shared, programmable, functional PEs and to working on a set of jobs which may be related or unrelated.

1.1 What is a Distributed Database?

Due to the information explosion and the need for more stringent require-ments, the design of efficient coordination schemes for the management of data on a DCS is a very critical problem. To indicate the amount of data processed, the typical database processing requirements for a ballistic missile defense system [DDP78] operating in a centralized environment are shown in Table 1.1. In order to manage the data on a computer system (centralized or distributed) and satisfy all the requirements, systematic techniques must be developed so that the system can be realized in a cost-effective way.

Data on a DCS are managed through a *Database* (*DB*), which is a collection of stored operational data used by the application systems of some particular enterprise [DAT77, FRY76]. A *Distributed Database* (*DDB*) can be thought of as the data stored at different locations of a DCS. It can be considered to exist only when data elements at multiple locations are interrelated and/or there is a need to access data stored at some locations

Table 1.1.   Typical Ballistic Missile Defense Database Processing Requirements in a Centralized Environment [DDB78]

Task	Number of independent tasks	20
Files	Number of dynamic files	117
	Local	30
	Global	87
	Dynamic file storage requirement	431K, 60 bits
	Local	26K, 60 bits
	Global	405K, 60 bits
	RTOS storage requirements	10K, 60 bits
Processing Environment	Processing speed	13.9 MIPS
	No. of reads/sec	7×10^6, 60 bits
	No. of writes/sec	3.4×10^6, 60 bits
	RTOS events/sec	24K

from another location. The prime concept of a generalized database system is based on the definition of a data format to store the data and on a generalized database management software for accessing the data. Due to the ever-increasing demand for on-line processing, there is a need for decomposing very large databases into physically or geographically dispersed units on a DCS and/or integrating existing databases held in physically isolated nodes of a DCS into a single, coherent database that will be available to each of the distributed nodes.

There are three major logical components in a database [BRA76]. First, there is the structured information or schema which describes the data structures and the validity criteria of the data. Second, there is the data itself. Finally, there are various programs or processes which control the operations of the database. A level below the schema is another structural component, the sub-schema. It describes the database as user applications see it. The control programs, together with the sub-schema, collectively form the Database Management System [FRY76, BAC75]. The Database Management System allows data sharing among a community of users, while ensuring the integrity of the data over time, and providing security against unauthorized access. It also provides the transparency of the data, in order to allow the data to be stored in different formats in different parts of the system. Finally, it provides an interface between the users and the system.

The database can be classified according to how these components are put together. In [ASC74], two classifications are proposed; the first is based on the number of Database Management Systems in the network and the second is based on the centralization or decentralization of the file directory and data. In [BOO76], the DDBs are classified into two structures, partitioned databases and replicated databases. A partitioned database is one that has been decomposed into physically separate units, and distributed across multiple nodes of a DCS. The partitioning will normally be based on the distribution of access requirements. In a replicated database, all or part of the database is replicated at multiple processing nodes. The amount of partitioning and replication depends on the architecture of the distributed system, the amount of traffic anticipated, and other requirements such as reliability and security.

1.2   Issues in Designing Distributed Database Systems

The issues associated with the design of a DDB can be classified from a user's viewpoint or from a system designer's viewpoint. The users are concerned with the type of organization and controls which can give efficient and reliable operations, and can satisfy their requirements. The users usually do not relate very closely other factors such as technology and architecture in their considerations. On the other hand, the designers are more concerned with the architecture of the system and its dependency on technology. However, the issues considered from both viewpoints are not independent and must be investigated jointly in the design of a DDB. We have, therefore, taken an integrated approach and have classified these issues into four categories. The classification is shown in Figure 1.1.

1.2.1   Issues in Logical Organization

These issues are related to the user-system interface and can be classified as:

(A) User Interface

The user interface may be defined as a boundary in the system below which everything is invisible to the user [DAT77]. The function of this interface is to provide the users with an efficient and powerful query language and to help the users to manipulate the data in the database. The query language must be powerful enough so that an entire set can be manipulated as a single object, instead of being restricted to one record at a time. The complexity of this interface depends on the required ease with which users wish to access the data and it directly governs the design of communication processors.

(B) Database Organization

A database is generally organized in one or more of the data models: relational, hierarchical, or network model, where a data model refers to a representation of the entire information content of the database in a form that is somewhat abstract in comparison with the way in which data is

Figure 1.1. Classification of Issues in Distributed Databases

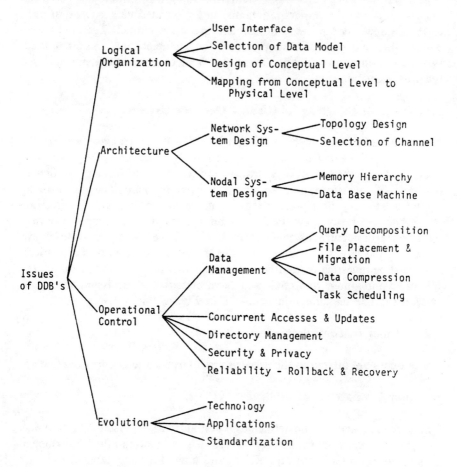

physically stored [DAT77]. There are other models like the binary association model and the external set model which are not especially popular. Each user views the database through an external model which may be one of the above data models. The database should, therefore, be able to support multiple data models for different users and to provide users with transparent accesses. The efficiency of a DDB is very much dependent on the type of organization since it affects the storage organization, access mechanisms, and communication requirements. The criterion for designing and selecting a model has not yet been well understood or established, nor is it likely to be established in the near future. The designers of a DDB are, therefore, confronted with two decisions: which data model to utilize and how to structure the data for a chosen model [SIL76]. Further, there is the problem of mapping the different external models onto the conceptual level.

(C) Design of the Conceptual Level

The conceptual level is a level of indirection between the external level, which consists of different data models and language interfaces, and the internal level, which consists of the physically stored data. The conceptual level actually maps the users' views onto physical data and is intended to provide a solid and enduring foundation for the total operation of the DDB. Its design depends on how the data are stored, the physical storage media, the number of different data models, the way that data are distributed on the DCS, and other user requirements. It is important to construct a conceptual schema at a suitable level of abstraction in the design stage [DAT77]. Many of the techniques in artificial intelligence have been applied successfully in this design.

1.2.2 Issues in Architecture

(A) Network System Design

The DCS is made up of nodal processors interconnected together through an interconnection network. There are many database related issues associated with the design of network systems in addition to the design issues of efficient nodal systems. Among these are: the selection of network topology to support DDB requests; the selection of the channel type; the design of network control strategies; and the design of communication processors. Some of these issues have been studied [RAM76, RAM79b].

(B) Nodal System Design

The design of the nodal architecture to support a DDB is concerned with the design of a fast storage sub-system whose function is to provide the nodal processor sub-system and users with fast retrievals and accesses to the stored data. The storage sub-system usually consists of a memory hierarchy that is divided into levels. These levels are made up of memory elements of varying speeds, and the fastest level is interfaced to the processor sub-system. Further, intelligence has been distributed to the various levels of the hierarchy. One such design is the database machine [HSI77]. Issues like the selection of the number of levels and the size of each level of the memory hierarchy, the design of virtual memory for automatic file management, the utilization of new memory technologies, the hardware design for supporting database operations in a database machine, and the interconnection structure between memories and processors, must be considered in the design.

1.2.3.   Issues in Operational Control

These issues are concerned with the efficient, correct, reliable, and secure operations of the database. They can be classified into:

(A) Resource Management of Data

These are issues related to the management of data and files as resources of the system so that multiple users can share the files on the database efficiently [RAM79a]. The control of files as resources is not only applied at the file level, where the files have to be placed at nodes easily accessible to users and the data have to be compressed for efficient communication and storage, but it ranges from the users' level to the physical level. On the users' level, the queries have to be processed and sequenced so that the amount of data movements is minimal. On the physical level, the individual file requests have to be sequenced so that maximum hardware parallelism can be achieved. Some of these issues are the focus of study in this research.

(B) Concurrent Accesses and Updates

In a DDB where users share the same data, there are several problems associated with multiple accesses and updates. When users try to access common data, there would be interference among the accesses, and the communication protocol should be designed to minimize this interference. Another problem related to consistency arises when data elements with multiple copies at different locations are to be updated. Simple locking mechanisms cause excessive delays and throughput degradation in the DCS.

Efficient updating schemes are needed and the architectures would be very much influenced by such schemes [ESW76].

(C) Directory Management

The directory is a special file in which the addresses for various files on the system are provided. Each access to a file must first access the directory. Due to the high intensity of the accesses on the directory, special attention must be paid to its design. In particular, the designer has to consider the directory structure which is the most suitable for his application, and whether the directory should be replicated or partitioned. In general, a combination of replication and partition is used. Further, reliability considerations must be made in the design of the directory [ROT77].

(D) Security and Privacy

Another important issue in the design of a DDB is security and privacy. Security refers to the protection of data against deliberate or accidental destruction, unauthorized access, or modification of data. On the other hand, privacy refers to the right of an individual user to determine for himself what personal information to share with others as well as what information to receive from others. As the size of the database increases, the threat to security and privacy increases. In addition, it is increasingly difficult to implement effective measures in a DDB. Additional techniques such as data encryption would affect the transmission efficiency and communication mechanisms [BAD78, DOW77].

(E) Reliability—Rollback and Recovery

The determination of the necessary hardware for reliable operations, the data redundancy, and the reconfiguration strategies are major issues in the design of a DDB. Multiple copies of database realm offer fast recovery; checkpointing of realms, dumping and journal rollback and roll-forward offer a slower but cheaper recovery. The effect of any recovery mechanism and reconfiguration strategy on the response time and the associated overhead must be weighted against the reliability requirements [KRI78].

1.2.4. Issues in Evolution

In order for the system to be able to adapt to new application requirements and technology advancements, evolutionary measures must be incorporated into the system at the design stage. Three of the issues in evolution are:

Figure 1.2. The Density Growth of Large Scale Integrated Circuits

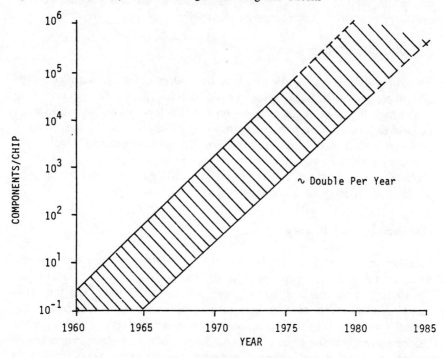

Figure 1.3. The Exponential Growth of CPU Speed

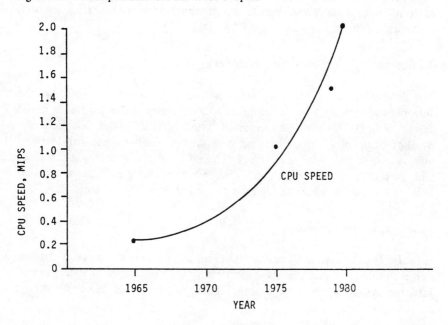

(A) Technology Dependence

Technology is one of the most important driving forces for the success of a computer system. As seen in Figures 1.2 and 1.3, the number of components per chip is approximately doubling each year, and the CPU speed is growing exponentially each year. These faster and denser logics, together with a variety of device manufacturing technologies [MOE78], offer a variety of semiconductor memories with different access times and prices [THE78, UPT78, FET76]. In Table 1.2, the typical access time and power consumption for several semiconductor memory types are shown. Given the diverse types of memories available on the market, the designer must decide at the design stage the most suitable memory to use. Moreover, magnetic device technologies have also improved significantly. With the improvement of disks, drums, and tapes; the invention of bubble memories [BOB71] and electron beam access memories (EBAMs) [HUG75], it is now possible to provide inexpensive secondary and archival storage to the computer system (Figure 1.4).

Table 1.2. Typical values for LSI Semiconductor RAMs (1978)
(Price is shown for quantities of 100)

Memory Type	Access Time (nsec)	Power Consumption (mw)	Approx. Price (¢/bit)
16K MOS dynamic	125-300	400-600	0.30
4K NMOS dynamic	150-350	460	0.33
4K ECL static	30	1000	0.85
4K I^2L dynamic	120	450	0.59
4K TTL static	50-70	600-900	0.80-1.00
4K MOS static	55-170	30-500	0.61-0.92
1K CMOS static	150	4	1.02
1K TTL static	40-100	500-800	0.95
1K ECL static	35-60	500-800	1.30

With these evolving technologies, there are three significant impacts on the design of computers. First, new technologies add extra design alternatives which allow a system to be designed with improved performance and decreased system complexity. An example is shown by the recent developments of bubble memories, CCD memories, and EBAMs which have emerged to fill the "access gap" between the two traditional memory technologies (Figure 1.4). The access gap is the region characterized by an access time between 10^{-6} sec. (MOS memories) and 10^{-3} sec. (fixed head magnetic disk). Much time and effort is expended in finding efficient ways to accomplish at minimum cost the necessary transfers of information across the access gap. With the utilization of "gap-filler" technologies, improved performance and less complex transfer algorithms can be envisioned.

Figure 1.4. Availability of New Memory Technologies

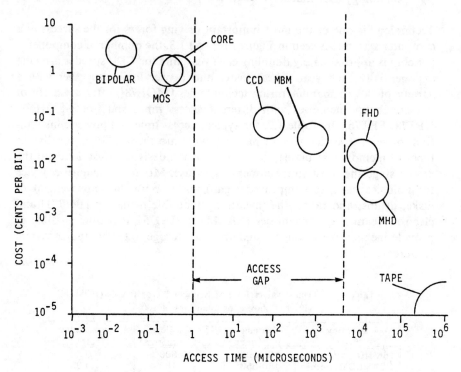

Second, improved integrated circuit technologies allow the designer to incorporate more logical capabilities into the storage sub-system in addition to the storage capabilities. These logical capabilities include abilities to execute arithmetic operations like summation and averaging, as well as logical operations like maximum/minimum searches and equality search.

The last impact of changing technologies on computer system design is the increasing speed mismatch among the elements of a computer system. With the development of high speed processors such as the CRAY-1 and multi-processor systems such as the C.mmp, there is an increasing need for higher bandwidth from the supporting memory sub-system. In order to improve the bandwidths of memories, it is necessary to have intelligent architectural designs and efficient access algorithms for supporting retrieval operations, in addition to the utilization of faster memory components. Special emphases should, therefore, be placed on the utilization of new technologies, the design of new memory architectures, and the study of efficient access algorithms.

Evolving technology allows the user more freedom in specifying and operating the system. More stringent requirements can be specified and many of the systems' functions can be designed in hardware. However, the dependence of a system on evolving technologies is usually a severe constraint on the designer, and the evolutionary capabilities of a system depend very heavily on how well the designer can predict the future technologies.

(B) Application Dependence

Because the size and complexity of applications change with time, the design of the system may have to be altered after the system has been deployed. However, much too often, systems are designed without taking into account provision for future changes. When the system evolves, the changes are incorporated into the system in a very disorganized manner. As a result the structurelessness of the system increases enormously [BEL77] and leads to a regenerative, highly non-linear increase in the effort and cost of the system maintenance [LEH76]. In addition to this, the reliability and the integrity of the system are also jeopardized greatly. One provision is to have a systematic design and development methodology which provides guidelines for the systematic design and construction of DDB and allows the system to evolve as the application requirements and technology change [RAM78b, RAM79b].

(C) Standardization

One of the major inhibiting factors in the development and evolution of DDBs is the lack of standardization in areas such as programming languages, user interface commands, data models, concurrency control mechanisms, hardware components (e.g. disks, tapes), data formats, and network protocols. Standardization of hardware and software components allow modular expansion of the system. On the other hand, with a highly evolving technology, standardization may cause costly refitting later and may even hinder acceptance of new ideas.

We have outlined some of the issues in the design of a distributed system supporting a DDB. These issues are by no means complete and other issues, both design and operational, have to be considered. Alternative solutions to these issues provide the options to be decided upon by the designer during the design phase of the system.

1.3   Architecture of the System Supporting a DDB

The memory sub-system of a DCS is made up of nodal memories connected together by a network and communicates via the connected processors (Fig. 1.5a). Each node in the system, which consists of a set of processing elements and the supporting storage sub-system, may be active or passive. If the node is active, it acts as a requesting source and can access the memories at other nodes via the communication sub-system. Each active node in the system has the following functions in addition to the local file accesses.

(1)   Remote access control

This module detects all remote access requests originating from this node and is responsible for processing them. When a remote request is detected, this module looks up the network directory, and assesses the file status. If the file exists on the network and is accessible by this request, the request will then be transmitted.

(2)   Local access control

This module is responsible for processing all remote requests received from other nodes in the network. It acts as a security filter and :ermines whether the file is accessible. If so, the local file is accessed and the data will be transmitted.

(3)   Redundant file maintenance control

> This module coordinates all the local and remote updates at this node and manages the multiple copies of files on the system. In coordinating updates, if the update originates from a remote node, the status of the file is checked. In case a conflict occurs and the data cannot be updated, a status message is sent. On the other hand, if no conflict occurs, the file is updated. In addition, if the update originates locally this module looks up the network directory and sends out remote updates to every redundant copy on the system.

The relation of these modules to each other in an active node is shown in Fig. 1.5b. The logical issues in a DDB, such as security and privacy, concurrency control, etc., are resolved in these modules.

On the other hand, the physical storage sub-system at a node comprises a memory hierarchy that stores programs and data. It has been realized for a long time that the conflicting requirements for a high performance and low cost storage sub-system at a node can be satisfied by a combination of expensive high performance devices with inexpensive low performance devices which results in a memory hierarchy. The spectrum of storage devices ranges from bulk store and magnetic tape, to the fast register storage and cache memory in the CPU (Figure 1.6).

Many issues have to be considered when these elements of different speeds are put together. These include: the selection of some physical parameters such as the number of levels in the hierarchy and the size and speed of each level [RAM70, WAR76]; the design of the interconnection mechanism among levels [SMI76, POH75]; the design of efficient scheduling algorithms and record/file distribution and migration algorithms [MUN74, STR77]; and the provision of virtual memory support for an automatic file management system [TUE76, POH75, DEN70, BAS70]. The last issue is particularly important because the success of a database is very much dependent on the efficiency of the virtual memory. A file on a database is likely to be large and cannot reside entirely in the main memory. The use of virtual memory can relieve the user from the laborious task of storage management. Research is urgently needed in this area.

There is also an increasing tendency to distribute the processing in the CPU to the various levels of the storage sub-system. One example of this is the database machine (Figure 1.7) [HSI77]. The database machine may be a separate member of the storage sub-system or it may represent a level of the memory hierarchy with additional intelligence. The use of a database machine relieves the processing load of the central processor and allows more parallelism in the processing of database requests. Further, processing

Figure 1.5. Architecture of a DDB System

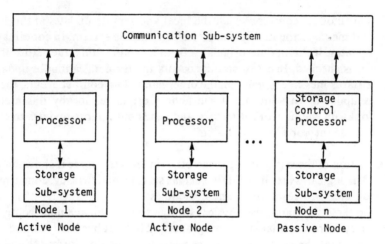

(a) A DCS Memory System

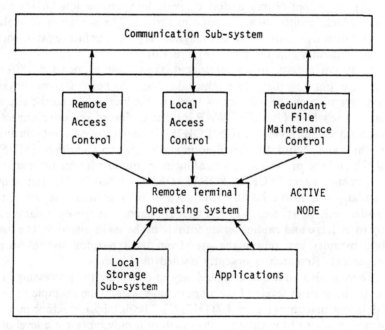

(b) Functional Design of an Active Node

Figure 1.6. Storage Hierarchy (With Typical Sizes shown for 1975 and 1985)

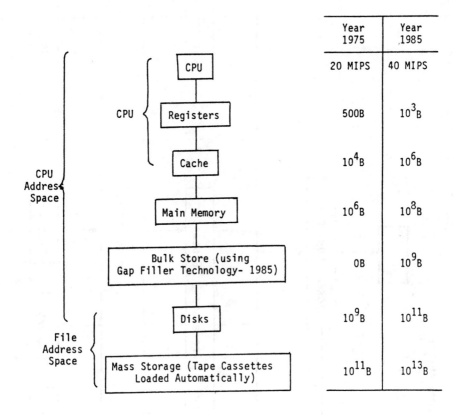

	Year 1975	Year 1985
CPU	20 MIPS	40 MIPS
Registers	500B	10^3B
Cache	10^4B	10^6B
Main Memory	10^6B	10^8B
Bulk Store (using Gap Filler Technology- 1985)	0B	10^9B
Disks	10^9B	10^{11}B
Mass Storage (Tape Cassettes Loaded Automatically)	10^{11}B	10^{13}B

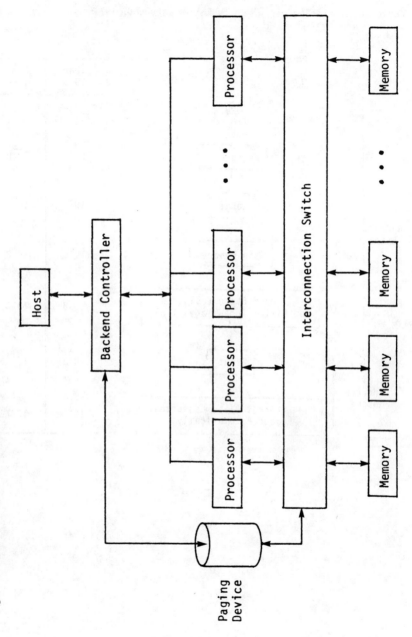

Figure 1.7. Architecture of a Database Machine

on large file systems are often I/O bound and many of the file operations are quite simple. A significant communication overhead is incurred in transferring the file to a level of the memory hierarchy where the processor can access it. By distributing the intelligence to the different levels of the memory hierarchy, the database machine can allow parallel processing with very little communication overhead.

Although database machines have been successfully designed or implemented, e.g. database computer (DBC) [BAU76], context addressed segment sequential storage (CASSM) [LIP78], relational associative processor (RAP) [OZK77], rotating associative memory for relational database applications (RARES) [LIN76], Datacomputer [MAR75], etc., the design of database machines is still plagued by many issues. Examples of these issues are: deciding on the kind and degree of parallelism; selecting the appropriate technologies for implementing the storage media; designing the hardware and software interface; building the storage structure and backend primitives; and designing the control algorithms. These issues are very important because the storage sub-system is very expensive and can be more than 50% of the total hardware cost [SCH78]. The design of a database machine is proposed in Chapter 5 of this study.

This section has described some of the necessary architectures in supporting DDB applications. Database processing generally has some special characteristics and these allow the architecture to be designed differently than conventional architectures. In the next section, the issues of resource management of data on a DDB are discussed.

1.4 Objectives and Contributions of this Research

1.4.1 Problem Statement

The primary objective of this research effort is the development of a realistic, comprehensive, analytical approach for the management of data as resources on a DDB. This design problem encompasses the issues of establishing a systematic way of classifying the different levels of resource management in a DDB, design of performance measures for each level, and development of procedures for the optimal solution of certain problems in each level. We hope to provide a strong framework for future research for problems associated with these large scale systems as well as the solutions to some specific design problems.

1.4.2 Approach

In order to achieve the global objective, the resource management issues are classified into four related levels, namely, the query level, the file level, the task level, and the hardware support level. The specific data management issues investigated are:

(1) Query Decomposition on DDBs

A *query* is an access request made by a user or a program in which one or more files have to be accessed. When multiple files are accessed by the same query on a DDB, these files usually have to reside at a common location before the query can be processed. Substantial communication overhead may be involved if these files are geograph- ically distributed and a copy of each file has to be transferred to a common location. It is therefore necessary to decompose the query into sub-queries so that each sub-query accesses a single file. These sub- queries may then be processed in parallel at any location which has a copy of the required file. The results after the processing are sent back to the originating location. It is generally true that the amount of communication needed to transmit the results is much smaller than the amount needed to transmit the files. This approach has been proposed in the design of the centralized version of INGRES [WON76] and is extended to the design of SDD-1 [WON77], and distributed INGRES [EPS78]. However, in some cases, decomposition is impossible and some file transfers are still necessary. Two techniques are proposed in Chapter 2 to reduce the overall operational costs of the system.

(2) File Placement and Migration

This issue relates to the distribution and migration of database components, namely, files and control programs, on a DDB with the objective of minimizing the overall storage, migration, updating, and access costs on the system. A file assignment algorithm is proposed in Chapter 3.

(3) Task Scheduling

Requests on a DDB must be scheduled so that high parallelism and overlap can be achieved. The request may be a single word fetch or a page or file access. This parallelism is important because in order to attain high throughput, the parallel hardware and resources must be efficiently utilized. The control of task scheduling can be distributed or centralized. In distributed control, each node may act independently and coordinate with each other through inter-processor communica- tions. In centralized control, there is a primary node in which all scheduling controls are performed. The decision of which is a better control mechanism depends very heavily on the interconnection structure and the communication overhead involved. This issue is discussed in Chapter 4.

(4)   Hardware Support

In addition to studying the logical data management techniques, the design of the hardware support is also very important. This hardware does not necessarily implement a solution to one of the data management issues such as file placement, but it provides auxilliary support to these solutions so that they can be implemented efficiently. The particular hardware supports studied are the associative memory and the database machine. These are discussed in Chapter 5.

The relationships among the various data management issues are shown in Figure 1.8 where a relation $\rightarrow$ is said to exist between two design issues $\bar{a}$, $\bar{b}$, i.e. $\bar{a} \rightarrow \bar{b}$, if the solution of $\bar{b}$ is transparent to the solution of $\bar{a}$. That is, the solution of $\bar{a}$ is not affected by the solution to $\bar{b}$, but not vice versa. The solution to $\bar{a}$ can therefore be developed independent of $\bar{b}$.

In Figure 1.5, it is seen that, generally, task scheduling is transparent to file placement and migration which, in turn, could be transparent to query decomposition. Further, hardware support is transparent to all these logical issues and is generally developed after the algorithms for the logical issues have been designed. Due to the independency, algorithms for query decomposition can be developed independently.

In developing algorithms for file placement and migration, the solutions for query decomposition should be taken into account. However, in most cases, assumptions can be made about their solutions and the file placement and migration problem can be solved independently. For example, it may be assumed that all queries which access multiple files may be decomposed into sub-queries that access single files. This assumption is only true in some circumstances, an example of which is shown in Chapter 2. The file placement and migration problem for multiple files is, therefore, decomposed into many single file optimization sub-problems. It must be noted that other operational control requirements may also impose restrictions on the solutions to the data management issues. For instance, different reliability requirements may demand different lower bounds on the number of copies of a file on a DDB; different concurrency control mechanisms may have different costs on the file placement problem; etc. Reasonable assumptions must be made about these requirements in order to determine their effects on the resource management issues and to solve these issues independently.

Figure 1.8.   Relationships Among Various Data Management Issues

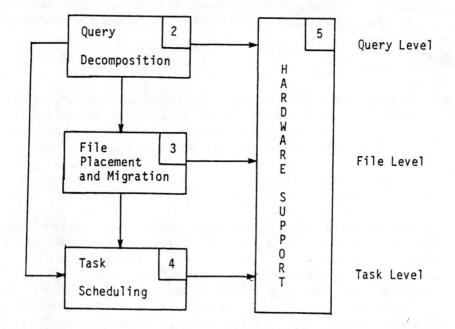

1.4.3   Contributions of this Research

Some specific contributions of this research, arranged in the order of discussion, are listed below.

(A)   A model for query decomposition on relational databases has been developed. It is shown that the optimization of placements of multiple relations can be achieved independently for each relation.

(B)   Two cost reduction models have been designed to reduce the operational costs of a relational database. The first model reduces the retrieval cost, but increases the update cost. The second model reduces the update cost but increases the retrieval cost. These two cost reduction models can be combined to reduce the operational costs of DDBs. Further, it is shown that the optimization of placements of multiple relations under the use of these techniques can be done independently for each relation.

(C)   The isomorphism between a limited version of the file placement problem and a limited version of the single commodity warehouse location problem has been proved. Due to this isomorphism, it is shown that some conditions and techniques developed in computer science to solve the file placement problem are weaker than the corresponding conditions and techniques developed in operations research to solve the warehouse location problem, and vice versa. Further, the techniques developed in both problems are inter-changeable.

(D)   A file placement heuristic has been developed. While not necessarily yielding optimal system design, this heuristic yields solutions of lower cost than those generated by other currently available heuristics.

(E)   A model for the scheduling of tasks on a distributed system has been developed. This model assumes that global control is infeasible and all the scheduling decisions have to be made locally at each node. It is shown that the scheduling of tasks in this model, when all the task processing times are deterministic, is a NP-complete problem. A heuristic has been developed and the performance of this heuristic has been verified using simulations.

(F)   A restricted model for the scheduling of tasks on a DCS has been proposed. By using the additional constraints, it is shown that the optimal scheduling problem is polynomially solvable. This model actually represents an organization of an interleaved memory system. The performance of the scheduling algorithm has been verified using simulations.

(G)   An associative memory has been designed which is capable of searching the maximum and minimum in a time independent of the number of words in the memory. It is also capable of doing equality search, threshold searches, and proximity search. The design is very efficient and has a complexity of 17 gates per cell. The design is asynchronous and utilizes a word-parallel and bit-serial algorithm. The delay is one to four gate delays across each bit slice.

(H) The associative memory concept is extended to the design of a database machine. DIALOG—a database machine which uses distributed and associative processing and utilizes current memory technologies for implementation is proposed. The memory devices are enhanced with additional processing logic for associative processing and join processing. The memory modules are connected by a hierarchical interconnection network.

2

Query Decomposition on a Distributed Relational Database

In this chapter, the problem of query decomposition and its association with the optimal placements of relations on a distributed relational database are studied. Our objectives are to study techniques which allow query decomposition to be effected more efficiently and to investigate properties on the optimal placements of multiple copies of relations or segments of relations on a DCS that minimize the total operational cost of the system (such as storage cost, multiple update cost, retrieval cost, query processing cost, file migration cost).

The theme of this chapter is to demonstrate that the placements of multiple relations on a distributed relational database can be optimized for each relation independently. It is assumed that a technique exists to find the optimal placements of multiple copies of a single relation on a DDB, an example for which is shown in Chapter 3.

In this chapter, two methods have been proposed to reduce the operational costs of the system. The first method utilizes additional redundant information on the DDB in order to reduce the total retrieval cost and increase the total update cost. The second method uses file partitioning to reduce the total update cost and increase the total retrieval cost. It is shown by an example database that under certain conditions, either method, or a combination of both methods, can reduce the total operational costs of the system. A relational data model is chosen in this discussion because it is very popular and the results obtained would be more specific. However, the techniques proposed in this chapter can be generalized to any type of data model and file system.

2.1 Queries on a Relational Database

In a relational database [COD70], data is viewed as relations of varying degree, the degree being the number of distinct domains in the relation. Each instance of a relation is known as a tuple, which has a value for each domain

Figure 2.1. Relations S and SP

(a) Relation S

S	s#	sname	city	inventory
	1	Supplier A	New York	1500
	3	Supplier B	San Francisco	700
	5	Supplier C	Chicago	2500

(b) Relation SP

SP	s#	p#
	1	A1
	2	A1
	3	A2
	4	A2
	5	P2

of the relation. Thus a relation can simply be represented in tabular form with columns as domains and rows as tuples.

A *Query* is an access request made by a user or a program, in which one or more relations have to be accessed. A query on a relational database consists of two parts: the part specifying the domain(s) of the relation to be retrieved and the part specifying the predicate which is a quantification representing the defining properties of the set to be accessed. Let S be a relation of domains s#, sname, city, inventory; and SP be a relation of domains s#, p# (Figure 2.1). The queries on a relational database can be classified into the following categories [DAT77]:

(1) Retrieval Operations
  (a) Single Relation Retrieval: The predicate representing the defining property of the set to be retrieved is defined on the same relation as the set.
      E.g. GET (S.sname): (S.city = "Paris" AND S.inventory > 1000)
  (b) Multiple Relation Retrieval: The predicate, as well as the set to be retrieved, may be defined over multiple relations.
      E.g. GET (S.sname): (S.s# = SP.s# AND SP.p# = "P_2")
      Relations S and SP must be available simultaneously before the retrieval can be processed.
(2) Storage Operations
  (a) Single Relation Update;
  (b) Multiple Relation Update;

(c) Insertion;
(d) Deletion.
(3) Library Functions
These represent more complicated operations in the predicate than the equality operations, such as counting the number of occurrences, selecting the maximum/minimum, etc.

Single relation queries can be processed very easily on a distributed relational database. When the relation is geographically distributed, the query can be sent to a node that has a copy of the relation and be processed there. The results after the processing are sent back to the originating node. It is generally true that the amount of communication needed to transmit the results is much smaller than the amount needed to transmit the entire relation.

On the other hand, the processing of a multi-relation query is more complicated. When multiple relations are accessed by the same query on a DDB, these relations usually have to reside at a common location before the query can be processed. Substantial communication overhead may be involved if these relations are geographically distributed and a copy of each relation has to be transferred to a common location. It is therefore necessary to decompose the query into sub-queries so that each sub-query accesses a single relation. This technique has been proposed in the design of the centralized version of INGRES [WON76], and is extended to the design of SDD-1 [WON77] and distributed INGRES [EPS78].

Specifically, the technique consists of two steps. The first step is to select a site with the minimum amount of data movements before the query can be processed. This is used as a starting point for the second step of the algorithm which determines the sequence of moves that results in the minimum cost. The algorithm used is a greedy algorithm and only local optima can result from such an algorithm.

Hevner and Yao [HEV79] have followed a similar approach and have developed two optimal algorithms for arranging data transmissions and local data processing with the minimal response time and minimal total time, for a special class of queries. These optimal algorithms are used as a basis to develop a general query processing algorithm for a general query in which each required relation may have any number of joining domains and output domains, and each node may have any number of required relations. This general algorithm is a heuristic which uses an improved exhaustive search to find efficient query distribution strategies.

Ghosh also proposed a model of data distribution on a database which facilitates query processing [GHO76]. Specifically, the model consists of a database with multiple target segment types and where queries with multiple target segment types exist. The objective is to distribute the segments on the database in order to maximize the number of segments that the queries can retrieve in parallel from different nodes. The model looks at the problem from a retrieval point of view only and no cost is associated with retrieving a segment from a node.

Most of the previous work addresses the problem from two separate viewpoints. The first one is concerned about the questions of the processing sequence of the query and where it should be processed. The second viewpoint is concerned about where the files should be placed so that they can be accessed efficiently. These two viewpoints are not entirely independent and should be investigated together. Further, there exist queries which are non-decomposable. For example, the query:

$$\text{GET (S.sname): (S.s\# = SP.s\# AND SP.p\# = ``}P_2\text{")}$$

is not decomposable into single relation retrievals because there is a logical relation "=" which is defined over a common domain s# of the relations S and SP. These relations must be available simultaneously at a common location before the retrieval or update operations can be performed.

Instead of solving the problem of query decomposition, we study two techniques to reduce the processing and communication costs for non-decomposable queries in this chapter. It is shown later that, by the introduction of some redundant information on the database and by the use of file partitioning, non-decomposable queries may be made decomposable (see also [RAM79a, RAM79c]). The basic assumption made here is that all the required relations are moved to the node at which the query originates, before the processing of the query begins. It is possible to consider a sequence of moves which will minimize the total amount of data transferred. However the problem is very complicated and the intention of this chapter is to demonstrate the usefulness of the techniques of using redundant information and file partitioning.

Before the techniques are discussed, the problem of placement of relations on a DDB is first formulated.

2.2   The Placements of Relations on a DDB

In this section, a model for the placements of multiple relations on a DDB is formulated. The model is shown for the special case of two relations and is generalized later to the case of more than two relations.

Consider two relations a and b, the retrieval and the update rates at node i are (see Figure 2.2)[1]:

$q_{i,a}{}^a(q_{i,b}{}^b)$ = rate of access at node i for a single relation retrieval accessing relation $a(b)$;

$q_{i,a,b}{}^{a,b}$ = rate of access at node i for a multi-relation retrieval accessing both relations a and b;

$u_{i,a}{}^a(u_{i,b}{}^b)$ = rate of update at node i for a single relation query updating relation $a(b)$;

$u_{i,a}{}^{a,b}(u_{i,b}{}^{a,b})$ = rate of update at node i for a multi-relation query accessing both relations a and b before updating relation $a(b)$.

The costs for each unit of access are:

$S_{i,j}{}^a(S_{i,j}{}^b)$ = communication and processing costs per unit query of accessing relation $a(b)$ from node i to node j;

$M_{i,j}{}^a(M_{i,j}{}^b)$ = communication and processing costs per unit update of multiple updating relation $a(b)$ from node i to node j.

We differentiate between the costs of retrievals and updates because in some applications, retrievals are more important than updates and would have a higher cost (e.g. inventory system). In other real-time applications, updates may be more frequent and, therefore, more critical (e.g. airline reservation system). Let:

n = number of nodes of the DCS;

$l_a(l_b)$ = size of relation $a(b)$;

$f_{i,a}(f_{i,b})$ = per unit cost of storing relation $a(b)$ at node i.

We define from the characteristics of the queries initiated from node i, the following symbols:

(1) Single relation retrievals:

$\alpha_{i,a}{}^a(\alpha_{i,b}{}^b)$ = fraction of relation $a(b)$ that is put into the result relation due to the execution of a single relation retrieval on $a(b)$;

---

1. The conventions of the symbols used are as follows: i,j represent indexes for nodes; a,b represent indexes for relations; the superscripts represent the list of relations that the query must access before the query can be processed; the subscripts represent the nodes concerned and the target list of relations for the query. Note that other versions of this work have used a slightly different notation than this edition. The first section of equation 2.1 (2.1a), which would have been represented as

$$\sum_{r=a,b} \sum_{i=1}^{n} \sum_{j=1}^{n} q_{i,r}^r \ \alpha_{i,r}^r \ l_r \ X_{i,j}^r \ S_{i,j}^r$$

will be represented in this work as

$$\Sigma_{r=a,b} \ \Sigma_{i=1}{}^n \ \Sigma_{j=1}{}^n \ q_{i,r}{}^r \alpha_{i,r}{}^r l_r X_{i,j}{}^r S_{i,j}{}^r.$$

Figure 2.2. Retrieval and Update Rates on a 2-Relation DDB from
Node i

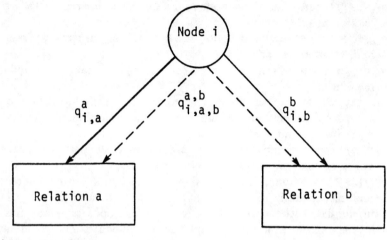

(a) Retrievals

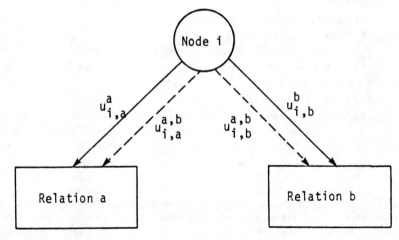

(b) Updates

⟶ Single Relation Accesses

- - -▶ Multi-Relation Accesses

(2) Multi-relation retrievals:

$\alpha_{i,a}{}^{a,b}(\alpha_{i,b}{}^{a,b})$ = fraction of relation $a(b)$ that is needed to process a multi-relation retrieval on a and b;

(3) Single relation updates:

$\beta_{i,a}{}^{a}(\beta_{i,b}{}^{b})$ = fraction of relation $a(b)$ that will be updated by a single relation update;

(4) Multi-relation updates:

$\nu_{i,a}{}^{a,b}(\nu_{i,b}{}^{a,b})$ = fraction of a relation $a(b)$ that is needed to process a multi-relation update before the updates can be performed;

$\beta_{i,a}{}^{a,b}(\beta_{i,b}{}^{a,b})$ = fraction of relation $a(b)$ that will be updated by a multi-relation update after relations a and b have been accessed.

In processing a multi-relation update, the relations a and b must be accessed first in order to determine the actual updates that have to be made. This is measured by the parameters $\nu_{i,a}{}^{a,b}$ and $\nu_{i,b}{}^{a,b}$. The part of relations a and b to be updated after they have been determined are measured by the parameters $\beta_{i,a}{}^{a,b}$ and $\beta_{i,b}{}^{a,b}$.

The parameters defined above can be estimated from the characteristics of the different types of queries that are made on the DDB and the probability distribution of the data stored in the relations.

The control variables governing the file locations and the routing discipline are defined as follows:

$$Y_i^a(Y_i^b) = \begin{cases} 0 & \text{if relation } a(b) \text{ does not exist at node } i \\ 1 & \text{otherwise} \end{cases}$$

$X_{i,j}{}^a(X_{i,j}{}^b)$ = fraction of queries made at node i on relation $a(b)$ that are routed to node j.

It is true that if $X_{i,j}^r > 0$, then $Y_j^r = 1$ for $r = a,b$.

The optimization problem of placing relations a and b on the DDB can be formulated in the following linear program:

min   (2.1)

$$\sum_{r=a,b} \sum_{i=1}^{n} \sum_{j=1}^{n} q_{i,r}{}^{r} \alpha_{i,r}{}^{r} l_r X_{i,j}{}^{r} S_{i,j}{}^{r} \tag{2.1a}$$

$$+ \sum_{r=a,b} \sum_{i=1}^{n} \sum_{j=1}^{n} q_{i,a,b}{}^{a,b} \alpha_{i,r}{}^{a,b} l_r X_{i,j}{}^{r} S_{i,j}{}^{r} \tag{2.1b}$$

$$+ \sum_{r=a,b} \sum_{i=1}^{n} \sum_{j=1}^{n} u_{i,r}{}^{r} \beta_{i,r}{}^{r} l_r M_{i,j}{}^{r} Y_j^{r} \tag{2.1c}$$

$$+ \Sigma_{r=a,b} \, \Sigma_{i=1}^{n} \, \Sigma_{j=1}^{n} \, u_{i,r}^{a,b} \, [\Sigma_{s=a,b} \, v_{i,s}^{a,b} \, l_s \, X_{i,j}^{s} \, S_{i,j}^{s} \tag{2.1d}$$

$$+ \beta_{i,r}^{a,b} \, l_r \, M_{i,j}^{r} \, Y_{j}^{r} \,]$$

$$+ \Sigma_{r=a,b} \, \Sigma_{i=1}^{n} \, f_{i,r} \, l_r \, Y_{i}^{r} \tag{2.1e}$$

subject to the following constraints:

$$\Sigma_{i=1}^{n} \, Y_{i}^{r} \geqslant 1 \qquad r = a,b \tag{2.1f}$$

$$\Sigma_{j=1}^{n} \, X_{i,j}^{r} = 1, \qquad r = a,b, \, i = 1,2,\ldots,n \tag{2.1g}$$

$$nY_{j}^{r} \geqslant \Sigma_{i=1}^{n} \, X_{i,j}^{r} \geqslant 0, \qquad r = a,b, \, j = 1,2,\ldots,n \tag{2.1h}$$

$$Y_{i}^{r} = 0,1, \qquad r = a,b, \, i = 1,2,\ldots,n. \tag{2.1i}$$

Eq. 2.1a represents the access cost for single relation retrievals; Eq. 2.1b represents the access cost for multi-relation retrievals; Eq. 2.1c represents the update cost for single relation updates; Eq. 2.1d represents the update cost for multi-relation updates and Eq. 2.1e represents the storage cost of relations on the DDB. Condition 2.1f assures that at least one copy of the relation exists; condition 2.1g assures that all the queries are serviced; condition 2.1h assures that the relation must exist at a node if a route is defined to access it at that node and condition 2.1i assures that the control variables Y_i^r are integral.

LEMMA 2.1

The above optimization problem can be partitioned into two independent optimization sub-problems, one for each relation:

(a) min   (2.2)

$$\Sigma_{i=1}^{n} \, \Sigma_{j=1}^{n} \, Q_{i}^{a} \, X_{i,j}^{a} \, S_{i,j}^{a} \, + \, \Sigma_{i=1}^{n} \, \Sigma_{j=1}^{n} \, U_{i}^{a} \, M_{i,j}^{a} \, Y_{j}^{a}$$

$$+ \, \Sigma_{i=1}^{n} \, F_{i}^{a} \, Y_{i}^{a}$$

where

$$Q_{i}^{a} = (q_{i,a}^{a} \, \alpha_{i,a}^{a} + q_{i,a,b}^{a,b} \, \alpha_{i,a}^{a,b} + u_{i,a}^{a,b} \, v_{i,a}^{a,b}$$

$$+ u_{i,b}{}^{a,b} \; v_{i,a}{}^{a,b}) l_a$$

$$U_i{}^a = (u_{i,a}{}^a \; \beta_{i,a}{}^a + u_{i,a}{}^{a,b} \; \beta_{i,a}{}^{a,b}) l_a$$

$$F_i{}^a = f_{i,a} \, l_a$$

subject to:

$$\Sigma_{i=1}{}^n \; Y_i{}^a \geqslant 1$$

$$\Sigma_{j=1}{}^n \; X_{i,j}{}^a = 1 \qquad i = 1, \ldots, n$$

$$n Y_j{}^a \geqslant \Sigma_{i=1}{}^n \; X_{i,j}{}^a \geqslant 0 \qquad j = 1, \ldots, n$$

$$Y_i{}^a = 0,1 \qquad i = 1, \ldots, n.$$

(b) min $\hspace{9cm}$ (2.3)

$$\Sigma_{i=1}{}^n \; \Sigma_{j=1}{}^n \; Q_i{}^b \; X_{i,j}{}^b \; S_{i,j}{}^b + \Sigma_{i=1}{}^n \; \Sigma_{j=1}{}^n \; U_i{}^b \; M_{i,j}{}^b \; Y_j{}^b$$

$$+ \Sigma_{i=1}{}^n \; F_i{}^b \; Y_i{}^b$$

where

$$Q_i{}^b = (q_{i,b}{}^b \; \alpha_{i,b}{}^b + q_{i,a,b}{}^{a,b} \; \alpha_{i,b}{}^{a,b} + u_{i,a}{}^{a,b} \; v_{i,b}{}^{a,b}$$

$$+ u_{i,b}{}^{a,b} \; v_{i,b}{}^{a,b}) l_b$$

$$U_i{}^b = (u_{i,b}{}^b \; \beta_{i,b}{}^b + u_{i,b}{}^{a,b} \; \beta_{i,b}{}^{a,b}) l_b$$

$$F_{i,b} = f_{i,b} \, l_b$$

subject to:

$$\Sigma_{i=1}{}^n \; Y_i{}^b \geqslant 1$$

$$\Sigma_{i=1}^{n} X_{i,j}^{b} = 1 \qquad i = 1,\ldots,n$$

$$nY_{j}^{b} \geqslant \Sigma_{i=1}^{n} X_{i,j}^{b} \geqslant 0 \qquad j = 1,\ldots,n$$

$$Y_{i}^{b} = 0,1 \qquad i = 1,\ldots,n.$$

Proof

We notice in optimization problem (2.1) that there are no cross product terms in the control variables of relations a and b. Therefore, the objective function of (2.1) can be written as a sum of objective functions of optimization problems (2.2) and (2.3), and similarly, the constraints can be partitioned into two independent sets. The solution to (2.2) will therefore be a constant in (2.1) which implies that (2.3) can be solved independently. Similarly, the solution to (2.3) will be a constant in (2.1) and this implies that (2.2) can be solved independently.

Q.E.D.

We conclude that the optimization problem 2.1 for relations a and b can be carried out as two optimization sub-problems for relations a and b independently.

A further simplification of the integer programs (2.2) and (2.3) is to first solve for $X_{i,j}^{r}$, $r = a,b$, and substitute it into the integer programs. It is shown in [ALC76] that,

$$X_{i,j}^{r} = \begin{cases} 1 & \text{if } S_{i,j}^{r} = \min_{k, Y_{k}^{r}=1} S_{i,k} \\ 0 & \text{otherwise.} \end{cases}$$

The detailed proof will not be shown here.

A generalization of Lemma 2.1 is to allow any number of relations in the DDB. This is shown in the following theorem.

THEOREM 2.1

The general problem of optimizing the placements of multiple relations on a DDB can be decomposed into multiple sub-problems, one for the placement of each relation.

The proof, which requires some symbols to be defined and can be done by an obvious generalization of the proof of Lemma 2.1, will not be shown here.

The importance of Theorem 2.1 is that the original optimization problem of placing multiple copies of m relations on a DDB, which has a complexity of the order of $O(2^{nm})$, is reduced to m simpler optimization sub-problems of placing multiple copies of each relation on the DDB, each of which has a complexity of the order of $O(2^n)$. There are many techniques developed to place multiple copies of a relation on a DDB, e.g. [CAS72, LEV74, MOR77]. Some of these techniques are exhaustive and give optimal solutions, e.g. [CAS72, LEV74, MOR77]; others give sub-optimal solutions and have a polynomial execution time, an example of which is shown in Chapter 3 of this study. In the remainder of this chapter, we discuss two techniques to minimize the operational costs of a DDB. The costs with and without the application of these techniques are compared.

2.3 Cost Reduction on the Placements of Relations on a DDB by Utilizing Redundant Information

In section 2.1, the technique of query decomposition was briefly described. In query decomposition, optimization is performed on the processing of a single query which originates at a node. The objective is to decompose a multi-relation query into as many single relation sub-queries as possible so that the total amount of data (relation) movements is minimized. However, there exist non-decomposable queries which require all the relations that they access to be present at a common location. A large number of relation transfers may be needed if these relations are geographically distributed. In order to avoid these extra relation transfers, we propose a technique utilizing redundant information. Instead of decomposing queries that access multiple relations, it may be sufficient to provide redundant information in each relation so that not every relation has to reside at a single location before the query can be processed. For example, in processing the query:

GET (S.sname): (S.s# = SP.s# AND SP.p# = "P_2")

on two geographically separated relations, S and SP (Figure 2.1), it may be necessary to transfer relation S to the node where SP resides and then process the query there or vice versa. However, if the information (S.s# = SP.s#) is compiled beforehand into the two relations (Figure 2.3), then the above query can be decomposed into two single relation sub-queries:

GET (S.s#, S.sname): (S.s# = SP.s#) and

GET (SP.s#): (S.s# = SP.s# AND SP.p# = "P_2").

Figure 2.3.   Relations *S* and *SP* with (S.s#=SP.s#)
information compiled into the relations

(a) Relation S

S	s#	S.s#= SP.s#	sname	city	inventory
	1	1	Supplier A	New York	1500
	3	1	Supplier B	San Francisco	700
	5	1	Supplier C	Chicago	2500

(b) Relation SP

SP	s#	S.s#= SP.s#	p#
	1	1	A1
	2		A1
	3	1	A2
	4		A2
	5	1	P2

In this case, the processing can be done in parallel and the amount of information transfers is much smaller.

This technique poses several problems. First, it is necessary to take one extra bit for each tuple in order to compile this piece of information. If the amount of information to be added is large (e.g. when the number of different predicates defined on a common domain of two relations is large), the size of the extra storage space may be significant. Second, when the common domain of one relation is modified, it is necessary to "multiple update" the redundant information in all the common domains of the other relations in the DDB. Referring to Figure 2.3, if an extra tuple with s# = "2", sname = "Supplier D", city = "Boston" and inventory = "3000" is added to relation S, then it is necessary to find out the changes that have been made on the redundant information (S.s# = SP.s#) in both relations S and SP, and to update these changes in addition to the original update. In this case, the (S.s# = SP.s#) information has to be changed in relations S and SP because relation SP contains a tuple with s# = 2. If updating activities are frequent, the "multiple update" cost is large. The net effect of this technique is, therefore, to reduce the total retrieval cost and to increase the total update cost of the system. Further, the response time in reflecting an update on the DDB may be longer in this case because of the need to update the redundant information. Third, this technique requires that the database designer be able to estimate the amount of additional information to be compiled into the relations. A possible way is to pre-analyze the type of predicates used in retrievals and updates and to determine the essential information to be compiled into the relations. A compromise should be made between introducing extra information with additional storage space and higher cost in multiple updates, and reducing the amount of relation transfers. It would be advantageous for the more frequently used predicates and less advantageous for the others.

In the remainder of this section, a model is developed for deciding the amount of redundant information that is needed on a DDB in order for this technique to be cost effective. We first examine the strategies that have to be used for retrievals and updates.

The strategies on retrievals of a geographically distributed relation are the same as the strategy when no redundant information is used. The necessary information to be used in processing a single relation query is first projected onto temporary files before they are sent to the originating node. In the case of a non-decomposable multi-relation query, all the required relations are sent to the originating node before the query is processed. On the other hand, the strategy on updates is different from the case of no redundant information because it is also necessary to check whether the redundant information is updated. There are two variations of the update strategy:

(1) The updates are first sent to the multiple copies of the file to be updated;

The necessary information on all the relations, which is needed to determine if any redundant information has to be updated, is sent to a common node;

The updates to be made on the redundant information are determined there;

The updates on the redundant information are sent out to all the affected relations.

(2) The necessary information on all the relations, which is needed to determine if any redundant information has to be updated, is sent to the node where the update originates (actually, it can be sent to any other node, but the control overhead in doing this would usually be greater);

The update to be made on the redundant information is determined at this node;

The updates on the target relation as well as the updates on the redundant information, are sent out to all the relations.

The advantage of strategy (1) is that the updates on the target relation are reflected on the DDB in a shorter time than strategy (2). But strategy (1) involves more control overhead and the response time in reflecting the updates on the redundant information is longer than strategy (2). In general, strategy (2) will have a shorter overall response time. We assume that strategy (2) is used in our model.

Figure 2.4. Retrieval And Update Rates On a 2-Relation DDB From Node i Using Additional Redundant Information

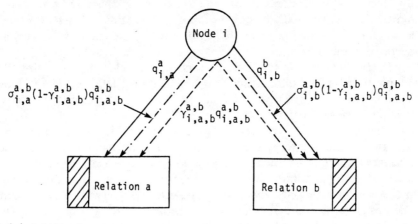

(a) Retrievals

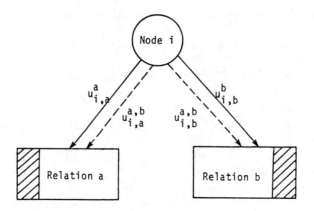

(b) Updates

 Single Relation Accesses

Multi-Relation Transformed Single Relation Accesses, Due To The Use Of Redundant Information

Multi-Relation Accesses

Redundant Information

As before, the model for determining the use of redundant information is first developed for the special case of two relations and is generalized to the case of more than two relations later.

Consider two relations a and b, the retrieval and the update rates, using the notations defined earlier, are shown in Figure 2.4. There are two additional types of single relation retrievals which are decomposed from part of the multi-relation retrievals due to the use of redundant information. In describing the model, the following symbols are defined:

$\gamma_{i,a,b}{}^{a,b}$ = fraction of non-decomposable multi-relation retrievals on a and b from node i that remain non-decomposable even with the use f redundant information;

$$\frac{\sigma_{i,a}{}^{a,b}}{(\sigma_{i,a}{}^{a,b} + \sigma_{i,b}{}^{a,b})} \quad \left[\frac{\sigma_{i,b}{}^{a,b}}{(\sigma_{i,a}{}^{a,b} + \sigma_{i,b}{}^{a,b})} \right]$$

= fraction of multi-relation-reduced-single-relation retrievals from node i on $a(b)$ due to the use of redundant information;

$(1 - \gamma_{i,a,b}{}^{a,b})q_{i,a,b}{}^{a,b}$ is the rate of multi-relation retrievals that is decomposable with the use of redundant information.

$(1 - \gamma_{i,a,b}{}^{a,b})q_{i,a,b}{}^{a,b}(\sigma_{i,a}{}^{a,b} + \sigma_{i,b}{}^{a,b})$ is the total rate of multi-relation-reduced-single-relation retrievals to relations a and b after the decomposition.

It is generally true that $\sigma_{i,a}{}^{a,b} + \sigma_{i,b}{}^{a,b} \geq 1$, that is, the total rate of additional single relation retrievals after the use of redundant information, is greater than the reduction in multi-relation retrieval rate. The access rate of multi-relation-reduced-single-relation retrievals on relation r is $(1 - \gamma_{i,a,b}{}^{a,b})q_{i,a,b}{}^{a,b}\sigma_{i,r}{}^{a,b}$ for $r = a,b$.

$\varepsilon_{i,a}{}^{a,b}(\varepsilon_{i,b}{}^{a,b})$ = fraction of relation $a(b)$ that is put into the result relation due to a multi-relation-reduced-single-relation retrieval on $a(b)$;

$\delta_{i,a}{}^{a,b}(\delta_{i,b}{}^{a,b})$ = fraction of non-decomposable multi-relation updates on $a(b)$ from node i that remain non-decomposable even with the use of redundant information;

$\eta_{i,a,b}{}^{a}(\eta_{i,a,b}{}^{b})$ = fraction of updates on relation $a(b)$ from node i that will update redundant information on relations a and b;

$\xi_{i,a}{}^{a}(\xi_{i,b}{}^{b})$ = fraction of relation $a(b)$ in which the redundant information has to be updated due to updates originating from node i;

$l'_a(l'_b)$ = size of relation $a(b)$ after the use of redundant information. In our model, although the amount of storage is greater after redundant information is used, i.e. $l'_r > l_r$ ($r = a,b$), but the effect on communication is very small because the redundant information does not have to be transferred over the network in processing a query.

The optimization problem of placing relations a and b on the DDB after the use of redundant information can be formulated in the following linear program:

min   (2.4)

$$\Sigma_{r=a,b} \Sigma_{i=1}^{n} \Sigma_{j=1}^{n} q_{i,r}^{r} \alpha_{i,r}^{r} l'_{r} X_{i,j}^{r} S_{i,j}^{r} \tag{2.4a}$$

$$+ \Sigma_{r=a,b} \Sigma_{i=1}^{n} \Sigma_{j=1}^{n} (1 - \gamma_{i,a,b}^{a,b}) q_{i,a,b}^{a,b} \sigma_{i,r}^{a,b}$$

$$\epsilon_{i,r}^{a,b} l'_{r} X_{i,j}^{r} S_{i,j}^{r} \tag{2.4b}$$

$$+ \Sigma_{r=a,b} \Sigma_{i=1}^{n} \Sigma_{j=1}^{n} \gamma_{i,a,b}^{a,b} q_{i,a,b}^{a,b} \alpha_{i,r}^{a,b} l'_{r} X_{i,j}^{r} S_{i,j}^{r} \tag{2.4c}$$

$$+ \Sigma_{r=a,b} \Sigma_{i=1}^{n} \Sigma_{j=1}^{n} u_{i,r}^{r} \beta_{i,r}^{r} l'_{r} M_{i,j}^{r} Y_{j}^{r} \tag{2.4d}$$

$$+ \Sigma_{r=a,b} \Sigma_{i=1}^{n} \Sigma_{j=1}^{n} u_{i,r}^{a,b} [\delta_{i,r}^{a,b} \Sigma_{s=a,b} v_{i,s}^{a,b} l'_{s} X_{i,j}^{s} S_{i,j}^{s}$$

$$+ \beta_{i,r}^{a,b} l'_{r} M_{i,j}^{r} Y_{j}^{r}] \tag{2.4e}$$

$$+ \Sigma_{r=a,b} \Sigma_{i=1}^{n} \Sigma_{j=1}^{n} \eta_{i,a,b}^{r} (u_{i,r}^{r} + u_{i,r}^{a,b}) [\Sigma_{s \neq r} \alpha_{i,s}^{a,b} l'_{s}$$

$$X_{i,j}^{s} S_{i,j}^{s} + \Sigma_{t=a,b} \xi_{i,t}^{t} l'_{t} M_{i,j}^{t} Y_{j}^{t}] \tag{2.4f}$$

$$+ \Sigma_{r=a,b} \Sigma_{i=1}^{n} f_{i,r} l'_{r} Y_{i}^{r} \tag{2.4g}$$

subject to:

$$\Sigma_{i=1}^{n} Y_{i}^{r} \geq 1 \qquad r=a,b$$

$$\Sigma_{j=1}^{n} X_{i,j}^{r} = 1 \qquad r=a,b \qquad i=1,\ldots,n$$

$$nY_{j}^{r} \geq \Sigma_{i=1}^{n} X_{i,j}^{r} \geq 0 \qquad r=a,b \qquad j=1,\ldots,n$$

$$Y_{i}^{r} = 0,1 \qquad r=a,b \qquad i=1,\ldots,n .$$

Most of the terms in Eq. 2.4 are the same as in Eq. 2.1, except in this case Eq. 2.4b represents the access cost of multi-relation-reduced-single-relation retrievals using redundant information; and Eq. 2.4f represents the update cost for the redundant information. The term $\eta_{i,a,b}{}^r(u_{i,r}{}^r + u_{i,r}{}^{a,b})$ for $r = a,b$ represents the access rate of updates that may have effects on the redundant information. In determining whether the redundant information will be updated, it is necessary to perform a multi-relation retrieval on the relations concerned. In this case, since we know the updates to be made on relation r, we can obtain a copy of all other relations $s \neq r$ and move the copies to node i. This cost is represented by the term $\Sigma_{s \neq r}\, \alpha_{i,s}{}^{a,b}l'_s X_{i,j}{}^s S_{i,j}{}^s$ in Eq. 2.4f. After the updates on the redundant information have been determined, the actual updates, together with the updates on the redundant information are sent to all the nodes which have a copy of the relation. This cost is represented by the term $\Sigma_{l=a,b}\, \xi_{i,t}{}^l l'_t M_{i,j}{}^l Y_j^l$ in Eq. 2.4f.

A similar lemma and theorem can be proved for this problem.

LEMMA 2.2

Optimization problem 2.4 can be partitioned into two independent optimization sub-problems, one for each relation:

(a)
$$\min_{j,\,Y_j^a = 1} \Sigma_{i=1}{}^n\, Q_i^a \min\, S_{i,j}{}^a + \Sigma_{i=1}{}^n \Sigma_{j=1}{}^n\, U_i^a M_{i,j}{}^a Y_j^a$$

$$+ \Sigma_{i=1}{}^n\, F_i^a\, Y_i^a \tag{2.5}$$

where

$$Q_i^a = [q_{i,a}{}^a\, \alpha_{i,a}{}^a + (1 - \gamma_{i,a,b}{}^{a,b})\, q_{i,a,b}{}^{a,b}\, \sigma_{i,a}{}^{a,b}\, \epsilon_{i,a}{}^{a,b}$$

$$+ \gamma_{i,a,b}{}^{a,b}\, q_{i,a,b}{}^{a,b}\, \alpha_{i,a}{}^{a,b} + u_{i,a}{}^{a,b}\, \delta_{i,a}{}^{a,b}\, v_{i,a}{}^{a,b}$$

$$+ u_{i,b}{}^{a,b}\, \delta_{i,b}{}^{a,b}\, v_{i,a}{}^{a,b} + \eta_{i,a,b}{}^b\, (u_{i,b}{}^b + u_{i,b}{}^{a,b})\, \alpha_{i,a}{}^{a,b}]\, l'_a$$

$$U_i^a = [u_{i,a}{}^a\, \beta_{i,a}{}^a + u_{i,a}{}^{a,b}\, \beta_{i,a}{}^{a,b} + \eta_{i,a,b}{}^a\, (u_{i,a}{}^a + u_{i,a}{}^{a,b})\, \xi_{i,a}{}^a$$

$$+ \eta_{i,a,b}{}^b\, (u_{i,b}{}^b + u_{i,b}{}^{a,b})\, \xi_{i,a}{}^a]\, l'_a$$

$$F_i^a = f_{i,a}\, l'_a$$

subject to:

$$\Sigma_{i=1}^{n} \, Y_i^{a} \geqslant 1$$

$$Y_i^{a} = 0,1 \qquad i=1,\ldots,n$$

(b) $\min \Sigma_{i=1}^{n} \, Q_i^{b} \, \min_{j, Y_j^{b}=1} \, S_{i,j}^{b} + \Sigma_{i=1}^{n} \, \Sigma_{j=1}^{n} \, U_i^{b} \, M_{i,j}^{b} \, Y_j^{b}$

$$+ \Sigma_{i=1}^{n} \, F_i^{b} \, Y_i^{b} \qquad\qquad\qquad\qquad (2.6)$$

where

$$Q_i^{b} = [q_{i,b}^{b} \, \alpha_{i,b}^{b} + (1- \gamma_{i,a,b}^{a,b}) \, q_{i,a,b}^{a,b} \, \sigma_{i,b}^{a,b} \, \epsilon_{i,b}^{a,b}$$

$$+ \gamma_{i,a,b}^{a,b} \, q_{i,a,b}^{a,b} \, \alpha_{i,b}^{a,b} + u_{i,a}^{a,b} \, \delta_{i,a}^{a,b} \, v_{i,b}^{a,b}$$

$$+ u_{i,b}^{b} \, \delta_{i,b}^{a,b} \, v_{i,b}^{a,b} + \eta_{i,a,b}^{a} \, (u_{i,a}^{a} + u_{i,a}^{a,b}) \alpha_{i,b}^{a,b}] l_b'$$

$$U_i^{b} = [u_{i,b}^{b} \, \beta_{i,b}^{b} + u_{i,b}^{a,b} \, \beta_{i,b}^{a,b} + \eta_{i,a,b}^{a} \, (u_{i,a}^{a} + u_{i,a}^{a,b}) \, \xi_{i,b}^{b}$$

$$+ \eta_{i,a,b}^{b} \, (u_{i,b}^{b} + u_{i,b}^{a,b}) \, \xi_{i,b}^{b}] l_b'$$

$$F_i^{b} = f_{i,b} \, l_b'$$

subject to:

$$\Sigma_{i=1}^{n} \, Y_i^{b} \geqslant 1$$
$$Y_i^{b} = 0,1 \qquad i=1,\ldots,n.$$

THEOREM 2.2

The general problem of optimizing the placements of multiple relations on a DDB using additional redundant information can be decomposed into multiple sub-problems, one for the placement of each relation.

The proofs of Lemma 2.2 and Theorem 2.2 are very similar to that of Lemma 2.1 and Theorem 2.1 and will not be illustrated here.

We demonstrate the use of this technique in the next section with a simple example.

2.4 A Numerical Example to Illustrate the Use of Redundant Information on a DDB

In this section, we show by the use of a numerical example, the cost improvement when redundant information is introduced in a DDB.

Consider a DCS of 3 nodes with two relations, S and SP, on the DDB. Let S have domains s#(1), sname(10), city(5), inventory(2) and SP have domains s#(1), p#(1)[2]. Assume that S has 500 tuples and SP has 10000 tuples. The following parameters are also assumed:

$$[S_{i,j}] = [M_{i,j}] = \begin{bmatrix} 0 & 1 & 2 \\ 1 & 0 & 1.5 \\ 2 & 1.5 & 0 \end{bmatrix} * 10^{-3}$$

$$f_{i,S} = f_{i,SP} = 0$$

$$l_S = l'_S = 500*18 = 9000 \text{ (words)}[3]$$

$$l_{SP} = l'_{SP} = 10000*2 = 20000 \text{ (words)}[3]$$

Node	Parameters						
i	$q^S_{i,S}$	$u^S_{i,S}$	$u^{S,SP}_{i,S}$	$q^{SP}_{i,SP}$	$u^{SP}_{i,SP}$	$u^{S,SP}_{i,SP}$	$q^{S,SP}_{i,S,SP}$
1	100	20	115	80	120	40	100
2	50	100	50	100	25	35	50
3	75	15	35	50	15	10	75

and for all $i \in \{1,2,3\}$,

$$\alpha_{i,S}^{S} = \alpha_{i,SP}^{SP} = v_{i,S}^{S,SP} = v_{i,SP}^{S,SP} = 0.1$$

$$\epsilon_{i,S}^{S,SP} = \epsilon_{i,SP}^{S,SP} = 0.05$$

---

2. The number in the parenthesis indicates the length in words in each domain.
3. Note that $l_r = l'_r$ (r=S,SP) because in this case, we do not consider the cost of storage on the DDB ($f_{i,r}=0$, $r=S,SP$) and the redundant information usually does not have to be sent over the network in order to process a query.

$$\alpha_{i,S}{}^{S,SP} = \alpha_{i,SP}{}^{S,SP} = 0.3$$

$$\beta_{i,S}{}^{S} = \beta_{i,SP}{}^{SP} = \beta_{i,S}{}^{S,SP} = \beta_{i,SP}{}^{S,SP} = 0.25$$

$$\sigma_{i,S}{}^{S,SP} = \sigma_{i,SP}{}^{S,SP} = 0.6$$

$$\xi_{i,S}{}^{S} = \xi_{i,SP}{}^{SP} = 0.05.$$

These parameters have been chosen based on some estimated distribution of the data stored in the relations and the characteristics of the queries made on these two relations. They have been set independent of the nodes and the relations for easy understanding. The fixed cost of storage on the system has been neglected because the storage cost is usually very small as compared to the communication cost. It is intended to show by this example, the amount of redundant information needed in order for this technique to be cost effective.

In Figures 2.5 and 2.6, two graphs are plotted to show the ratio of cost with redundancy and cost without redundancy against $\delta_{i,r}{}^{S,SP}$[4]. In Figure 2.5, the graph is plotted for various values of $\gamma_{i,S,SP}{}^{S,SP}$[4], with $\eta_{i,S,SP}{}^{r}$[4] fixed at 0.5. Similarly, in Figure 2.6, the graph is plotted for various values of $\eta_{i,S,SP}{}^{r}$[4], with $\gamma_{i,S,SP}{}^{S,SP}$[4] fixed at 0.5. It is seen from these two graphs that whenever sufficient redundant information is added to the DDB so that over half of the non-decomposable queries or updates become decomposable, the resultant operational costs are less than the costs without the use of redundant information. Further, it is seen from Figure 2.6 that when the fraction of updates that will update the redundant information is less than 0.5, there is, in general, a cost improvement.

The results we have shown in the example are for illustration. More detailed evaluations are necessary before any definite conclusions can be drawn.

2.5 Cost Reduction on the Placements of Relations on a DDB by File Partitioning

In section 2.3 we have shown a technique by which the total operational costs can be reduced by decreasing the total retrieval cost and increasing the total update cost. We study in this section, the dual of the previous technique, that is, a technique by which the total operational costs can be

---

4. It is assumed that for r=S, SP, the variables $\delta_{i,r}{}^{S,SP}$, $\eta_{i,S,SP}{}^{r}$ are independent of i and r and the variables $\gamma_{i,S,SP}{}^{S,SP}$ are independent of i.

Figure 2.5. A Plot of Cost Ratio with respect to γ for various values of δ under the use of redundant information (it is assumed that γ, δ and η are independent of $r=S$, SP and i)

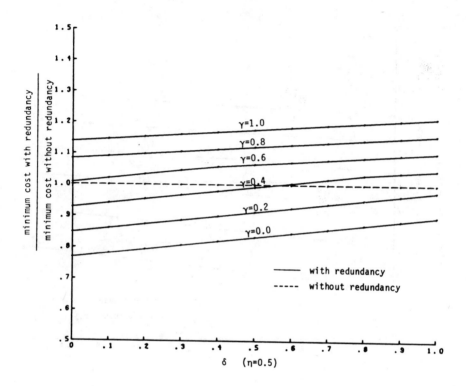

Figure 2.6. A Plot of Cost Ratio with respect to η for various values
of δ under the use of redundant information (it is
assumed that γ, δ and η are independent of $r=S$, SP
and i)

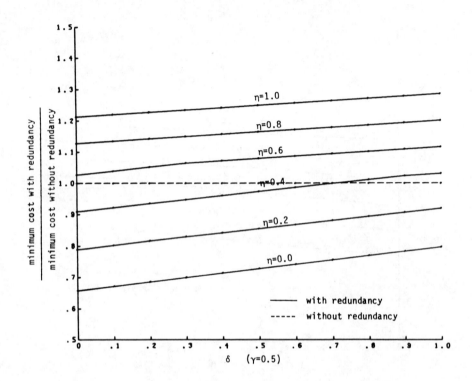

reduced by decreasing the total update cost and increasing the total retrieval cost. Before the technique is described, the characteristics of an update are first studied.

Updates on a relation can broadly be divided into two types. The first type updates only a small segment of the relation and the second type updates all the tuples in the relation. As an example, consider an employee relation. The first type can be an update which increases the salary of a particular employee and the second type can be an update which increases the salary of all the employees in the relation. If the first type is more prevalent, and there is a locality of the updates on the DDB, then the total update cost can be reduced by partitioning the relation into segments and distributing the segments to the various nodes of the DDB where there is a large amount of local updates on the segments. On the other hand, the entire relation usually has to be accessed in a retrieval or in a multi-relation update in which the target information to be updated must first be determined. The relation must be searched tuple by tuple in order to determine the set of tuples satisfying the predicate. If a relation is partitioned and distributed on the DDB, all the segments have to be searched and the results assembled before the retrieval can be made. This cost is likely to be greater than the cost of accessing a copy of the entire relation on the DDB. The effect of file partitioning is, therefore, an increase in the total retrieval cost and a decrease in the total update cost. The use of file partitioning is further illustrated in Figure 2.7.

The problems that are related to file partitioning are twofold: how to partition the relations; and after the relations are partitioned, how to distribute the segments on the DDB. The first problem can be solved by studying the characteristics of the updates made at different nodes of the DCS and partitioning the relation according to these characteristics. There exist algorithms to solve this problem, e.g., by clustering [JAR71, BON64]. We are more concerned with the problem of distributing the segments of the relations on the DDB after they have been partitioned. In this section, the case with no extra redundant information is first considered and the case with additional redundant information is considered in section 2.7. The model developed here is shown for the special case of two relations and is generalized later to the case of more than two relations.

In addition to the symbols defined in section 2.2, we define the following symbols here. Let

$P_a(P_b)$ = number of segments that relation $a(b)$ is partitioned into;

$a_j(b_j)$ = the jth segment of relation $a(b)$, $j = 1, \ldots, P_a(P_b)$;

P = $\{a_1, a_2, \ldots, a_{P_a}\} \cup \{b_1, b_2, \ldots, b_{P_b}\}$.

Figure 2.7. The Retrievals and Updates on a DDB (2 Nodes) With
and Without File Partitioning

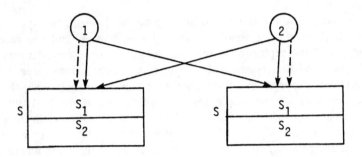

(a) Multiple Copies of Relation S Without File Partitioning

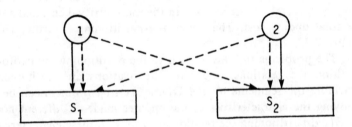

(b) Single Copy of Segments of Relation S With File Partitioning

———▶ Updates

---▶ Retrievals

For single relation queries,

$fr(a_j | q_{i,a}{}^a)[fr(b_j | q_{i,b}{}^b)]$ = fraction of retrievals accessing the *j*th segment of relation *a(b)* given that the retrieval rate is $q_{i,a}{}^a$ $(q_{i,b}{}^b)$;
$fu(a_j | u_{i,a}{}^a)[fu(b_j | u_{i,b}{}^b)]$ = fraction of updates on the *j*th segment of relation *a(b)* given that the update rate is $u_{i,a}{}^a$ $(u_{i,b}{}^b)$;

For multi-relation queries,

$fr(a_j | q_{i,a,b}{}^{a,b})$ $[fr(b_j | q_{i,a,b}{}^{a,b})]$ = fraction of multi-relation retrievals accessing the *j*th segment of relation *a(b)* given that the retrieval rate is $q_{i,a,b}{}^{a,b}$;
$fr(t_j | u_{i,a}{}^{a,b}$ $[fr(t_j | u_{i,b}{}^{a,b})]$ = fraction of multi-relation updates that have to access the *j*th segment of relation *t* ($t = a,b$) in order to determine the actual updates, given that the update rate is $u_{i,a}{}^{a,b}(u_{i,b}{}^{a,b})$;
$fu(a_j | u_{i,a}{}^{a,b})$ $[fu(b_j | u_{i,b}{}^{a,b})]$ = fraction of multi-relation updates on the *j*th segment of relation *a(b)* given that the update rate is $u_{i,a}{}^{a,b}(u_{i,b}{}^{a,b})$.

It is further assumed that the parameters α, β, γ, f are independent of the effects of partitioning. The optimization problem of placing P_a segments of relation *a* and P_b segments of relation *b* on the DDB can be formulated in the following linear program.

min (2.7)

$$\Sigma_{s=a,b} \Sigma_{k=1}{}^{P_s} \Sigma_{i=1}{}^{n} \Sigma_{j=1}{}^{n} q_{i,s}{}^{s} fr(s_k | q_{i,s}{}^{s}) \alpha_{i,s}{}^{s} l_{s_k} X_{i,j}{}^{s_k} S_{i,j}{}^{s} \quad (2.7a)$$

$$+ \Sigma_{s=a,b} \Sigma_{k=1}{}^{P_s} \Sigma_{i=1}{}^{n} \Sigma_{j=1}{}^{n} q_{i,a,b}{}^{a,b} fr(s_k | q_{i,a,b}{}^{a,b})$$

$$\alpha_{i,s}{}^{a,b} l_{s_k} X_{i,j}{}^{s_k} S_{i,j}{}^{s} \quad (2.7b)$$

$$+ \Sigma_{s=a,b} \Sigma_{k=1}{}^{P_s} \Sigma_{i=1}{}^{n} \Sigma_{j=1}{}^{n} u_{i,s}{}^{s} fu(s_k | u_{i,s}{}^{s}) \beta_{i,s}{}^{s} l_{s_k} M_{i,j}{}^{s} Y_{j}{}^{s_k} \quad (2.7c)$$

$$+ \Sigma_{s=a,b} \Sigma_{k=1}{}^{P_s} \Sigma_{i=1}{}^{n} \Sigma_{j=1}{}^{n} u_{i,s}{}^{a,b} [\Sigma_{t=a,b} \Sigma_{e=1}{}^{P_t} fr(t_e | u_{i,s}{}^{a,b})$$

$$v_{i,t}{}^{a,b} l_{t_e} X_{i,j}{}^{t_e} S_{i,j}{}^{t} \quad (2.7d)$$

$$+ fu(s_k | u_{i,s}{}^{a,b}) \beta_{i,s}{}^{a,b} l_{s_k} M_{i,j}{}^{s} Y_{j}{}^{s_k}]$$

$$+ \Sigma_{s=a,b} \, \Sigma_{k=1}^{P_s} \, \Sigma_{i=1}^{n} \, f_{i,s} \, l_{s_k} \, Y_i^{s_k} \qquad\qquad (2.7e)$$

subject to

$$\Sigma_{i=1}^{n} \, Y_i^{p} \geqslant 1 \qquad\qquad (2.7f)$$

$$\Sigma_{j=1}^{n} \, X_{i,j}^{P} = 1 \qquad\qquad (2.7g)$$

$$n Y_j^{p} \geqslant \Sigma_{i=1}^{n} \, X_{i,j}^{P} \geqslant 0 \qquad\qquad (2.7h)$$

$$Y_i^{p} = 0, 1 \qquad\qquad (2.7i)$$

$$1 \leqslant \Sigma_{j=1}^{P_s} \, fr(s_j | q_{i,s}^{s}) \leqslant P_s \qquad\qquad (2.7j)$$

$$1 \leqslant \Sigma_{j=1}^{P_s} \, fr(s_j | q_{i,a,b}^{a,b}) \leqslant P_s \qquad\qquad (2.7k)$$

$$1 \leqslant \Sigma_{j=1}^{P_s} \, fu(s_j | u_{i,s}^{s}) \leqslant P_s \qquad\qquad (2.7l)$$

$$1 \leqslant \Sigma_{j=1}^{P_s} \, fr(s_j | u_{i,t}^{a,b}) \leqslant P_s \qquad\qquad (2.7m)$$

$$1 \leqslant \Sigma_{j=1}^{n} \, fu(s_j | u_{i,s}^{a,b}) \leqslant P_s \qquad\qquad (2.7n)$$

where $s,t \; \epsilon \; \{a,b\}$, $i,j \; \epsilon \; \{1,2, \ldots, n\}$ and $p \; \epsilon \; \{a_1, \ldots, a_{P_a}\} \cup \{b_1, \ldots, b_{P_b}\}$.

Eq. 2.7a to Eq. 2.7i are similar to the corresponding equations in Eq. 2.1. Eq. 2.7j to Eq. 2.7n represent the conditions that one or more of the segments may have to be accessed when a relation is queried. A lemma and theorem similar to Lemma 2.1 and Theorem 2.1 can be proved for this problem.

LEMMA 2.3

Optimization problem 2.7 can be partitioned into $P_a + P_b$ independent optimization sub-problems, one for each segment. The optimization sub-problem for segment s_k where $s \; \epsilon \; \{a,b\}$, $k \; \epsilon \; \{1, \ldots, P_s\}$ is:

$$\min \Sigma_{i=1}^{n} Q_i^{s_k} \min_{j, Y_j^{s_k}=1} S_{i,j}^{s} + \Sigma_{i=1}^{n} \Sigma_{j=1}^{n} U_i^{s_k} M_{i,j}^{s} Y_j^{s_k} + \Sigma_{i=1}^{n} F_i^{s} Y_i^{s_k}$$

$$+ \Sigma_{i=1}^{n} F_i^{s} Y_i^{s_k} \tag{2.8}$$

where

$$Q_i^{s_k} = [q_{i,s}^{s} fr(s_k | q_{i,s}^{s}) \alpha_{i,s}^{s} + q_{i,a,b}^{a,b} fr(s_k | q_{i,a,b}^{a,b}) \alpha_{i,s}^{a,b}$$

$$+ \Sigma_{t=a,b} u_{i,t}^{a,b} fr(s_k | u_{i,t}^{a,b}) v_{i,s}^{a,b}] l_{s_k}$$

$$U_i^{s_k} = [u_{i,s}^{s} fu(s_k | u_{i,s}^{s}) \beta_{i,s}^{s} + u_{i,s}^{a,b} fu(s_k | u_{i,s}^{a,b}) \beta_{i,s}^{a,b}] l_{s_k}$$

$$F_i^{s_k} = f_{i,s} l_{s_k}$$

subject to

$$\Sigma_{i=1}^{n} Y_i^{s_k} \geqslant 1$$

$$Y_i^{s_k} = 0,1 \qquad i=1,\ldots,n.$$

A generalization of Lemma 2.3 is to allow any number of relations in the DDB. This is shown in the following theorem.

THEOREM 2.3

The general problem of optimizing the placements of multiple relations on a DDB using file partitioning can be decomposed into multiple sub-problems, one for the placement of each partition independently.

The proofs of Lemma 2.3 and Theorem 2.3 are very similar to those of Lemma 2.1 and Theorem 2.1 and will not be illustrated here.

We demonstrate the use of this technique in the next section with the example from section 2.4.

2.6 A Numerical Example to Illustrate the Use of File Partitioning on a DDB

Using the same example in section 2.4, we assume that both relations S and SP are partitionable into two segments each, with:

$$P_S = P_{SP} = 2.$$

$$l_{S_1} = l_{S_2} = 4500.$$

$$l_{SP_1} = l_{SP_2} = 10000.$$

We further assume that when a retrieval is made on a relation, all the segments of the relation must be accessed, that is, for $s, t \in \{S, SP\}$, $i \in \{1, 2, 3\}$ and $j \in \{1, 2\}$,

$$fr(s_j | q_{i,s}{}^S) = 1.$$

$$fr(s_j | q_{i,S,SP}{}^{S,SP}) = 1.$$

$$fr(s_j | u_{i,t}{}^{S,SP}) = 1.$$

We are interested in the effects of varying the fraction of updates that have to access multiple segments. For $i \in \{1, 2, ,3\}$, let

$$fu^1 = fu(S_1 | u_{i,S}{}^S) = fu(S_2 | u_{i,S}{}^S) = fu(SP_1 | u_{i,SP}{}^{SP})$$

$$= fu(SP_2 | u_{i,SP}{}^{SP})$$

and

$$fu^2 = fu(S_1 | u_{i,S}{}^{S,SP}) = fu(S_2 | u_{i,S}{}^{S,SP}) = fu(SP_1 | u_{i,SP}{}^{S,SP})$$

$$= fu(SP_2 | u_{i,SP}{}^{S,SP}).$$

That is, the fraction of updates that will access a particular segment of the relation is independent of the relation, but is dependent on the type of the updates, namely, single relation updates or multi-relation updates. The relationship between fu^1 and fu^2 is shown in Figure 2.8. It is seen that the total operational costs after partitioning are always less than the cost without partitioning. However, due to the fact that there is a higher overhead in maintaining a larger number of files on the DDB, all the curves in Figure 2.8 will shift upward. Depending on the additional cost in the overhead, a threshold in fu^1 and fu^2 can be found, below which the scheme is cost-effective.

Figure 2.8. A Plot of Cost Ratio with respect to f_u^1 for various values of f_u^2 under File Partitioning

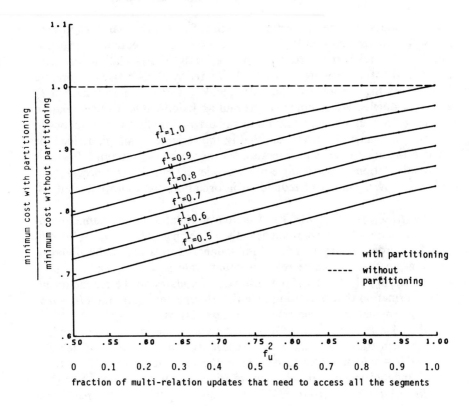

2.7 Cost Reduction on the Placement of Relations on a DDB by Utilizing Redundant Information and File Partitioning

The techniques described in sections 2.3 and 2.5 can be combined together to give a further reduction in the operational costs. Extra redundant information is first added to the relations in the DDB. These relations are then partitioned before they are allocated. Using the symbols defined before, we first discuss the case of two relations, a and b, which are partitioned in P_a and P_b segments. We assume that the multi-relation-reduced-single-relation queries behave in a similar fashion as the original multi-relation queries in accessing a segment of a relation, that is, the variables fr and fu defined for the multi-relation queries are identical for the variables fr and fu defined for the multi-relation-reduced-single-relation queries. Further, it is necessary to define for the updating of redundant information, the following symbols:

$fr^{rd}(t_j \mid u_{i,a}{}^a) [fr^{rd}(t_j \mid u_{i,b}{}^b)] =$ fraction of updates on the redundant information that have to retrieve the jth segment of relation t ($t = a,b$) in order to determine the redundant information to be updated, given that the single relation update rate is $u_{i,a}{}^a$ ($u_{i,b}{}^b$);

$fu^{rd}(t_j \mid u_{i,a}{}^a) [fu^{rd}(t_j \mid u_{i,b}{}^b)] =$ fraction of updates on the redundant information that have to update the jth segment of relation t ($t = a,b$) given that the single relation update rate is $u_{i,a}{}^a$ ($u_{i,b}{}^b$).

$fr^{rd}(t_j \mid u_{i,a}{}^{a,b}) [fr^{rd}(t_j \mid u_{i,b}{}^{a,b})] =$ fraction of updates on the redundant information that have to retrieve the jth segment of relation t ($t = a,b$) in order to determine the redundant information to be updated given that the multi-relation update rate is $u_{i,a}{}^{a,b}$ ($u_{i,b}{}^{a,b}$).

$fu^{rd}(t_j \mid u_{i,a}{}^{a,b}) [fu^{rd}(t_j \mid u_{i,b}{}^{a,b})] =$ fraction of updates on the redundant information that have to update the jth segment of relation t ($t = a,b$) given that the multi-relation update rate is $u_{i,a}{}^{a,b}$ ($u_{i,b}{}^{a,b}$).

$l'_{t_j} =$ size of segment j ($j = 1, \ldots, P_t$) of relation t ($t = a,b$) after the redundant information has been added.

The optimization problem of placing the segments on the DDB is:

min $\hspace{8cm}$ (2.9)

$$\Sigma_{s=a,b} \, \Sigma_{k=1}^{P_s} \, \Sigma_{i=1}^{n} \, \Sigma_{j=1}^{n} \, q_{i,s}{}^s \, fr(s_k \mid q_{i,s}{}^s) \alpha_{i,s}{}^s \, l'_{s_k} \, X_{i,j}{}^{s_k} S_{i,j}{}^s$$

$$+ \Sigma_{s=a,b} \, \Sigma_{k=1}^{P_s} \, \Sigma_{i=1}^{n} \, \Sigma_{j=1}^{n} \, (1-\gamma_{i,a,b}{}^{a,b}) q_{i,a,b}{}^{a,b} fr(s_k \mid q_{i,a,b}{}^{a,b})$$

$$\sigma_{i,s}{}^{a,b} \, \epsilon_{i,s}{}^{a,b} \, l'_{s_k} \, X_{i,j}{}^{s_k} S_{i,j}{}^s$$

$$+ \sum_{s=a,b} \sum_{k=1}^{P_s} \sum_{i=1}^{n} \sum_{j=1}^{n} \gamma_{i,a,b}^{a,b} \, q_{i,a,b}^{a,b} \, fr(s_k | q_{i,a,b}^{a,b})$$

$$\alpha_{i,s}^{a,b} \, l'_{s_k} \, X_{i,j}^{s_k} \, S_{i,j}^{s}$$

$$+ \sum_{s=a,b} \sum_{k=1}^{P_s} \sum_{i=1}^{n} \sum_{j=1}^{n} u_{i,s}^{s} \, fu(s_k | u_{i,s}^{s}) \beta_{i,s}^{s} \, l'_{s_k} \, M_{i,j}^{s} \, Y_{j}^{s_k}$$

$$+ \sum_{s=a,b} \sum_{k=1}^{P_s} \sum_{i=1}^{n} \sum_{j=1}^{n} u_{i,s}^{a,b} \, [\delta_{i,s}^{a,b}$$

$$\sum_{t=a,b} \sum_{e=1}^{P_t} \, fr(t_e | u_{i,s}^{a,b}) \, v_{i,t}^{a,b} \, l'_{t_e} \, X_{i,j}^{t_e} \, S_{i,j}^{t}$$

$$+ fu(s_k | u_{i,s}^{a,b}) \beta_{i,s}^{a,b} \, l'_{s_k} \, M_{i,j}^{s} \, Y_{j}^{s_k}]$$

$$+ \sum_{s=a,b} \sum_{i=1}^{n} \sum_{j=1}^{n} \eta_{i,a,b}^{s} \, u_{i,s}^{s} \, [\sum_{t \neq s} \sum_{e=1}^{P_t} fr^{rd}(t_e | u_{i,s}^{s})$$

$$\alpha_{i,t}^{a,b} \, l'_{t_e} \, X_{i,j}^{t_e} \, S_{i,j}^{t}$$

$$+ \sum_{t=a,b} \sum_{e=1}^{P_t} fu^{rd}(t_e | u_{i,s}^{s}) \xi_{i,t}^{t} \, l'_{t_e} \, M_{i,j}^{t} \, Y_{j}^{t_e}]$$

$$+ \sum_{s=a,b} \sum_{i=1}^{n} \sum_{j=1}^{n} \eta_{i,a,b}^{s} \, u_{i,s}^{a,b} \, [\sum_{t \neq s} \sum_{e=1}^{P_t} fr^{rd}(t_e | u_{i,s}^{a,b})$$

$$\alpha_{i,t}^{a,b} \, l'_{t_e} \, X_{i,j}^{t_e} \, S_{i,j}^{t}$$

$$+ \sum_{t=a,b} \sum_{l=1}^{P_t} fu^{rd}(t_e | u_{i,s}^{a,b}) \xi_{i,t}^{t} \, l'_{t_e} \, M_{i,j}^{t} \, Y_{j}^{t_e}]$$

$$+ \sum_{s=a,b} \sum_{k=1}^{P_s} \sum_{i=1}^{n} f_{i,s} \, l'_{s_k} \, Y_{i}^{s_k}$$

subject to the constraints 2.7f to 2.7n with four additional constraints:

$$1 \leqslant \sum_{j=1}^{P_s} fr^{rd}(s_j | u_{i,t}^{t}) \leqslant P_s \qquad s,t \in \{a,b\}, i \in \{1,\dots,n\}$$

$$1 \leqslant \sum_{j=1}^{P_s} fu^{rd}(s_j | u_{i,t}^{t}) \leqslant P_s \qquad s,t \in \{a,b\}, i \in \{1,\dots,n\}$$

$$1 \leqslant \sum_{j=1}^{P_s} fr^{rd}(s_j | u_{i,t}^{a,b}) \leqslant P_s \qquad s,t \in \{a,b\}, i \in \{1,\dots,n\}$$

$$1 \leqslant \Sigma_{j=1}^{P_s} \, {}^s\!fu^{rd}(s_j | u_{i,t}{}^{a,b}) \leqslant P_s \qquad s,t \in \{a,b\}, i \in \{1, \ldots, n\},$$

The explanation of each term of Eq. 2.9 is similar to the corresponding term of Eq. 2.7.

A lemma and theorem similar to Lemma 2.1 and Theorem 2.1 can be proved for this problem.

LEMMA 2.4

Optimization problem 2.9 can be partitioned into $P_a + P_b$ independent optimization sub-problems, one for each segment. The optimization sub-problem for segment s_k where $s \in \{a,b\}$, $k \in \{1, \ldots, P_s\}$ is

$$\min \Sigma_{i=1}^n \, Q_i{}^{s_k} \min_{j, Y_j^{s_k}=1} \, S_{i,j}{}^s + \Sigma_{i=1}^n \Sigma_{j=1}^n \, U_i{}^{s_k} M_{i,j}{}^s \, Y_j{}^{s_k}$$

$$+ \Sigma_{i=1}^n \, F_i{}^s \, Y_i{}^{s_k} \tag{2.10}$$

where

$$Q_i{}^{s_k} = [q_{i,s}{}^s \, fr(s_k | q_{i,s}{}^s) \, \alpha_{i,s}{}^s + (1 - \gamma_{i,a,b}{}^{a,b}) \, q_{i,a,b}{}^{a,b} \, fr(s_k | q_{i,a,b}{}^{a,b})$$

$$\sigma_{i,s}{}^{a,b} \, \epsilon_{i,s}{}^{a,b} + \gamma_{i,a,b}{}^{a,b} \, q_{i,a,b}{}^{a,b} \, fr(s_k | q_{i,a,b}{}^{a,b}) \alpha_{i,s}{}^{a,b}$$

$$+ \Sigma_{t=a,b} \, u_{i,t}{}^{a,b} \, \delta_{i,t}{}^{a,b} \, fr(s_k | u_{i,t}{}^{a,b}) \nu_{i,s}{}^{a,b}$$

$$+ \eta_{i,a,b}{}^{\bar{s}} \, u_{i,\bar{s}}{}^{\bar{s}} \, fr^{rd}(s_k | u_{i,\bar{s}}{}^{\bar{s}}) \alpha_{i,s}{}^{a,b}$$

$$+ \eta_{i,a,b}{}^{\bar{s}} \, u_{i,\bar{s}}{}^{a,b} \, fr^{rd}(s_k | u_{i,\bar{s}}{}^{a,b}) \alpha_{i,s}{}^{a,b}] \, l'_{s_k}$$

$$U_i{}^{s_k} = [u_{i,s}{}^s \, fu(s_k | u_{i,s}{}^s) \beta_{i,s}{}^s + u_{i,s}{}^{a,b} \, fu(s_k | u_{i,s}{}^{a,b}) \beta_{i,s}{}^{a,b}$$

$$+ \Sigma_{t=a,b} \, \eta_{i,a,b}{}^t \, u_{i,t}{}^t \, fu^{rd}(s_k | u_{i,t}{}^t) \xi_{i,s}{}^s$$

$$+ \Sigma_{t=a,b} \, \eta_{i,a,b}{}^t \, u_{i,t}{}^{a,b} \, fu^{rd}(s_k | u_{i,t}{}^{a,b}) \xi_{i,s}{}^s] \, l'_{s_k}$$

$$F_i^{s_k} = f_{i,s} \, l'_{s_k}$$

$\bar{s}, t \in \{S, SP\}$ and $t \neq s$

subject to

$$\Sigma_{i=1}^n \, Y_i^{s_k} \geqslant 1$$

$$Y_i^{s_k} = 0,1 \qquad i = 1, \ldots, n.$$

A generalization of Lemma 2.4 is to allow any number of relations in the DDB. This is shown in the following theorem.

THEOREM 2.4

The general problem of optimizing the placements of multiple relations on a DDB using additional redundant information and file partitioning can be decomposed into multiple sub-problems, one for the placement of each partition.

    The proofs of Lemma 2.4 and Theorem 2.4 are very similar to those of Lemma 2.1 and Theorem 2.1 and will not be illustrated here.

    The next section demonstrates the use of the combined technique with the same example discussed in section 2.4

2.8 A Numerical Example to Illustrate the Use of Redundant Information and File Partitioning on a DDB

Using the same values defined in sections 2.4 and 2.6, we further assume for $s, t \in \{S, SP\}$, $i \in \{1,2,3\}$ and $j \in \{1,2\}$, that

$$fr^{rd}(t_j | u_{i,s}^{s}) = 1$$

$$fr^{rd}(t_j | u_{i,s}^{a,b}) = 1$$

$$fu^1 = fu^{rd}(s_i | u_{i,s}^{s}) = fu^{rd}(s_i | u_{i,t}^{t})$$

$$fu^2 = fu^{rd}(s_i | u_{i,s}^{S,SP}) = fu^{rd}(s_i | u_{i,t}^{S,SP}).$$

Figure 2.9. A Plot of Cost Ratio with respect to γ for various values of δ under the use of Redundancy and Partitioning $(f_u{}^1=f_u{}^2=0.75)$

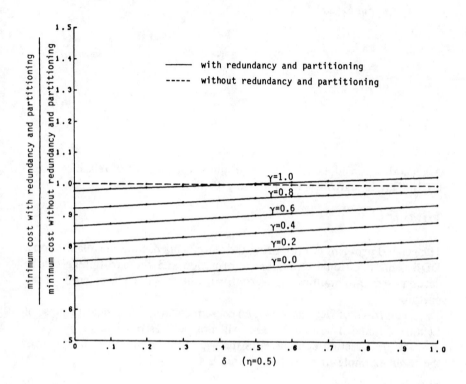

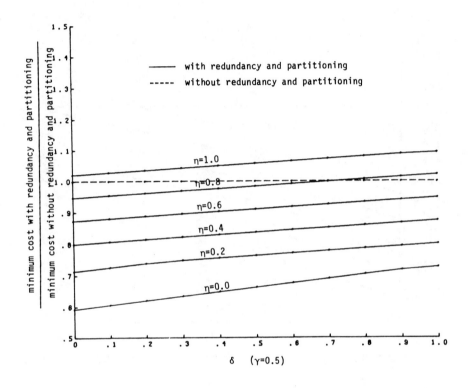

Figure 2.10. A Plot of Cost Ratio with respect to η for various values of δ under the use of Redundancy and Partitioning ($f_u{}^1 = f_u{}^2 = 0.75$)

Figure 2.11. A Plot of Cost Ratio with respect to f_u^1 for various values of f_u^2 under the use of Redundancy and Partitioning ($\delta=\eta=\gamma=0.5$)

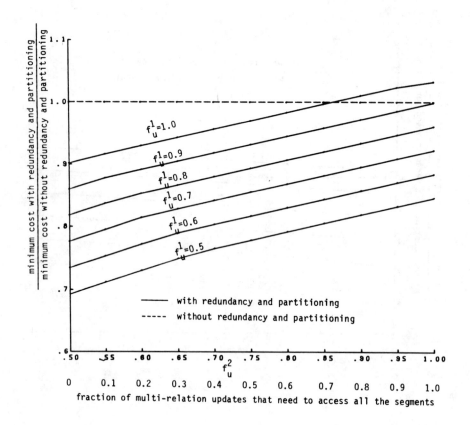

Figure 2.12. A Plot of Cost Ratio with respect to f_u^1 for various
values of f_u^2 under the use of Redundancy and
Partitioning ($\delta=\eta=\gamma=0.4$)

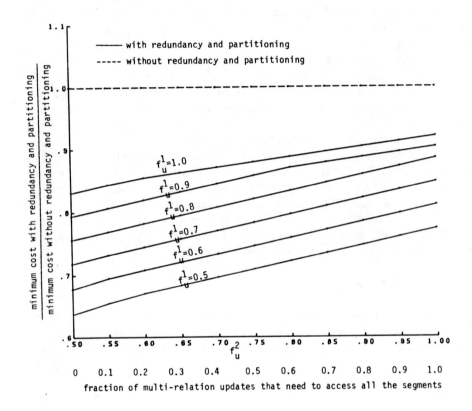

The evaluations of the combined technique are shown in Figures 2.9 to 2.12. Comparing Figures 2.9 and 2.10 with Figures 2.5 and 2.6 under the assumption of $fu^1=fu^2=0.75$ (that is, 50% of the updates have to access the two segments together), it is seen that the combined technique gives a larger cost decrease than when redundancy is used alone. In fact, as seen from Figures 2.9 and 2.10, it is "almost" true that the combined technique is always more cost effective than the case when none of the techniques are used. On the other hand, the curves plotted in Figure 2.11 where $\delta=\eta=\gamma=0.5$, have a higher cost ratio than the curves plotted in Figure 2.8. This means that the use of the combined technique is worse than the case when partitioning is used alone. The explanation for this is because there is a large update cost for the additional redundant information and this is not offset by the cost decrease due to partitioning. However, if sufficient redundant information can be added to the system so that the retrieval cost can be further reduced, the total operational costs may drop. This is shown in Figure 2.12, where $\delta=\eta=\gamma$ have been reduced to 0.4. The curves in Figure 2.12 indicate a smaller cost than the curves in Figure 2.8.

We conclude that the combined technique is always better than the technique of using redundancy alone and is better than the partitioning technique only when δ, γ and η are "small enough."

2.9   Conclusion

In this chapter, we have studied the problem of optimal relation placements on a distributed relational database. The objective of the problem is to minimize the total operational costs of the system and to allow query decomposition to be effected more efficiently. The type of queries that can be made on a distributed relational database are classified. It is seen that non-decomposable queries cause a lot of communication overhead on the system.

Two techniques and a combination of these two techniques are analyzed in this chapter. By pre-analyzing the type of queries made on the DDB and the probability distribution of the data in the relations, the first technique introduces additional redundant information on the DDB so that non-decomposable queries can be made decomposable. The result is a decrease in the total retrieval cost and an increase in the total update cost. The second technique partitions the relations on the DDB into smaller segments which results in a decrease in the total update cost and an increase in the total retrieval cost. The third technique combines the above two techniques. The total operational costs drop if the total cost increase is offset by the total cost decrease. It is proven that the problem of optimal relation (or segment of relation) placement on a DDB can be decomposed into multiple sub-problems, one for the placement of each relation (or segment). The underlying assumption about this decomposition is that multi-relation queries are always processed at a single node rather than in a sequence. The result is a significant reduction in the complexity of the optimization problem. A simple example is used to illustrate some of the properties of these techniques. It must also be noted that a lot of generality is introduced in the development of these techniques and a lot of parameters are defined. However, most of these parameters are identical in general, and therefore, as illustrated in the examples, the number of parameters to be estimated on the system is relatively small.

After decomposing the placements of multiple relations into the placements of individual relations, it is necessary to study algorithms to perform the placements. This is the topic of discussion in Chapter 3.

3

The Placement and Migration of Multiple Copies of a File on a DCS

3.1 Introduction

In the previous chapter, we studied the placement of multiple relations on a DCS and decomposed the problem into multiple sub-problems of placing multiple copies of each relation independently. In this chapter, we develop the theory and algorithms to place and to migrate multiple copies of a single file on the DCS. This is done by first showing that a limited version of the file allocation problem and the dynamic file allocation problem (or file migration problem), which have been studied extensively in computer science, are isomorphic to two equally well known problems in operations research, called the single commodity warehouse location problem and the single commodity dynamic warehouse location problem. Due to this isomorphism, it is found that many techniques which have been developed for one problem can be applied to solve the other problem. Further, it is found that some techniques developed for one problem match very closely with techniques developed for the other. The implications of such a proof of isomorphism are further shown in sections 3.6 and 3.7. By combining some conditions developed in both the file allocation problem and warehouse location problem, we have developed a file placement heuristic which performs better than other heuristics proposed. The heuristic is tested on sample problems whose optimal solutions have been established previously in the literature. In studying the file migration problem, we proved that it is NP-complete and developed some conditions to indicate when file migration should be carried out.

3.2 Definition of the Problem

On a DCS, one of the important problems is to distribute the files on the different computers so that they can be accessed efficiently. The optimal file allocation problem, which was first studied by Chu [CHU69], is defined as follows: given a number of computers that process common information files, how can one allocate the files so that the allocation yields minimum overall operating costs. This problem is directed toward the optimal allocation of multiple files on a multiprocessor system. Subsequently, a lot of work has been done in partitioning the multiple file allocation problem to multiple single file allocation sub-problems, e.g. [CAS72, LEV74, MOR77, RAM79]. This single file allocation problem has been coined by Eswaran as the file allocation problem (FAP) [ESW74]. A more general problem is the dynamic file allocation problem (DFAP) or the file migration problem in which the files are allowed to migrate over time in order to adapt to changing access requirements. It is usually assumed that the period for migration is fixed ahead of time.

There are others who have studied variations of the general process and file allocation problem. Among them are Stone and Jenny, who have studied the allocations of processes on a multi-processor system [STO77, STO78a, STO78b, JEN77, HOF78]; Loomis and Popek, who have introduced additional parameters such as the capability of a node on their model [LOO75, LOO76]; Mahmoud and Riordon, who have considered jointly the file placements and capacity assignments for links [MAH76]. We concentrate in this chapter on the FAP defined by Eswaran (multiple copies of single file allocation problem) and the DFAP (an extension of FAP in which the placements vary over time).

3.3   Motivations for File Placement and Migration

The major reason that multiple copies of a file are allocated to a limited part of the system at certain times is because users have localities of access. At any particular time, a file may be used by a group of users, and it will continue to be used by the same group for a certain length of time. For a particular user, the file that he wants to access may be available locally, in which case, he can access the file with very little cost. If the file is not available locally, he would have to pay a cost in terms of delay in accessing the file and also additional traffic in the network before he can make the access. It is under this situation that we should consider moving a copy of the file to his node. Introducing a new copy would also increase the cost in terms of storage space and the extra overhead in locking and concurrency control. Therefore, the decision of whether to introduce a new copy of a file involves a balance of the cost between the two cases.

The costs, such as communication costs and storage costs, are a function of the topology of the system, the storage sub-system at a node, the type of communication protocols used, and, most importantly, the extensiveness of usage at a particular node. Some examples of the tariff for the usage of the Telenet Data Communication Network are shown in Table 3.1 [TEL78]. For example, suppose the user uses a public dial-in service with local dial at 1200 bps, the cost that he has to pay (assuming 100% line utilization with 30% overhead) is $4.009 for 1 Kbyte of data. On the other hand, the storage costs on the system, with the advances of low cost mass storage, are much smaller as compared with the communication costs. As an example, it costs $1.00/month to store 24 Kbytes of data on the disk of the CDC 6400 at the University of California, Berkeley. Therefore, the minimization of communication traffic on the DCS, in the expense of using additional storage by having multiple copies of the data, is a more important problem.

Before we show the proof of the isomorphism, we survey in the next two sections, some of the previous work on file allocation and warehouse location.

Table 3.1. Examples of Communication Costs on Telenet Data Communication Network (July 1, 1978) [TEL78]

Type of Service	Port Speed	Installation Charge ($)	Usage Charge ($)
Dedicate Access Facilities	50-300 bps 1200 bps 9600 bps	400 500 800	300/month 340/month 1100/month
Public Dial-in Service	Local Dial 110-300 bps Local Dial 1200 bps In-WATS 110-300 bps In-WATS 1200 bps	0 0 0 0	3.25/hr* 3.25/hr* 15.00/hr 15.00/hr
Private Dial-in Service	110-300 bps 1200 bps TWX	320 340 300	160/month* 215/month* 210/month*
Private Dial-out Service	75-300 bps TWX	420 420	300/month* 300/month*

3.4 Previous Work on the File Allocation Problem

Most of the previous work on file allocation is based on static distribution, that is, the allocation does not change with time. A typical method in dynamic distribution involves the application of a static algorithm whenever need arises. Levin has applied dynamic programming to migrate copies of a file over a multi-period horizon [LEV74]. He has also developed some conditions in order to reduce the number of solution vectors that have to be generated in each period. However, the static algorithms are usually very expensive to run in real time. Grapa and Belford remarked that a particular solution to this problem solved a thirty node problem in one hour on an

Table 3.2. A Summary of the Previous work in File Placement/Migration

	Mathematical Programming & Exhaustive Searches					Heuristic	
	Chu [CHU69]	Casey [CAS72]	Levin & Morgan [LEV74, LEV75, MOR77]	Ghosh [GHO78]	Foster et. al. [FOS77]	Loomis & Popek [LOO75, LOO76]	Mahmoud & Riordon [MAH78]
	Complete relations among objects; File access is poisson.	All objects independent	Only program-data relations exist between objects.	All objects independent.	Star network; All objects independent.	Complete Probabilistic relations among objects.	Independent objects; Query and return traffic divided equally among allocated nodes.
	Storage cost; Transmission cost; File length; Request rate between files; Update rate between files; Maximum allowable access time; Storage capacity.	Storage cost; Query transmission cost; Update transmission cost; Query rate between nodes; Update rate between nodes.	Communication cost for query; Communication cost for update; Traffic rate for query/update from a node to a file via a program; Inter-period file migration cost.	Data base with multiple target segment types; Queries with multiple target segment types.	Queueing time & service time for transactions; Storage capacity; Average number of messages in network; Average local processing; Average file length; Access frequency; Hardware.	Inter-node transmission cost; Node capability; File length; Processing needs of file; Probability of a request accessing an object; Probability that a request/update	Communication cost; File storage cost; Query/update traffic & corresponding return traffic for each file at each node; Availability requirements.

Integer Programming	Path search on cost graph	Path search on cost graph; dynamic programming	Combinatorial search through possible solutions	Queueing network algorithm; Integer programming	Clustering	Add-drop heuristic
				software characteristics.	is incident on a node; Probability of 2 objects processed in parallel.	
Algorithm very complex; Consider delay from network queueing approach.	Algorithm efficient; Independence of objects reduces allocation of multiple files into single file.	Algorithm efficient; Definite access relations among objects reduce the allocation of multiple files to single file; Define conditions to reduce dynamic programming search	Maximize number of segments that query can retrieve in parallel from different nodes; Do not model communication delays.	Minimize difference from optimal branching probabilities; Algorithm complex.	Dynamic network behavior ignored; Maximize potential for parallelism.	Obtain both capacity assignment for links & file placements; Should consider query to be routed to nearest node & not distributed equally among all nodes.

IBM 360/91 computer [GRA77b]. The difficulty in optimization is also exemplified in [SIC77]. Moreover, the problem has been shown to be NP-complete [ESW74], i.e., a class of problems for which there is no known optimal algorithm with a computation time which increases polynomially with the size of the problem [KAR72]. The computation times for all known optimal algorithms for this class of problem increase exponentially with the problem size, i.e., if n represents the size of the problem, then the computation time goes up as k^n where $k > 1$. A summary of the previous work in file allocation is shown in Table 3.2. Some of these studies introduce additional constraints on the model (e.g. link capacity, node capability). Basically, the algorithms for statically allocating multiple copies of a single file can be divided into two types: (1) mathematical programming and exhaustive searches, and (2) heuristics.

(1) Mathematical Programming and Exhaustive Searches

This technique has been used by Chu [CHU69], Casey [CAS72], Levin and Morgan [LEV74, LEV75, MOR77], and Mahmoud and Riordon [MAH76]. Using the notations defined in Chapter 2, and repeated here in Table 3.3, the formulation of the FAP is as follows[1]:

Table 3.3. Mapping between the Defined Notations in this Study and Casey's Notations [CAS72]

Notations defined in this thesis for file a	Casey's notations	Explanation
I	I	= index set of nodes with a copy of the file;
n	n	= number of nodes in the DCS;
U_j	ψ_j	= update load originating at node j per unit time;
Q_j	λ_j	= query load originating at node j per unit time;
$S_{j,k}$	$d_{j,k}$	= cost of communication of one query unit from j to k;
$M_{j,k}$	$d_{j,k}$	= cost of communication of one update unit from j to k;
F_k	σ_k	= storage cost of file at k per unit time.

---

1. Since we are considering a single file a, and without ambiguity, all the subscripts and superscripts for a will be deleted in the formulation.

An optimal allocation for a given file is then defined as an index set I which minimizes the cost function.

$$C(I) = \sum_{j=1}^{n} [\sum_{k \in I} U_j M_{j,k} + Q_j \min_{k \in I} S_{j,k}] + \sum_{k \in I} F_k.$$

By defining a control variable Y_j such that

$$Y_j = \begin{cases} 0 & j \notin I \\ 1 & j \in I \end{cases}.$$

The cost function can be written as:

$$C(I) = \sum_{j=1}^{n} [\sum_{k=1}^{n} U_j M_{j,k} Y_k + Q_j \min_{k \in I} S_{j,k}] + \sum_{k=1}^{n} F_k Y_k.$$

The optimization problem for file placements is:

min

$$C(I) = \sum_{j=1}^{n} Q_j \min_{k \in I} S_{j,k} + \sum_{k=1}^{n} G_k Y_k \qquad (3.1)$$

subject to

$$Y_k = 0 \text{ or } 1 \text{ (integer)} \quad k = 1,...,n$$

and

$$G_k = F_k + \sum_{j=1}^{n} U_j M_{j,k}. \qquad (3.2)$$

The quantity G_k has been introduced as Z_k in [GRA77b]. Optimization problem (3.1) can be solved by using integer programming techniques [GEO72]. Casey [CAS72] and Levin and Morgan [LEV74, MOR77] have used the hypercube technique to enumerate over a reduced set of possible solutions in order to find the optimum. However, the approach of using integer programming or exhaustive enumeration is only suitable when the problem size is small. Due to this difficulty, Grapa and Belford have done some pioneering work in developing three simple conditions to check whether a copy of a file should be placed at a node [GRA77b]. This reduces the complexity of the problem tremendously because many alternatives can be eliminated.

(2) Heuristics

Heuristics are "reasonable" search strategies which do not guarantee that the optimum solution can be found. Heuristics are usually interactive algorithms. A feasible solution can be generated. Users or some decision algorithm then have to decide whether to improve the solution or not and how to improve it. The decision algorithm is usually an add-drop algorithm in which perturbations are induced on the existing solution to see if a better solution can be obtained. Three of the most commonly used heuristics are (1) hierarchical designs; (2) clustering algorithms; and (3) add-drop algorithms.

(a) Hierarchical designs

This is a heuristic procedure in which attention is first restricted to the more important features of a system. In a file allocation problem, attention can first be restricted to geographical regions. After analysis has been performed and the files have been distributed to different geographical regions, attention can be directed to the less important details such as allocating files within a geographical region. This stepwise refinement procedure can continue down many levels. At each level of optimization, it is hoped that the effects on the optimization of the current level from the levels above and the levels below are very small. Nevertheless, iterations and design cycles may exist to refine the solution.

(b) Clustering algorithms

Clustering algorithms are horizontal design processes which have an objective similar to hierarchical algorithms, namely, to reduce the complexity of the analysis in a large system. In a DDB, clusters can be formed from the geographical distribution of access frequencies. The files are then allocated to clusters. The file allocation within a cluster may further be refined as in hierarchical algorithms [LOO75, LOO76].

(c)   Add-drop algorithms

In applying this algorithm, a feasible distribution of files is first found. The total cost of the system can be improved by successive addition or deletion of file copies. When a feasible solution with a lower cost is found, it is adopted as a new starting solution and the process continues. Eventually, a local optimum is reached in which any new addition or deletion does not reduce the cost. The whole procedure can be repeated with a different starting feasible solution and several local optima can be obtained. By taking the minimum of all the local minima obtained, it is hoped that we can get very close to the global optimum [MAH76].

The disadvantages of all these heuristics are that they usually find a local optimum instead of a global optimum and the validation of the performance is very difficult. The goodness of a heuristic is often measured by its computational complexity and by its average and worst case behavior. Because the average and the worst case performance are difficult to solve analytically, evaluations are generally done by simulations. Therefore, it is possible that the heuristic performs satisfactorily for some example problems, but it may perform unpredictably for some other problems. Using the add-drop principle, a heuristic for the FAP is shown in section 3.8.

3.5 Previous Work on the Single Commodity Warehouse Location Problem

The problem of warehouse location has been studied extensively by operation researchers. As early as 1951, Dantzig used the simplex method to solve the transportation problem [DAN51]. In 1958, Baumol described a problem called the warehouse location problem [BAU58]. The problem was then studied by many other people. There are several variations of the problem and all of them consider a single type of commodity.

(1) Simple plant location problem:

Given a set of plants which can supply customers with goods and with no constraints on the amount shipped from any source, the problem is to determine the geographical pattern of plants' locations which are most profitable to the company. The optimization is done by equating the marginal cost of warehouse operation with the transportation cost savings and incremental profits resulting from more rapid delivery. This problem has been studied in [MAN64, EFR66, SPI69, SNY71, ALC76]. Manne studied the use of "steepest ascent one point move algorithm" [MAN64]. Efroymson and Ray, Spielberg, Alcouffe and Muratet studied enumerative optimal algorithms [EFR66, SPI69, ALC76]. Snyder studied a special case of the plant location problem in which the paths connecting two plant locations lie on a rectangular grid [SYN71].

(2) Single Commodity Warehouse Location Problem (SCWLP):

Given a set of factories, a set of customers, and a set of possible warehouse locations, the problem is to locate the warehouses so that the fixed and the operational costs of the system are minimum. A special form of the problem is to neglect the transportation costs from the factories to the warehouses and to consider only the transportation costs from the warehouses to the customers. This problem then becomes the simple plant location problem and has been studied in [KUE63, FEL66, KHU72, ERL78, COR77]. Keuhn and Hamburger developed the add-drop heuristic for the problem [KUE63]. Feldman and Ray extended Keuhn and Hamburger's work to include non-linear fixed costs [FEL66]. Khumawala further extended Efroymson and Ray's work [EFR66] and applied a branch and bound algorithm to solve the problem [KHU72]. A linear programming dual formulation was proposed by Erlenkotter [ERL78] which produces optimal solutions when augmented with a branch and bound technique. Cornuejols, Fisher, and Nembauser proposed a greedy algorithm for the bank account location problem with a proved worse case bound [COR77].

(3) Single Commodity Dynamic Warehouse
    Location Problem (SCDWLP):

This is a dynamic version of the simple plant location problem or the warehouse location problem, except that the locations of plants or ware-houses are allowed to change over a planning horizon of r periods in order to adapt to the changing demands of the customers. This problem, first proposed by Francis [FRA63], has been studied in [WES73, ERL74, SWE76, RAO77]. Wesolowsky and Erlenkotter studied the single facility migration problem [WES72, ERL74]. Sweenly and Tatham applied dynamic programming to solve the multi-facility migration problem [SWE76]. Rao and Rutenberg studied a dynamic multi-location problem in which time is continuous and demand can change at different rates [RAO77].

(4) Capacitated warehouse location problem:

Consider a set of warehouses with a finite and fixed capacity; the problem is to determine the warehouses' locations so that the customers' needs can be satisfied and the operational costs of the system are minimum. This problem has been studied in [SA69, GIG73, AKI77]. Sa, Akinc and Khumawala solved the problem using a branch and bound technique [SA69, AKI77].

Giglio solved a special case of the SCDWLP in which capacity constraints are taken into account and demands are assumed to be growing at a decreasing rate.

(5) Quadratic assignment problem:

Given a set of plants in which certain fixed quantities of a single type of commodity are to be shipped between the plants, and a set of possible plant locations, the problem is to assign the plants to locations so that the total operational costs of the system are minimum. This problem appears in [KOO57, GIL62, ARM63, LAW63, HIL66b, GRA70, RIT72]. Armour and Buffa have presented a heuristic which considered pairwise exchanges of work centers and locations [ARM63]. Gilmore and Lawler have developed optimal algorithms which are computationally feasible for small problems [GIL62, LAW63]. Lawler's solution requires a large number of linear assignment problems to be solved. Hiller and Connors modified Gilmore and Lawler's algorithms and obtained a more efficient but sub-optimal algorithm [HIL66b]. Graves and Whinston solved the problem using a probabilistic branch and bound algorithm [GRA70].

Some of the problems defined above are more general than others. In fact, problem (1) is a subset of problem (2) which in turn is a subset of problem (3). Problem (4) also contains problems (1) and (2). We are concerned in this paper with problems (1), (2), and (3). The formulations of problems (1) and (2) are identical. Using the notations of Efroymson and Khumawala [EFR66, KHU72], the SCWLP, with m potential warehouses (with unlimited capacity) and n customers, can be formulated as a mixed integer program as follows.

minimize

$$Z = \Sigma_{i,j} \; D_j t_{i,j} X_{i,j} + \Sigma_i \; F_i Y_i$$

subject to

$$\Sigma_{i \epsilon N_j} \; X_{i,j} = 1 \qquad j = 1, \ldots, n$$

$$0 \le \Sigma_{j \epsilon P_i} \; X_{i,j} \le n_i Y_i \qquad i = 1, \ldots, m$$

$$Y_i = 0 \text{ or } 1 \text{ (integer)} \qquad i = 1, \ldots, m$$

where

$t_{i,j}$ = the per unit cost which includes the FOB cost at the warehouse
(*i*), the warehouse handling cost and the transportation cost from
the warehouse to the customer (*j*);
D_j = the demand of customer *j*;
$X_{i,j}$ = the portion of D_j supplied from warehouse *i*;
F_i = the fixed cost associated with warehouse *i*;
N_j = set of warehouses which can supply customer *j*;
P_i = set of those customers that can be supplied by warehouse *i*;
n_i = number of elements in P_i;

$$Y_i = \begin{cases} 1 & \text{if warehouse exists at site } i. \\ 0 & \text{otherwise} \end{cases}$$

We assume that $m=n$ and that every warehouse can supply every customer.
Let:

I = index set of sites with a warehouse.

It has been shown in [ALC76] for $j=1, \ldots, n$ that:

$$X_{i,j} = \begin{cases} 1 & \text{if } t_{i,j} = \min_{k \in I} t_{k,j}, \; i \in I \\ 0 & \text{otherwise}. \end{cases}$$

That is, the commodity will be shipped to a customer from a warehouse with
the minimum transportation costs. The optimization problem can be
rewritten as:

minimize

$$Z = \Sigma_{j=1}^{n} D_j \min_{k \in I} t_{k,j} + \Sigma_{i=1}^{n} F_i Y_i \qquad (3.3)$$

subject to

$$Y_i = 0,1 \; (\textit{integer}) \qquad i=1,\ldots,n.$$

3.6   The Isomorphism between File Allocation and Single Commodity Warehouse Location

After defining the (D)FAP and the SC(D)WLP, we are ready to prove the
following theorem.

THEOREM 3.1

The FAP and the SCWLP are isomorphic and the DFAP and the SCDWLP are isomorphic.

Proof

The theorem can be proved by associating the variables of the FAP with the variables of the SCWLP and similarly, the variables of the DFAP with the variables of the SCDWLP. This association is shown in Table 3.4. An alternative way to prove the theorem is to notice that Eq. 3.1 and 3.3 are actually identical with only a change of variables. The mapping of the variables is also shown in Table 3.4.

Q.E.D.

Table 3.4. Mapping between the (D)FAP and the SC(D)WLP

FAP		SCWLP	
Locations of computers	n	Possible warehouse sites	n
Locations of file	I	Locations of warehouse	I
Access for a file		Commodity flow	
Amount of access at j	Q_j	Customer demand at j	D_j
Per unit cost of communicating one query unit from j to k	$S_{j,k}$	Per unit cost of shipping commodity from plant to warehouse j and from warehouse j to customer k	$t_{j,k}$
File storage cost + multiple update cost for file at node k	C_k	Fixed cost of opening a warehouse at site k	F_k
File migration		Warehouse relocation	
Cost of migrating a copy of the file from j to k		Cost of relocating a warehouse from site j to site k	

Using the isomorphism result, we have shown the equivalence of these two problems. Therefore all the results available to operations researchers are available to computer scientists and vice versa. The implications are further illustrated in the next section.

3.7   Implications of the Isomorphism between the (D)FAP and the SC(D)WLP

Because the SCWLP has been studied extensively for a long time, techniques developed for the SCWLP can be used to solve the FAP. These include the add-drop technique used in [KUE63, ARM63, FEL66] which is a heuristic of complexity $O(n^4)$ and generates sub-optimal solutions; the branch and bound algorithms used in [EFR66, SA69, KHU72, AKI77] which exhaustively enumerate over a reduced set of possible solutions in order to obtain the optimal allocations and in which the running time depends on the bounding and the branching criteria used; the linear programming dual formulation proposed in [ERL78] which produces optimal solutions when augmented with a branch and bound algorithm; the probabilistic branch and bound algorithm used in [GRA70] which is similar to the branch and bound technique but uses probabilistic estimation to generate a lower bound; the direct search or implicit enumeration algorithm used in [SPI69, ALC76]; the steepest ascent algorithm used in [MAN64] which is a sub-optimal steepest ascent one point move algorithm; the dynamic programming method used in [SWE76] in which some conditions are developed to reduce the number of solution vectors searched; the heuristics developed in [HIL66] and [COR77]; and the polynomial algorithms for some special cases, e.g. a plant location problem on a grid-like network solved in [SNY71], a one facility plant migration problem solved in [WES73].

Similarly, there are techniques developed in the FAP and DFAP which can be used to solve the warehouse location problem. These include the hypercube technique developed in [CAS72, LEV74, MOR77] which is essentially the same as Alcouffe and Muratet's optimal algorithm [ALC76] and is an implicit enumeration with conditions to discontinue the search; the clustering technique used in [LOO75]; the dynamic programming method used in [LEV74] to solve the optimal migration sequence for copies of a file; and the max-flow-min-cut network flow technique used in [STO77, STO78a, STO78b], which can be used to solve a special case of the SCQAP[2]. Despite the similarities, there are several key functions in the general FAP which may not have any corresponding counterparts in the general SCWLP. The FAP used in the proof of isomorphism is a limited version of the general problem. In the general problem, the querying delays of accessing a file (or transmitting queries/updates) may not be an important issue in the SCWLP. In addition, the issue of updates and concurrency control in the general FAP does not have any similar counterparts in the general SCWLP. For these reasons, the technique developed in one problem has to be modified and extended before being applied to solve the general problem.

Besides the fact that techniques developed for both problems are interchangeable, there are instances where techniques developed for one problem match very closely with techniques developed for the other problem. These are stated in the following three corollaries.

---

2. The proof of this is shown in Appendix A.

COROLLARY 3.1

Two of the three conditions derived by Grapa and Belford [GRA77b] for a file to be placed or not to be placed at a node may be weaker than the conditions derived by Efroymson and Ray [EFR66] for a warehouse to be opened or closed.

Proof

Before the conditions can be stated, some additional symbols must be defined. Let:

$$K_0 = \{j: \ Y_j = 0\};$$
$$K_1 = \{j: \ Y_j = 1\};$$
$$K_2 = \{j: \ Y_j = \text{unassigned}\}.$$

In the FAP, K_1, K_0 represent the set of nodes with and without a copy of the file, and K_2 represents the remaining nodes in the system. In the SCWLP, K_1, K_0 represent the set of sites for which a warehouse is opened and closed and K_2 represents the set of the remaining sites.

Two of the three Grapa and Belford conditions for a file to be placed or not to be placed at a node are[3] [GRA77b]:

For $i \epsilon K_2$:

$$Y_i = 1 \text{ if } Q_i \min_{\substack{k \epsilon K_1 \cup K_2 \\ k \neq i}} (S_{i,k} - S_{i,i})_+ > G_i \tag{3.4}$$

$$Y_i = 0 \text{ if } \Sigma_{j=1}^{n} Q_j \max_{k \epsilon K_1 \cup K_2} (S_{j,k} - S_{j,i}) < G_i \tag{3.5}$$

where

$$(f)_+ = \begin{cases} f & \text{if } f \geq 0 \\ 0 & \text{if } f < 0. \end{cases}$$

---

3. Equation (3.4) has been augmented by the term $S_{i,i}$ on the R.H.S. because the original condition of Grapa and Belford is not correct when $S_{i,i} > 0$.

Two of the three Efroymson and Ray conditions for a warehouse to be opened or closed are[4] [EFR66]:

$$Y_i = 1 \text{ if } \Sigma_{j=1}^{n} \, Q_j \min_{\substack{k \in K_1 \cup K_2 \\ k \neq i}} (S_{j,k} - S_{j,i})_+ > G_i \qquad (3.6)$$

$$Y_i = 0 \text{ if } \Sigma_{j=1}^{n} \, Q_j \min_{k \in K_1} (S_{j,k} - S_{j,i})_+ < G_i. \qquad (3.7)$$

In order to show that condition (3.4) is weaker than condition (3.6) and condition (3.5) is weaker than condition (3.7), it is necessary to show:

(a) $\Sigma_{j=1}^{n} Q_j \min_{\substack{k \in K_1 \cup K_2 \\ k \neq i}} (S_{j,k} - S_{j,i})_+ \geq Q_i \min_{\substack{k \in K_1 \cup K_2 \\ k \neq i}} (S_{i,k} - S_{i,i})_+$

(b) $\Sigma_{j=1}^{n} Q_j \min_{k \in K_1} (S_{j,k} - S_{j,i})_+ \leq \Sigma_{j=1}^{n} Q_j \max_{k \in K_1 \cup K_2} (S_{j,k} - S_{j,i})$

To prove

(a) L.H.S. $= Q_i \min_{\substack{k \in K_1 \cup K_2 \\ k \neq i}} (S_{i,k} - S_{i,i})_+ + \Sigma_{\substack{j=1 \\ j \neq i}}^{n} Q_j \min_{\substack{k \in K_1 \cup K_2 \\ k \neq i}} (S_{j,k} - S_{j,i})_+$

$\geq Q_i \min_{\substack{k \in K_1 \cup K_2 \\ k \neq i}} (S_{i,k} - S_{i,i})_+$

$= \text{R.H.S.}$

(b) Comparing term by term, we would like to show that

$$\min_{k \in K_1} (S_{j,k} - S_{j,i})_+ \leq \max_{k \in K_1 \cup K_2} (S_{j,k} - S_{j,i}).$$

---

4. The variables in the following two conditions have been transformed into the corresponding variables in the FAP with the use of Table 3.3. In the original Efroymson and Ray conditions, $j \epsilon P_i$ which is the set of customers that can be supplied from plant (or warehouse) i. We have made the assumption that all the customers can be supplied from any plant and therefore $j \epsilon \{1, \ldots, n\}$. Note that $t_{j,k}$ in the SCWLP corresponds to $S_{k,j}$ in the FAP.

We consider three different relationships between $S_{j,i}$ and the set of values of $S_{j,k}$ with i, j fixed (note that $i \epsilon K_2$):

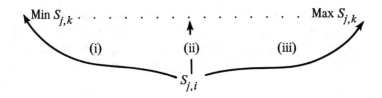

(i) If $\min\limits_{k \epsilon K_1} S_{j,k} \geqslant S_{j,i}$ then $\min\limits_{k \epsilon K_1} (S_{j,k} - S_{j,i})_+ = \min\limits_{k \epsilon K_1} (S_{j,k} - S_{j,i})$

$$\leqslant \max\limits_{k \epsilon K_1 \cup K_2} (S_{j,k} - S_{j,i}).$$

(ii) If $\min\limits_{k \epsilon K_1} S_{j,k} < S_{j,i} \leqslant \max\limits_{k \epsilon K_1} S_{j,k}$ then $\min\limits_{k \epsilon K_1} (S_{j,k} - S_{j,i})_+ = 0$

$$\leqslant \max\limits_{k \epsilon K_1 \cup K_2} (S_{j,k} - S_{j,i}).$$

(iii) If $\max\limits_{k \epsilon K_1} S_{j,k} < S_{j,i}$ then $\min\limits_{k \epsilon K_1} (S_{j,k} - S_{j,i})_+ = 0 = $ L.H.S.

But $\max\limits_{k \epsilon K_1 \cup K_2} (S_{j,k} - S_{j,i}) = \max [\max\limits_{k \epsilon K_1} (S_{j,k} - S_{j,i}), \max\limits_{k \epsilon K_2} (S_{j,k} - S_{j,i})]$

$= \max$ [Negative value (NV), Indefinite value (IV)]

$= \max$ [NV, IV] = R.H.S.

If R.H.S. = NV, then L.H.S. > R.H.S.

If R.H.S. = IV, then L.H.S. ? R.H.S.

From the above analysis, condition (3.5) is weaker than condition (3.7) if:

$$S_{j,i} \leqslant \max\limits_{k \epsilon K_1} S_{j,k}$$

or $\quad S_{j,i} > \max\limits_{k \epsilon K_1} S_{j,k}$ and $\max\limits_{k \epsilon K_2} S_{j,k} \geqslant S_{j,i}$

for all values of i.

Condition (3.7) will be applied if the above condition is satisfied, otherwise condition (3.5) should be applied instead.

This proves the corollary. It must be noted that the third condition derived by Grapa and Belford, which is shown as condition (d) in Table 3.5, has no corresponding counterparts in the SCWLP and, therefore, may be useful in the SCWLP. The summary of these conditions is shown in Table 3.5.

Q.E.D.

By using the stronger Efroymson and Ray conditions, a larger set of nodes can be pre-assigned to have or not to have a copy of the file than by using Grapa and Belford's conditions. This may save a lot of computation time in enumerating some possible assignments which cannot be pre-assigned using Grapa and Belford's conditions.

COROLLARY 3.2

The dynamic programming method is used by Levin [LEV74] to solve the file migration problem and by Sweenly and Tatham [SWE76] to solve the dynamic warehouse location problem.

Proof

In [LEV74], Levin has developed a method of dynamically migrating copies of a file over a multi-period horizon. The technique uses the basic dynamic programming procedure. Dominance conditions are defined in order to reduce the number of solution vectors that have to be generated in each period. The conditions are defined so that the reduced set of solution vectors always includes the optimum.

On the other hand, Sweenly and Tatham have also used dynamic programming to solve the multi-period warehouse location problem. In order to reduce the number of solution vectors that have to be generated in each period, an upper bound is determined first. All solution vectors with values less than the upper bound are generated and ranked for each period. Dynamic programming is applied to find a new upper bound v^*. If v^∞ is the sum of optimum solutions for each period without the relocation costs and $K=v^*-v^\infty$, then it is proven that additional solution vectors have to be generated for periods where the difference between the best and the worst solutions is less than K. A solution vector in a period is obtained by solving an integer program. It is difficult to determine the number of solutions to be generated in each period. However, some fixed number may be selected ahead of time based on the previous knowledge obtained.

Table 3.5. Summary of Conditions for Placement and Non-placement of a file at node $i \epsilon K_2$. (The first and the third conditions are from [EFR66]; the second condition is combined from both [EFR66] and [GRA77b]; the last condition is from [GRA77b].)

Condition	Rule
a	$Y_i = 1$ if $\displaystyle\sum_{\substack{j=1 \\ j \neq i}}^{n} Q_j \min_{k \epsilon K_1 U K_2} (S_{j,k} - S_{j,i})_+ > G_i$
b	$Y_i = 0$ if $\displaystyle\sum_{j=1}^{n} Q_j \min_{k \epsilon K_1} (S_{j,k} - S_{j,i})_+ < G_i$ or $\displaystyle\sum_{j=1}^{n} Q_j \max_{k \epsilon K_1 U K_2} (S_{j,k} - S_{j,i}) < G_i$
c	If $\displaystyle\min_{k \epsilon K_1} (S_{j,k} - S_{j,i}) < 0$ $j \epsilon \{1, \ldots, n\}$, then n_i is reduced by 1.
d	$Y_i = 0$ if $G_i - G_k > \displaystyle\sum_{j=1}^{n} Q_j (S_{j,k} - S_{j,i})_+$

Although no performance results on the number of solutions that have to be generated in each period are given for both techniques, it seems that Levin's solution is easier to apply because it is not necessary to solve an integer program in order to obtain a solution. However, a smaller number of solutions may be generated using Sweenly and Tatham's technique, although it may be necessary to go through several iterations before the optimum solution is contained in the solution vectors; whereas using Levin's technique, the reduced set of solution vectors always contains the optimum. The solutions that these two techniques give may not be identical and the practical benefits between these two methods can only be distinguished when they are applied on realistic problems. More evaluations are necessary before any quantitative judgment can be made between the two techniques.

Q.E.D.

COROLLARY 3.3

The hypercube technique developed by Casey [CAS72] and Levin and Morgan [LEV74, MOR77] and the condition used to discontinue the search, are identical to the algorithm and condition developed by Alcouffe and Muratet [ALC76].

Proof

The hypercube technique was first introduced by Casey [CAS72] (a later version was developed by Levin and Morgan [LEV74, MOR77]) to enumerate over all the possible combinations of allocations in order to find the optimal allocations. A condition is developed to discontinue the search whenever the objective function [CAS72] (the sum of the query and storage costs [LEV74, MOR77]) does not decrease after a file copy is added to an arbitrary assignment at a node. A similar condition is also developed by Alcouffe and Muratet [ALC76]. However, the algorithm used by Alcouffe and Muratet is slightly different. They started their search from an assignment in which every warehouse is opened. This corresponds to the case in which every node has a copy of the file. In Casey's or Levin's algorithm, the search is started with the assignment in which every node does not have a copy of the file. However, the basic underlying principle of these two algorithms is still identical.

Q.E.D.

In conclusion, as a result of the proof of isomorphism, we have found that many techniques developed for the two problems are inter-changeable and that some techniques developed for one problem match very closely with techniques developed for the other. It is, therefore, possible to study these two problems in an integrated fashion in the future. In the next section, we will use the conditions in Table 3.5 to develop a heuristic for the FAP.

3.8   A Heuristic for the FAP—Algorithm 3.1

In this section, we propose a heuristic to solve the FAP using the combined conditions in Table 3.5. The heuristic is a greedy algorithm which extends the assignment in the best possible way without backtracking on the previous assignment. The solution obtained depends on the criterion used in the extension. Because the previous assignment is never backtracked, a wrong decision may have been made earlier and the solution obtained may not be optimal. Several alternative selection criteria are, therefore, investigated.

Essentially, the heuristic starts with all the nodes unassigned. It first applies the conditions of Table 3.5 to see if any node can be assigned. This can be done very fast. After all these nodes have been assigned, it has to select a node from the set of unassigned nodes and decide whether to assign a copy of the file there. The current assignment is extended by one node. For each of these extended assignments, there are two possibilities; either to assign or not to assign a copy of the file there. Therefore, there are altogether $2*|K_2|$ possible assignments which results in $2*|K_2|$ candidate problems. (The state of a candidate problem is made up of the states of allocation of the multiple copies to the n different nodes on the DCS. In general, the n nodes of the DCS can be partitioned into three sets, K_0, K_1, and K_2.) For each of the candidate problems, a representative value is calculated. The function of the representative value is to estimate the minimum value of the candidate problem without actually enumerating over all the possible allocations for the unassigned nodes. Based on these $2*|K_2|$ representative values, the selection criterion selects the node and decides whether or not to assign a copy of the file there. After this assignment has been made, the algorithm comes to a point at which it is ready to check for the conditions of Table 3.5 again and therefore it repeats the steps described above until all the nodes have been assigned. The general steps of the algorithm are shown in Figure 3.1. We discuss these steps briefly here.

M-1   This is to initialize the algorithm—all nodes are unassigned at this point. The candidate list, which is a list of states made up of the sets K_0, K_1, K_2, and its corresponding representative value, is assigned the empty set.

M-2-5   These four steps essentially achieve the following: a node is selected from the unassigned set, K_2, and is assigned a copy or not assigned a copy of the file. A representative value is calculated for each of the

Figure 3.1. File Assignment Algorithm

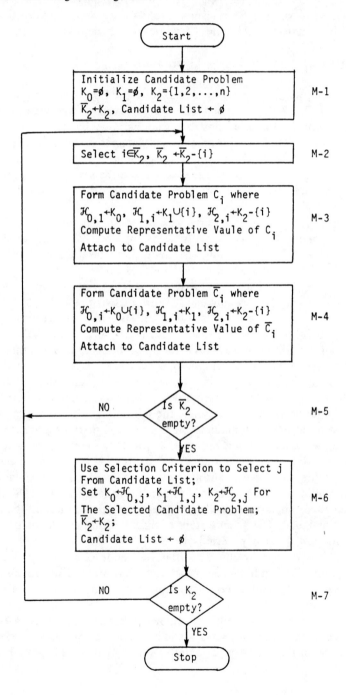

candidate problems. The computed representative value and the corresponding assignments are attached to the candidate list. These steps are then repeated for each node in K_2.

M-6   This step selects, from the candidate list, the candidate problem and the corresponding assignment of nodes using the selection criterion, and uses it for the next iteration. Steps M-2 to M-6, therefore, have selected a node and have decided whether a copy should be placed at that node. This node is removed from the K_2 list.

M-7   The steps M-2 to M-6 are repeated until the K_2 list is empty.

There are two basic parts of the algorithm discussed here: the selection criterion and the computation of the representative value.

S1   The selection criterion;

  S1a   Select from the candidate list, the candidate problem with the minimum representative value;

  S1b   Select from the candidate list, the two candidate problems for which node i is extended, that is, $Y_i=0$ and $Y_i=1$, that have the maximum difference between the representative values. From these two candidate problems, select the candidate problem with the minimum representative value.

R1   The computation of the representative value;

  R1a   A lower bound is computed by solving the linear program (Eq. 3.1) without the integrality constraints. (This has been derived earlier by Efroymson and Ray [EFR66]. See Appendix B for the derivation.);

  R1b   The expected value of the candidate problem is computed by assuming that each of the remaining unassigned nodes has an equal probability of having or not having a copy of the file (see Appendix C for the derivation);

Using the two selection criteria and the two types of representative values, there are four different versions of the algorithm:

1.   MINLB—minimum lower bound (S1a, R1a);
2.   MINE—minimum expected value (S1a, R1b);
3.   MAXDLB—minimum lower bound for a node i with the maximum difference in lower bounds between $Y_i=0$ and $Y_i=1$ $(i\epsilon K_2)$ (S1b, R1a);
4.   MAXDE—minimum expected value for a node i with the maximum difference in expected values between $Y_i=0$ and $Y_i=1$ $(i\epsilon K_2)$ (S1b, R1b).

To further illustrate the steps of the algorithm, it is applied on Casey's five-node example [CAS72].

Suppose the following matrix represents the query cost $S_{i,j}$ for a five-node system.

$$S = \begin{bmatrix} 0 & 6 & 12 & 9 & 6 \\ 6 & 0 & 6 & 12 & 9 \\ 12 & 6 & 0 & 6 & 12 \\ 9 & 12 & 6 & 0 & 6 \\ 6 & 9 & 12 & 6 & 0 \end{bmatrix}$$

Let

$$Q = [Q_i] = [24\ 24\ 24\ 24\ 24]$$
$$U = [U_i] = [2\ 3\ 4\ 6\ 8]$$
$$F = [F_i] = [0\ 0\ 0\ 0\ 0]$$

and

$$G = [G_i] = [168\ 180\ 174\ 126\ 123].$$

By enumerating the 2^5-1 possible allocations, it is found that a copy of the file should be allocated to nodes 1, 4, and 5 giving a cost of 705. The steps for the four possible variations of the algorithm are shown in Figures 3.2a, 3.2b, 3.2c, and 3.2d, respectively. It is seen that two of these variations give the optimal solution.

The algorithm is evaluated by applying it on the published examples in the FAP and the SCWLP[5]. The optimal solutions for these examples have been established in the literature. The deviation of the heuristic solutions from the optimal solutions can be used as an indication of the "goodness" of the heuristic. The heuristic is also compared against the add-drop algorithm of Keuhn and Hamburger [KEU63][6]. The evaluation results are shown in Table 3.6. The four proposed variations of the heuristic are all polynomial algorithms and each has a complexity of $O(n^4)$ (the same as the add-drop algorithm). The execution times on the CDC 6400 are shown in Table 3.7.

It is seen from Tables 3.6 and 3.7 that the algorithm MINLB gives the best results and has an execution time very small as compared with other

---

5. The first six sets of problems are taken from [CAS72]. Problems 7 to 18 are taken from [KEU63] and problems 19 to 22 are taken from problem 7 of [SA69, p. 1013].
6. Instead of directly using Keuhn and Hamburger's add-drop algorithm, which selects only 5 warehouse sites to be evaluated in each cycle, the add-drop algorithm used here allows for all the unassigned warehouse sites to be taken into consideration.

algorithms. In fact, algorithm MINLB obtains the optimal solutions more often than the add-drop algorithm in general, but the worst case behavior seems to be worse than the add-drop algorithm and the execution times are longer because the algorithm is more complex. On the other hand, algorithm MAXDLB produces more optimal solutions than algorithm MINLB, but its worst case behavior seems to be worse. Algorithms MINE and MAXDE are much worse than algorithms MINLB and MAXDLB. Improvements can be obtained if we use the estimated lower bound (by estimating the mean and the standard deviation and making an assumption of normal distribution), but the complexity of the algorithm will become $O(n^5)$ and it takes too long to produce a solution for any of these problems (> 600 seconds). However, we can still improve the heuristic solution by combining the results of the add-drop algorithm, the MINE algorithm, and the MAXDLB algorithm. In this case, over 80% of the problems will have optimal assignments and the complexity of the combined algorithm is still $O(n^4)$.

We have presented in this section a heuristic which can be used to obtain a file assignment with a value very close to the optimal solution. We show in the next section, that by including the migration cost into the cost function, the above heuristic is also applicable. Further, we prove some conditions for file migration on a DDB.

3.9 DFAP—The Migration of Files on a DCS

The model that we have discussed so far assumes that the access and update rates at each node do not vary with time. The query load (Q_j) and update load (U_j) defined in Table 3.3 are actually defined for a period of finite length. If they remain constant for every period, then the placements of files determined initially will remain static. However, it is generally true that the access and the update rates are time-varying. For example, a large DCS usually experiences different query and update rates at different parts of the system due to the different time zones in different geographic regions. The time varying characteristics of the query and the update rates should be taken into account in the placements of files on the DCS.

We assume in the following discussion that time is divided into periods and the file assignments remain static within the periods. The length of each period may not be identical. The shorter the period, the more adaptive the system would be to the time-varying retrieval and update rates, but the higher would be the costs of migration which include the relocation costs and the costs of executing the file assignment algorithm. The selection of the period length is, therefore, very application dependent and is governed by the rate of change of the query rates and the costs of migration. It is also

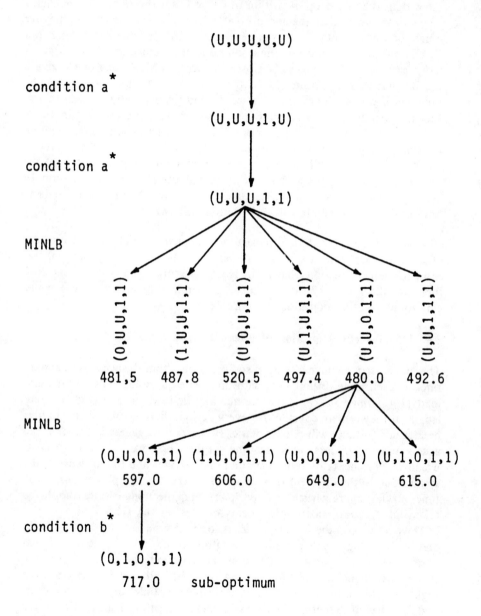

Figure 3.2a. Evaluation of Casey's 5 node Example using MINLB
(U indicates that the node is un-assigned)

* see Table 3.5

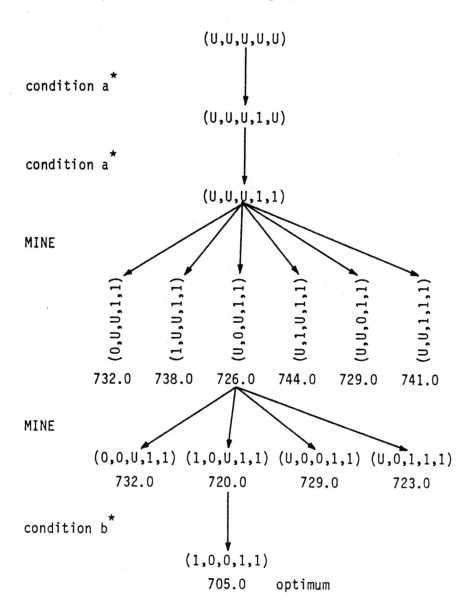

Figure 3.2b. Evaluation of Casey's 5 node Example using MINE
(U indicates that the node is un-assigned)

* see Table 3.5

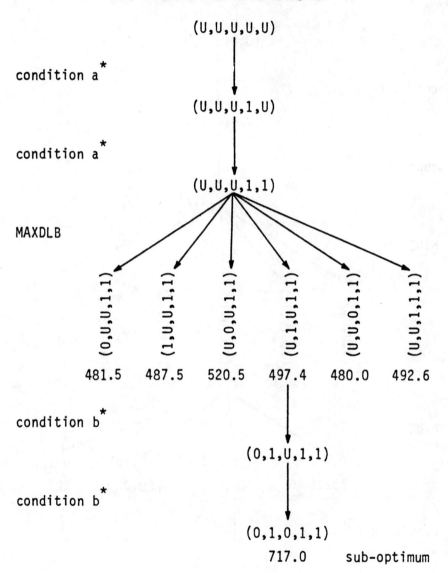

Figure 3.2c. Evaluation of Casey's 5 node Example using
MAXDLB (U indicates that the node is un-assigned)

* see Table 3.5

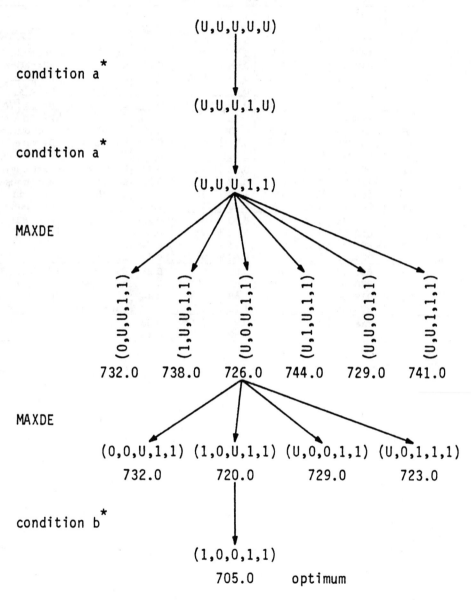

Figure 3.2d. Evaluation of Casey's 5 node Example using MAXDE
(U indicates that the node is un-assigned)

condition a*

condition a*

MAXDE

MAXDE

condition b*

* see Table 3.5

Table 3.6. % Deviations of File Allocation Heuristic from Optimal Solutions

Prob.	Optimum Sol.	Add-Drop	MINLB	MINE	MAXDLB	MAXDE	Comments	
1	117596	0	0	0	8.43	0	α=0.1	Casey's 19
2	188738	0.03	0.31	0.31	0.31	0.31	α=0.2	node file
3	242581	0	0	0.66	0	0.66	α=0.3	allocation
4	291790	0	1.39	0	1.39	0	α=0.4	problem
5	431720	0	0	0	0	0	α=1.0	[CAS72]
6	705	0.85	1.70	0	1.70	0	Casey's 5 no-	de ex. [CAS72]
7	796648	0.11	0	0.78	0	0.78	Factory	keuhn and
8	854704	0.15	0.09	0.89	0	0.89	at Ind-	Hamburger's
9	893782	0.14	0	0.71	0	0.71	ianapolis	24 ware-
10	928942	0	0.61	0.94	1.49	0.99		houses, 50
11	1092916	0.08	0	0.13	0.10	0.13	Factory	customers
12	1145923	0.13	0	0.22	0	0.22	at Jack-	warehouse
13	1188241	0.13	0	1.37	0	1.37	sonville	location
14	1244991	0.22	0.22	2.49	0	1.67		problem
15	614548	0.14	0	0.90	0	0.90	Factory	[KEU63]
16	859983	0	0.12	0.80	0	0.80	at Balt-	
17	690746	0.03	0	0.74	0	0.74	imore and	
18	724886	0	0	0.42	0	0.49	Ind'polis	
19	806145	0	0	0.88	0	0.38	Factory at	Problem 7
20	870792	0.15	0	0.67	0	0.67	Ind'polis,	of Sa
21	919994	0.11	0	1.46	0	0.44	but not	[SA 69]
22	970446	0	0.42	1.73	1.36	0.67	warehouse	
	mean	0.10	0.22	0.73	0.67	0.58		
	std.dev.	0.18	0.46	0.62	1.83	0.44		

Table 3.7. Execution Time of Heuristic in seconds on the CDC 6400

Prob.	Add-Drop	MINLB	MINE	MAXDLB	MAXDE	Comments	
1	0.57	11.45	22.79	11.42	103.71	α=0.1	Casey's 19
2	0.43	11.59	23.57	11.66	105.57	α=0.2	node file
3	0.43	11.77	23.60	11.76	105.50	α=0.3	allocation
4	0.43	11.80	23.48	11.79	105.26	α=0.4	problem
5	0.29	11.80	23.80	11.84	105.10	α=1.0	[CAS72]
6	0.04	0.08	0.09	0.06	0.24	Casey's 5 no-	de ex. [CAS72]
7	11.46	8.08	11.85	8.29	26.41	Factory	keuhn and
8	9.36	13.55	13.52	11.23	35.73	at Ind-	Hamburger's
9	5.34	20.89	13.91	20.99	37.61	ianapolis	24 ware-
10	3.61	8.48	8.29	8.50	21.42		houses, 50
11	12.08	6.40	9.13	6.39	17.74	Factory	customers
12	8.62	12.66	12.64	12.71	30.62	at Jack-	warehouse
13	7.82	22.16	21.26	22.83	62.03	sonville	location
14	7.02	40.18	33.47	40.33	112.93		problem
15	9.75	5.48	12.44	5.50	25.35	Factory	[KEU63]
16	7.33	5.49	4.37	4.64	7.90	at Balt-	
17	5.58	6.82	7.01	6.84	17.25	imore and	
18	3.79	2.66	3.75	2.68	7.26	Ind'polis	
19	12.24	4.94	9.16	4.95	16.04	Factory at	Problem 7
20	9.02	13.63	13.81	11.29	34.39	Ind'polis,	of Sa
21	6.76	23.27	22.05	20.97	67.74	but not	[SA 69]
22	5.94	22.79	28.81	22.02	73.40	warehouse	
mean	5.81	12.54	15.58	12.21	50.87		
std.dev.	4.11	8.92	8.83	8.84	39.27		

difficult to estimate the query rates precisely ahead of time. We assume that the query rates are estimated dynamically at the beginning of each period. This may be done by using a variation of the working set algorithm [DEN70] which estimates the query rates based on the rate of change of the query rates in the previous periods. With this assumption, it is possible to optimize the file allocations of each period independently and is not necessary to use dynamic programming to optimize the allocations for all the periods as done by Levin [LEV74] and Sweenly and Tatham [SWE76].

There are two approaches to migrate files on a DCS:

1. Apply stored decisions dynamically whenever migration is needed.

In such an approach, the decisions of how to migrate the files based on the dynamic state of the system is computed before hand. At the beginning of each period, it involves only a search of the appropriate migrations to be taken. This type of stored decision approach is very efficient because it is essentially a table look-up. However, the abundance of states usually prohibits the application of such an approach. In order to store the decisions, it is necessary to find a convex hull to an n-dimensional region where n is the number of nodes in the system. The number of points on this convex hull is of the order k^n where $k>1$. Present algorithms to find the equation of a convex hull in four dimensional regions have an expected behavior of $O(m^2)$ where m is the number of points on the hull [BEN77] and algorithms for higher dimensions do not exist. Therefore, it is unlikely that a general stored decision algorithm can be found at this time for file migration. However, by utilizing some special structure of the problem, it may be possible to find a feasible solution. This approach has been taken in communication and control systems, e.g. [CHU76, RUD77] and can be a useful and efficient heuristic if optimality requirements can be relaxed.

2. Apply static file assignment algorithm dynamically whenever restructuring is needed.

This is the approach taken generally and is the approach taken here. The disadvantage about this approach is the complexity of the optimal algorithm. However, by using a good heuristic, close to optimal results can still be obtained.

In the remainder of this section, we formulate the file migration problem for each period and show that the costs of file migration can be included into the fixed cost of the system. We define the following symbols with respect to a period.

T = current period of consideration;

$S_{j,k}{}^T$ = cost of communication of one query unit from j to k in period T;

$M_{j,k}^T$ = cost of communication of one update unit from j to k in period T;

$N_{j,k}^T$ = cost of moving a copy of file a from node j to node k in period T;

F_k^T = storage cost of file at node k per unit time in period T;

Q_j^T = query load originating at node j in period T;

U_j^T = update load originating at node j in period T;

C_{op}^T = estimated cost of running the file placement heuristic in period T;

I_T = index set of nodes with a copy of the file in period T;

I_{T-1} = index set of nodes with a copy of the file in period T-1.

By defining the control variable Y_j with respect to the period of consideration, we have:

$$Y_j^T = \begin{cases} 0 & j \notin I_T \\ 1 & j \in I_T. \end{cases}$$

The access and the update costs are the same as in Eq. 3.1 and 3.2 except that the costs per unit time are defined for period T specifically. Further, there is an additional component of the costs, the migration cost.

File Migration cost = $\Sigma_{k=1}^n Y_k^T \min_{j \in I_{T-1}} N_{j,k}^T$.

That is, if node k does not have a copy of the file in period T and it is necessary to migrate a copy of the file to node k, then a copy of the file is migrated from the nearest node in the assignments of period T-1. It is easily seen that optimization problem 3.1 can be written in the original form with only a change in the values of G_k (Eq. 3.2).

min

$$C(I) = \Sigma_{j=1}^n Q_j^T \min_{k \in I_T} S_{j,k}^T + \Sigma_{k=1}^n G_k^T Y_k^T \tag{3.8}$$

subject to

$$Y_k^T = 0 \text{ or } 1 \text{ (integer)} \qquad k = 1,\ldots,n$$

and

$$G_k^T = F_k^T + \Sigma_{j=1}^n U_j^T M_{j,k}^T + \min_{j \in I_{T-1}} N_{j,k}^T. \tag{3.9}$$

The importance of the above formulation is that the static file assignment algorithms developed in the literature and the file assignment heuristic described in section 3.8 are still applicable to solve the file assignment problem in each period although migration costs have been included in the formulation. At the beginning of each period, it is necessary to determine Q_j^T, U_j^T, and G_j^T for all $j\epsilon\{1,\ldots,n\}$ and the static file assignment algorithm can then be applied.

3.10   Conditions to Reduce the Complexity of the DFAP

In this section, we want to establish some general theorems on the DFAP which will aid in simplifying the problem. Specifically, we want to show the NP-completeness of the problem of selecting the migration points and to find an upper bound on the number of file migrations in period T.

3.10.1   The problem of selecting the times for migration is NP-complete. Since Eswaran has shown that the FAP is NP-complete [ESW74], the DFAP, which is a general case of the FAP, is also NP-complete. However, we want to show that the problem of selecting the points of migration in a multi-period time interval is also NP-complete. This means that we have to exhaustively enumerate over all the possibilities before we can decide when to initiate a file migration. We achieve this by reducing the knapsack problem to the problem of selecting the points of migration.

Knapsack Problem [KAR72]

Input: $(a_1, a_2, \ldots, a_n, b) \epsilon Z^{n+1}$; $Z =$ set of integers;
Property: $\Sigma a_j x_j = b$ has a 0-1 solution for x_j.

Problem of selecting the migration points—feasibility form

During a time period [0,t], at what points of time should migrations be initiated so that the total operating cost $=$ B?

We assume that the query rates are changing with time and that migrations can only be initiated at fixed discrete times, $t_1, t_2, \ldots, t_k$ within the period [0, t]. The last assumption is made because computer operations are governed by a clock which is discrete.

THEOREM 3.2

The problem of selecting the migration points is NP-complete.

Proof

First, we want to show that the problem ϵ NP. A non-deterministic Turing machine can guess the set of times at which the files in the system are to be migrated and, therefore, the problem ϵ NP

Second, we have to show that the satisfiability problem (SAT) is reducible to this problem (SAT $\propto$ the problem of selecting the migration points). We can do this by showing that the knapsack problem $\propto$ migration problem because SAT $\propto$ knapsack and by transitivity, SAT $\propto$ migration problem. Given an instance of the knapsack problem, we can construct (in polynomial time), an instance of the problem of selecting the migration points as follows:

Let

$$x_i = \begin{cases} 0 & \text{if no migration is initiated at } t_i \\ 1 & \text{otherwise.} \end{cases}$$

a_i = the costs of migration at time t_i. (The costs are not the same at different t_i's because the costs may be discounted to time t_0, or different costs may be associated with different times.)

$B = b$.

There are no other costs associated with the operation of the system.

The knapsack problem is therefore reducible to the problem of selecting the migration points. Since the knapsack problem is NP-complete, hence, we have proved the theorem.

Q.E.D.

After establishing that the problem of selecting the migration points is NP-complete, we are left with two alternatives: (1) exhaustively check the 2^k possibilities of whether to migrate at the k discrete time instances within the period $[0, t]$; or (2) establish some criteria for migration. The first alternative has been taken by Levin [LEV74] and Sweenly and Tatham [SWE76]. We investigate the second alternative here.

3.10.2 Criteria for initiating a migration. We want to establish in this section some criteria under which migration should be carried out. First, we want to find the maximum number of necessary file movements in any migration.

LEMMA 3.1

Given the allocations of the multiple copies of a particular file, the maximum number of file movements needed is $n-1$.

Proof

A file movement is needed for node i whenever $Y_i = 0$ before the migration and $Y_i = 1$ after the migration. Under no other cases should there be a file movement. It is also assumed that there is at least a copy of the file on the system. Therefore, the maximum number of file movements occur when there are $n-1$ nodes without a copy before the migration and these $n-1$ nodes have copies after the migration.

Q.E.D.

Given an allocation in period T, we are interested in finding a lower bound and an upper bound on the costs of p file movements, $p = 1, \ldots, n-1$ in period $T+1$.

Recall that:

$$K_0^T = \{j:\ Y_j^T = 0\}$$

$$K_1^T = \{j:\ Y_j^T = 1\}$$

and assume that all the nodes have been assigned, i.e. $K_2^T = \phi$.

Let

$C_L^p(C_U^p) = $ lower (upper) bound on the costs of p file movements. $1 \leq p \leq n - |K_1|$.

The following algorithm finds C_L^p, C_U^p.

Algorithm 3.2—To find the Lower and the Upper Bounds on the Costs of p file movements:

1. $C_L^p \leftarrow 0; C_U^p \leftarrow 0;$

$$K_{0,L}^{T+1} \leftarrow K_0^T; K_{1,L}^{T+1} \leftarrow K_1^T;$$

$$K_{0,U}^{T+1} \leftarrow K_0^T; K_{1,U}^{T+1} \leftarrow K_1^T;$$

2.   Do steps 3 and 4 p times;

3. $C_L{}^P \leftarrow C_L{}^P + \min\limits_{\substack{j \in K_{1,L}{}^T \\ k \in K_{0,L}{}^{T+1}}} N_{j,k}{}^T$;

$$K_{1,L}{}^{T+1} \leftarrow K_{1,L}{}^{T+1} \cup \{k\}, K_{0,L}{}^{T+1} \leftarrow K_{0,L}{}^{T+1} - \{k\};$$

4. $C_U{}^P \leftarrow C_U{}^P + \max\limits_{k \in K_{0,U}{}^{T+1}} \min\limits_{j \in K_{1,U}{}^T} N_{j,k}{}^T$;

$$K_{1,U}{}^{T+1} \leftarrow K_{1,U}{}^{T+1} \cup \{k\}, K_{0,U}{}^{T+1} \leftarrow K_{0,U}{}^{T+1} - \{k\}.$$

Note that $C_L{}^P \leqq C_L{}^{P+1}$ because all the costs involved are positive.

Having established the lower and upper bounds on the cost of p file movements, we want to compute the change in total system costs due to a perturbation in the access rate. When the change in total system cost is greater than a threshold, a file migration is necessary. The change in total system cost is given partially by the following theorem.

THEOREM 3.3

Let

$$R_j{}^T = Q_j{}^T + U_j{}^T;$$

$$r_j{}^T = Q_j{}^T / R_j{}^T;$$

$R_j{}^{T+1} = R_j{}^T + \omega_j{}^{T+1}$ where $\omega_j{}^{T+1}$ is the perturbation in the total number of accesses in period $T+1$ at node j and is proportionally divided between retrievals and updates;

$$C_\omega{}^T = \Sigma_j r_j{}^T \omega_j{}^{T+1} \min\limits_{k \in I_T} S_{j,k}{}^T + \Sigma_{j,k} (1-r_j{}^T) \omega_j{}^{T+1} M_{j,k}{}^T Y_k{}^T.$$

= Cost increase due to the perturbation.

(a)   If $\forall\ j, \omega_j{}^{T+1} \geqq 0$, then the upper bound of file movements that can be made on the system is $\tilde{p}$ where

$$\tilde{p} = \min\ \{p: C_L{}^P + C_{op}{}^T > C_\omega{}^T\} - 1; \tag{3.10}$$

(b) If $\exists\ j,\ \omega_j^{T+1}<0$, then the lower bound of file movements that can be made on the system is 0.

Proof

Let

$Y^T = (Y_1^T,\ Y_2^T,\ \ldots,\ Y_n^T)$ be the original optimal state of allocation in period T;

$Y^{T+1} = (Y_1^{T+1},\ Y_2^{T+1},\ \ldots,\ Y_n^{T+1})$ be the state of allocation after the perturbation in period $T+1$;

$C(Y^T)[C(Y^{T+1})]$ = cost of operation at state $Y^T(Y^{T+1})$.

We want to show:

(1) C_ω^T is an upper bound in the cost increase due to ω_j^{T+1} if $\forall\ j$, $\omega_j^{T+1}\geqq0$;

(2) C_ω^T is a lower bound in the cost saving due to ω_j^{T+1} if $\forall\ j,\ \omega_j^{T+1}\leqq0$;

(3)   if $\exists\ i,j$ s.t. $\omega_i^{T+1}>0,\ \omega_j^{T+1}<0$ and $C_\omega^T\leqq0$, then C_ω^T is a lower bound in the cost saving;

(4)   if $\exists\ i,j$ s.t. $\omega_i^{T+1}>0,\ \omega_j^{T+1}<0$ and $C_\omega^T>0$, then the lower bound in the cost saving is 0.

To prove:

(1)   We observe that $\exists\ Y^{T+1}$ s.t.

$$C(Y^T) \leqslant C(Y^{T+1}) - C_\omega^{T+1} \leqslant C(Y^{T+1}) \leqslant C(Y^T) + C_\omega^T$$

where

$$C_\omega^{T+1} = \Sigma_j\ r_j^T\ \omega_j^{T+1}\ \min_{k\in I_{T+1}} S_{j,k}^T + \Sigma_{j,k}\ (1-r_j^T)\ \omega_j^{T+1}\ M_{j,k}^T\ Y_k^{T+1}.$$

The first inequality can be proved by contradiction. If $C(Y^T) > C(Y^{T+1}) - C_\omega^{T+1}$, this means that $C(Y^{T+1}) - C_\omega^{T+1}$, which is the cost of operation at state Y^{T+1} without the cost of the perturbation; this has a lower cost than state Y^T. This implies that state Y^T cannot be the optimal state of allocation which contradicts the original assumption.

For the second inequality, $C(Y^{T+1}) \geq C(Y^{T+1}) - C_\omega^{T+1}$, we observe that $C_\omega^{T+1} \geq 0$ if all $\omega_i^{T+1} \geq 0$.

The third inequality, $C(Y^T) + C_\omega^T \geq C(Y^{T+1})$, can be proved by contradiction. If $C(Y^T) + C\omega^T < C(Y^{T+1})$, then it is not necessary to re-organize the database to state Y^{T+1} where the cost of operation is higher than the cost involved without the re-organization.

Therefore, $0 \leq C(Y^{T+1}) - C(Y^T) \leq C_\omega^T$ and C_ω^T is the upper bound in the cost increase.

(2) We observe that:

$$C(Y^{T+1}) - C_\omega^{T+1} \geq C(Y^T) \geq C(Y^T) + C_\omega^T \geq C(Y^{T+1}).$$

The proof is exactly the same as part (1) with an inter-change of Y^T and Y^{T+1}.

Therefore $C(Y^T) - C(Y^{T+1}) \geq -C_\omega^T$ and C_ω^T represents a lower bound in the cost savings.

(3) We observe a similar condition as part (2).

$$C(Y^{T+1}) - C_\omega^{T+1} \geq C(Y^T) \geq C(Y^T) + C_\omega^T \geq C(Y^{T+1})$$

Therefore, $C(Y^T) - C(Y^{T+1}) \geq -C_\omega^T$

(4) We can only establish a weaker condition in this case:

$$C(Y^T) \leq C(Y^{T+1}) - C_\omega^{T+1}$$

$$C(Y^{T+1}) \leq C(Y^T) + C_\omega^T.$$

These two inequalities can be proved similarly as before. We cannot prove any relation between $C(Y^{T+1}) - C_\omega^{T+1}$ and $C(Y^{T+1})$ because C_ω^{T+1} may be ≥ 0 or < 0.

In summary, we have proved for case(s)

(1) $0 \leq C(Y^T) - C(Y^{T+1}) + C_\omega^T \leq C_\omega^T$;

(2), (3), (4), $0 \leq C(Y^T) - C(Y^{T+1}) + C_\omega^T$.

We can now prove the theorem.

(a)   We observe that $C_L{}^p + C_{op}{}^T$ is a lower bound on the costs of running the optimization program and initiating p file movements, so in order for the reconfiguration to be cost-effective, we must have

$$C_\omega{}^T \geq C(Y^T) - C(Y^{T+1}) + C_\omega{}^T \geq C_L{}^p + C_{op}{}^T, \text{ where}$$

the upper bound on the number of file movements is

$$\tilde{p} = \min \{p: C_L{}^p + C_{op}{}^T > C_\omega{}^T\} - 1;$$

(b)   We note that the lower bound on the cost savings is ≥ 0, so the lower bound on the number of file movements is 0.

$$\text{Q.E.D.}$$

Although the above theorem does not provide us with an upper bound on the number of file movements when some or all of the $\omega_i{}^{T+1}$'s are less than zero, we can still find an upper bound on the number of file movements if we can establish a lower bound on the costs of operation for the perturbated state of accesses. In these cases, i.e., when some $\omega_i{}^{T+1} < 0$, we can estimate $\overline{C}(Y^{T+1})$, the lower bound on the optimal cost of operation after the perturbation without taking into account the cost of migration. Then

$$C_\Omega{}^T = C(Y^T) + C_\omega{}^T - \overline{C}(Y^{T+1}) \geq 0$$

is an upper bound on the cost savings due to migration.

The maximum number of file movements is therefore

$$\tilde{p} = \min \{p: C_L{}^p + C_{op}{}^T > C_\Omega{}^T\} - 1 \tag{3.11}$$

where

$$C_\Omega{}^T = \begin{cases} C_\omega{}^T & \text{if } \omega_j{}^{T+1} \geq 0 \ \forall \ j \in \{1,\dots,n\} \\ C(Y^T) + C_\omega{}^T - \overline{C}(Y^{T+1}) & \text{if } \exists \ j \in \{1,\dots,n\} \text{ s.t. } \omega_j{}^{T+1} < 0. \end{cases}$$

The problem that remains is to compute the lower bound $\overline{C}(Y^{T+1})$. This can be done by solving the optimization problem (3.1) without the integrality constraints (see Appendix B). Theorem 3.3, therefore, establishes the basis for the initiation of a file migration on the DDB. It has also taken into account the cost of running the optimization program for the FAP. It indicates that when it is very expensive to run the optimization program for the FAP, it is not cost effective to do file migration.

3.11 Conclusion

In this chapter, we have investigated some important properties and solution algorithms for the file allocation problem and the dynamic file allocation problem. First, we have proved the isomorphism between the (dynamic) file allocation problem and the single commodity (dynamic) warehouse location problem. Based on this property, we have found that many techniques developed for both problems are inter-changeable. Among these are algorithms developed in the warehouse location problem, such as the add-drop algorithm, the branch and bound algorithms, the probabilistic branch and bound algorithm, the integer programming technique, the steepest ascent algorithm, and the dynamic programming methods. These algorithms can be applied to solve the (dynamic) file allocation problem. On the other hand, there are algorithms developed in the file allocation problem which can be used to solve the warehouse location problem. These include the hypercube technique, the clustering technique, the dynamic programming methods, and the max-flow min-cut network flow technique.

We have also found that some techniques developed for one problem match very closely techniques developed for the other problem. This is shown by the fact that some of Grapa and Belford's conditions for locating a copy of the file at a node [GRA77b] are weaker than the conditions derived by Efroymson and Ray for opening or closing a warehouse [EFR66]. This implies that by using the stronger conditions of Efroymson and Ray, more nodes can be assigned initially to have or not to have a copy of the file. Similarly, the dynamic programming technique was applied by Levin to solve the dynamic file allocation problem [LEV74] and by Sweenly and Tatham to solve the dynamic warehouse location problem [SWE76]. Finally, the hypercube technique has been developed at different times by Casey [CAS72], Levin and Morgan [LEV74, MOR77], and Alcouffe and Muratet [ALC76]. We conclude that these two problems can be studied in an integrated fashion in the future.

Second, we have developed a heuristic to solve the file allocation problem. This heuristic uses the add-drop principle and different criteria on selection are compared. It is found that a combination of these criteria, together with the add-drop algorithm, is very promising and gives solutions very close to the optimum based on sample problems published in both the file allocation problem and warehouse location problem.

Third, we have studied some aspects of the file migration problem. It is shown that the problem of deciding when to migrate the files is NP-complete. This means that it is likely that an exhaustive enumeration is necessary before an optimal migration sequence can be found. We have also formulated the migration problem and have shown that the migration costs can be incorporated into the fixed cost of the system. This implies that the file allocation heuristic developed in this chapter can be applied to solve the file migration problem as well. Finally, we have developed a threshold to indicate when migration should be carried out.

4

Task Scheduling on Distributed
Computer Systems

4.1 Introduction

In the previous chapters, we have addressed the optimization problems of data management on the query and file level. The operations to be performed on the query and file level are a conglomerate of tasks, each of which may require the use of a different resource for a different amount of time. In this chapter, we address the problem of task scheduling on DCS's so that the hardware can be efficiently utilized and the requirements can be satisfied.

Although one of the motivations for the development of DCS's is the declining hardware costs, the problem of task scheduling is still an important topic of research because the parallel resources are more difficult to coordinate and, other constraints on the system such as deadlines and response time requirements must be satisfied. Further, the advantages of using parallel hardware are lost if the improvement over a conventional uni-processor system is small. It is the goal of this chapter to study the problem of task scheduling on DCS's.

A task is defined to be a simple request which uses a resource for a finite amount of time. A request is said to be simple if no other resource is needed during the processing of this request. A complex request can always be broken down into a sequence of simple requests. A resource on a DDB can be physical, such as a communication channel, a processor, etc., or it can be logical, such as a file. The tasks are usually governed by a precedence graph so that a task cannot be processed until its predecessor has finished processing.

For example, in order to handle a file request on a database, many processes, such as receive-message, create-transaction, assemble-reply, file-storage-I/O, etc., have to be activated. Another example is shown in the processing of user queries which are directed to different nodes on a DCS. Each query may be partitioned into a set of tasks. The general precedence

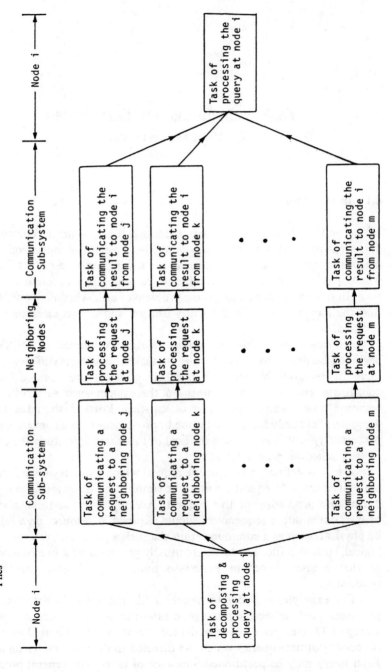

Figure 4.1. Task Precedence Graph for the Processing of a Query which requires the use of Geographically Distributed Files

graph for the processing of a query which requires the use of geographically distributed files is shown in Figure 4.1. On a DCS, the communication overhead, which includes time to set up the communication path and the queueing delay to transmit the messages, is usually much larger than the processing overhead of a query. Therefore, the time required to process a task at a node in Figure 4.1 is usually negligible when compared with the time to pass the results over the communication sub-system. There are also other queries on the system, each of which has its own task precedence graph. There may also be precedence constraints among the precedence graphs of the different queries.

The task scheduling problem that we are concerned with here, is to sequence the processing of tasks, subject to precedence constraints, so that some overall optimization criteria are satisfied. The criteria can be the maximum completion time of all the tasks if the objective is to maximize the throughput of the system; or the sum of the completion times of all the tasks if the objective is to minimize the average response time; or a combination of several optimization criteria.

We first describe a model of a DCS and state some tradeoffs which can be used to simplify the problem. We show that the problem of deterministic scheduling on this model is NP-complete. We proceed to study the problem by putting additional constraints on the model so that the problem is polynomially solvable. The resultant model we have obtained is an organization for an interleaved memory. We study in detail the performance of the interleaved memory and show that the polynomial scheduling algorithm we have developed is an optimal average behavior algorithm. That is, the polynomial algorithm will have the best average performance as compared with any other polynomial algorithms. Lastly, we return to the original model and show a heuristic for the scheduling of tasks on the general model. Some simulation results for this heuristic are also shown.

4.2 A Model for the Scheduling of Tasks on Distributed Systems

4.2.1 The Model

Flynn [FLY66] has classified methods of achieving parallel operations into four classes: the single instruction, single data stream (SISD), the single instruction, multiple data stream (SIMD), the multiple instruction, single data stream (MISD), and the multiple instruction, multiple data stream (MIMD).

A basic model of a computer system is the SIMD model. This model is shown in Figure 4.2. The control unit may represent the CPU. The N

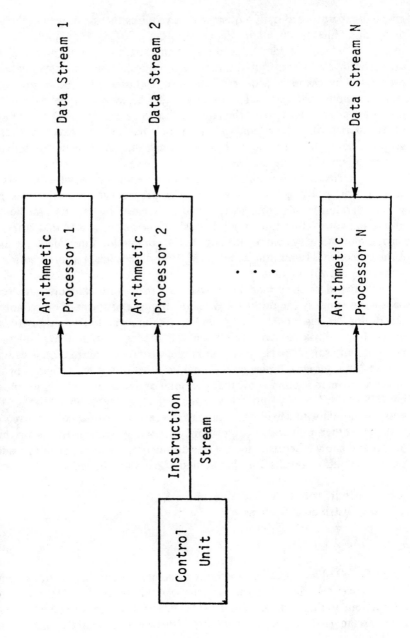

Figure 4.2. Model of an SIMD Computer System [STO75]

arithmetic processors may represent the peripheral processors or backend machines. An instruction may be a search for a particular item on the mass storage with the data streams coming directly from the disks. Another example of a SIMD architecture is the database machine [HSI77].

On the DCS level, the DCS may be represented by a job-shop model in which the basic building block within the job-shop model is the SIMD model. A job-shop is a model which has been used in industrial engineering and deterministic task scheduling [GRA77a]. The characteristic of the job-shop model is that a job or a request is made up of a set of tasks, each of which may be processed on a given machine or processor for a given amount of time. A conceptual model of a DCS is shown in Figure 4.3. The graph is actually a fully connected graph in which an arrow represents an instruction stream and the corresponding return data flow. This is a more restricted model than the general job-shop model because each job or request is only made up of a set of parallel tasks. The basic model at each node is the SIMD model.

The model we have discussed here can be more general. For example, each job or request may consist of a sequence of tasks to be scheduled on different nodes or computers instead of a set of parallel tasks to be scheduled on neighboring nodes. However, this scheduling problem can be solved only when the status of all the nodes of the DCS is known. This is possible when the scheduling is done by a centralized control and all the status changes are reported instantly to the centralized controller. In a geographically distributed DCS, the collection of global information for scheduling is usually very difficult and expensive if not impossible. As a result, we have restricted our study to the case in which the scheduling of tasks is done by using the local information available (distributed control), that is, a SIMD model at each node. The restricted model to be studied is shown in the dotted box in Figure 4.4. The notations used in Figure 4.4 are:

N—number of tasks to be scheduled (it may or may not fit entirely in the buffers of M_a);
M_a—Distributor on the first stage;
$M_{b,j}$—module or machine j on the second stage;
$P_i(M_j)$—Processing time requirement of task i on machine M'_j;
$buff(M_j)$—Amount of buffers for M_j.

The task precedence graph for request i is shown in Figure 4.5. The precedence graph in Figure 4.1 falls in the class of precedence graphs we discuss here if the tasks of communicating to and from node i and the task of processing at a neighboring node are combined into a single task. We assume that the optimization criterion is to minimize the finish time of all the tasks

Figure 4.3. Conceptual Model of a DCS (The direction of an arrow
represents the flow of an instruction stream and the
corresponding return data flow).

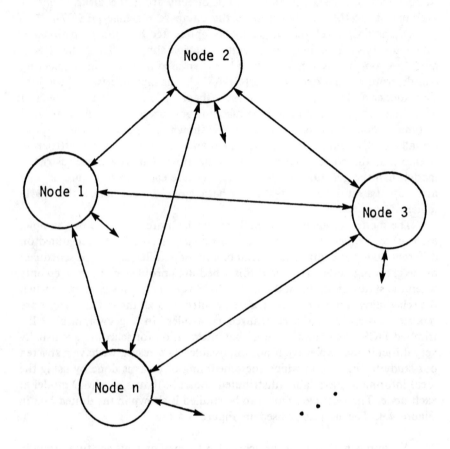

Figure 4.4. An SIMD Model for Task Scheduling on a DCS

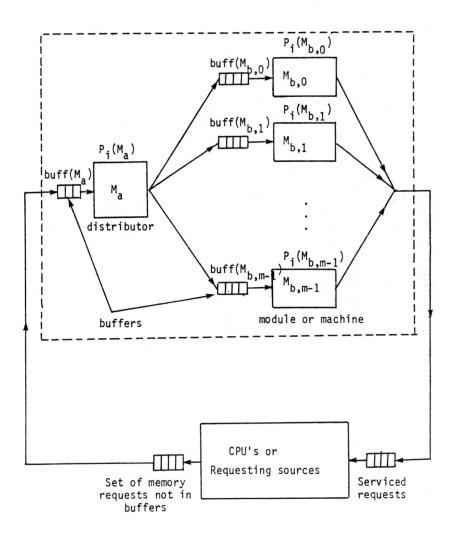

Figure 4.5. Precedence Graph of Tasks for Request i which can be
scheduled on the SIMD Model

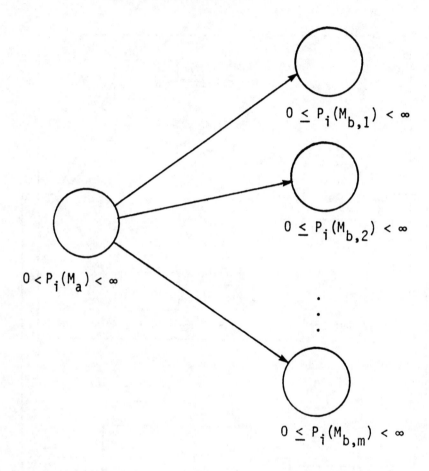

$$0 \leq P_i(M_{b,1}) < \infty$$

$$0 \leq P_i(M_{b,2}) < \infty$$

$$0 < P_i(M_a) < \infty$$

$$0 \leq P_i(M_{b,m}) < \infty$$

in the system. This is generally the assumption made when the objective is to maximize the throughput of the system.

It is also assumed that the amount of buffers on the second stage is finite and that the amount of buffers on the first stage may be infinite, that is,

$$0 \leq buff(M_a) \leq \infty;$$

$$0 \leq buff(M_{b,0}) = buff(M_{b,1}) = \ldots = buff(M_{b,m-1}) < \infty.$$

Further, it is assumed that precedence constraint may exist among the different requests and the tasks may have positive release dates. The analysis of this model is shown in section 4.3. We now discuss some assumptions which would allow the problem to be simplified.

4.2.2. Assumptions which allow the Task Scheduling Problem to be Simplified

Certain assumptions can be made so that the task scheduling problem can be simplified.

(1) Processing Overhead is ignored

The processing overhead is usually much smaller than the communication overhead and it is ignored. This assumption will eliminate many tasks in the precedence graph.

(2) Static Algorithms are used

Static algorithms schedule a set of tasks available at the time of scheduling and a set of tasks that are known to arrive at fixed future times. The schedule does not change during the duration of the processing of these tasks. On the other hand, dynamic algorithms are more flexible and they reschedule all the available tasks whenever a new task comes in. The advantage of dynamic algorithms is that they allow task initiations to be dynamic and do not restrict the schedule to the order determined initially, but have the disadvantage of larger overheads. In our model, we have assumed that static algorithms are used because they do not depend on the arrival process and are easier to optimize. The static algorithm developed can be used as a heuristic when the arrival process is indeterminate.

(3)   Deterministic Processing Times are assumed

The processing time of a task can be assumed to be deterministic or probabilistic. In the deterministic case it is possible to determine the order which can best satisfy the optimization criterion. The theory of scheduling developed now is mostly applicable to the deterministic case. A lot of work has been done in flow-shop and job-shop scheduling (see [GRA77a, LEN77] for a good survey). The theory developed there can be applied to solve the problem here. The algorithm developed in section 4.5 is actually extended from Johnson's optimal polynomial algorithm for a two stage flow-shop [JOH54]. One additional advantage about the deterministic assumption is that the difficulty of the scheduling problem can be assessed easily in most cases. NP-completeness of the problem can usually be shown or a polynomial algorithm can be found.

On the other hand, a lot of work in queueing theory has been done with respect to the "central server model" to evaluate its performance. For example, Baskett et al. have developed a closed form formula for the performance of a queueing network when certain conditions are satisfied [BAS75]; Sauer and Chandy have developed approximate analysis techniques for central server models [SAU75]; Chandy et al. have studied approximate analysis techniques for general queueing networks [CHA75]. Unfortunately, when a probabilistic assumption is made on the processing time of a job, the optimization criterion must be defined probabilistically, and the analysis may become very difficult. Some work has been done in finding a service schedule which minimizes the expected costs [MEI77, KON68, KLI74]. However, a general theory in this area is still lacking.

In the analysis presented in this chapter, the deterministic assumption is made because of its mathematical tractability. The general task scheduling problem on DCS's using our model can be shown to be NP-complete. Evaluation methods of scheduling algorithms are analysis augmented with simulations. We have not studied the solution of scheduling problems using approximation algorithms [WEI77] in this chapter.

Based on these assumptions, the NP-completeness of the general task scheduling problem is shown in the next section.

4.3   NP-Completeness of the Task Scheduling Problem

We prove in this section, the NP-completeness of the task scheduling problem on the model of Figure 4.4. It is assumed that we have identical processing orders on all machines, that is, the best permutation schedule has to be determined; and the amount of buffer space in all the machines is infinite. It is further assumed that no preemption is allowed in the schedule.

We only prove for the special case of two machines on the second stage (i.e., $m=2$).

THEOREM 4.1

The problem of deterministic task scheduling on the SIMD model with the following assumptions, is NP-complete:

(1) $m=2$ (two machines on the second stage);
(2)   Each request has the following task precedence graph:

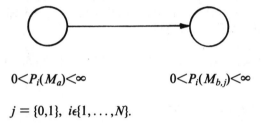

$$0<P_i(M_a)<\infty \qquad\qquad 0<P_i(M_{b,j})<\infty$$

$$j = \{0,1\}, \ i\epsilon\{1,\ldots,N\}.$$

That is, each request only requires the service of one machine on the second stage. There are no precedence constraints among requests;
(3)   The optimization criterion is to minimize C_{max}, the maximum task completion time.

Proof

Problem ϵ NP because a non-deterministic Turing machine can predict the sequence in polynomial time.

The problem is reducible from the Knapsack problem[1].

Let $n=t+2$

$$\forall \ i\epsilon T \ P_i(M_{b,1})=0; \ \Sigma_{i\epsilon T}P_i(M_a)=A; \ \Sigma_{i\epsilon T}P_i(M_{b,0})=B;$$

---

1.   The Knapsack problem is: "Given positive integers $a_1, \ldots, a_t, A = \Sigma_{i=1}^{t} a_i, B$, does there exist a subset $S \subset T = \{1, \ldots, t\}$ such that $\Sigma_{i\epsilon S} \ a_i = B.$"

Jobs are agreeable if for $S \subset T$ where S contains jobs $1, 2, \ldots, n-2$,

$$\Sigma_{S \subset T} P_i(M_a) \gtreqless a \text{ then } \Sigma_{S \subset T} P_i(M_{b,0}) \lesseqgtr b$$

$$P_i(M_a), \ P_i(M_{b,0}) \geqslant 0$$

$$P_{n-1}(M_a) = 1; \ P_{n-1}(M_{b,0}) = a; \ P_{n-1}(M_{b,1}) = 0;$$
$$P_n(M_a) = b - A + a; \ P_n(M_{b,0}) = 0; \ P_n(M_{b,1}) = B - b + A - a;$$
$$y = B + a + 1.$$

If Knapsack has a solution, then there exists a schedule with $\Sigma_{i \in S} P_i(M_a) = a$ and $C_{\max} = y$ as illustrated in Figure 4.6a. If Knapsack has no solution, then $\Sigma_{i \in S} P_i(M_a) - a = c \neq 0$ for each $S \subset T$ and we have a processing order $(J_{n-1};$ $\{J_i : i \in S\}; J_n; \{J_i : i \in T - S\})$ such that:

$$c > 0 \implies C_{max} = 1 + \Sigma_{i \in S} P_i(M_a) + P_n(M_a) + P_n(M_{b,1}) =$$
$$B + a + c + 1 > y$$

$$c < 0 \implies \text{see Figure 4.6b.}$$

If $\Sigma_{i \in S} P_i(M_{b,0}) < b$, then there exists overlap between the operation of $P_j(M_a)$ and $P_j(M_{b,0})$ for $j \in T - S$. The maximum finish time is:

$$C_{\max} = 1 + a + B + \delta > y.$$

It follows that Knapsack has a solution iff this problem has a solution with $C_{\max} \leqq y$. Since the Knapsack problem is NP-complete, the problem we are considering is also NP-complete.

Q.E.D.

THEOREM 4.2

The problem of deterministic task scheduling on the SIMD model with assumptions similar to Theorem 4.1 except for assumption (2), is NP-complete.

(2) Each request has the following task precedence graph:

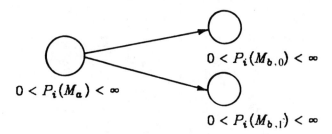

$$0 < P_i(M_{b,0}) < \infty$$

$$0 < P_i(M_a) < \infty$$

$$0 < P_i(M_{b,1}) < \infty$$

That is, each request requires the service of both machines on the second stage. There are no precedence constraints among requests.

Proof

Problem ϵ NP because a non-deterministic Turing machine can predict the sequence in polynomial time.

The problem is reducible from the Knapsack problem.
Let

$$n = t + 1$$

$$P_i(M_a) = 1; \quad P_i(M_{b,0}) = t^*a_i; \quad P_i(M_{b,1}) = 1; \quad (i \epsilon T);$$

$$P_n(M_a) = t^*b; \quad P_n(M_{b,0}) = 1; \quad P_n(M_{b,1}) = t(A - b) + 1;$$

$$y = t(A + 1) + 1;$$

The timing diagram is shown in Figure 4.7.

If Knapsack has a solution, then $\exists$ schedule with $\Sigma_{i \epsilon S} P_i(M_a) = b$ and $C_{max} = y$. If Knapsack has no solution, then $\Sigma_{i \epsilon S} P_i(M_a) - b = c \neq 0$ for each $S \subset T$, and we have a processing order $(\{J_i : i \epsilon S\}; J_n; \{J_i : i \epsilon T - S\})$ such that:

$$c > 0 => C_{max} > \Sigma_{i \epsilon S} P_i(M_a) + P_n(M_{b,1}) = t(\Sigma_{i \epsilon S} P_i(M_a)) + t(A - b) + 1$$

$$= t(A + c) + 1 \geqslant y$$

$$c < 0 => C_{max} > P_n(M_a) + P_n(M_{b,0}) + \Sigma_{i \epsilon T - S} P_i(M_{b,0})$$

Figure 4.6. Proof of Theorem 4.1

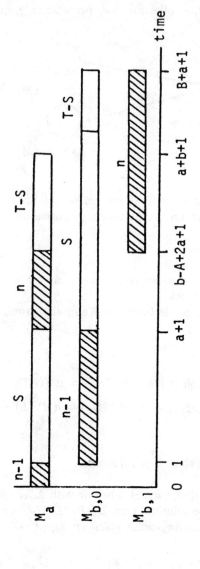

(a) Knapsack has a solution

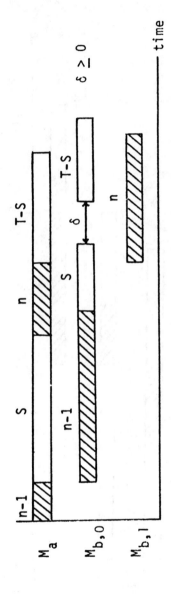

(b) Knapsack has no solution and $c < 0$

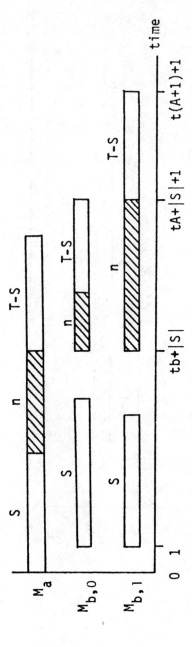

Figure 4.7. Timing Diagram for the Proof of Theorem 4.2

$$= t*b + 1 + t*A - t\, \Sigma_{i\in S}\, P_i(M_a)$$

$$= t(A - c) + 1 \geqslant y.$$

It follows that Knapsack has a solution iff this problem has a solution with $C_{max} \leqq y$. Since the Knapsack is NP-complete, the problem we are considering is also NP-complete.

Q.E.D.

THEOREM 4.3

The problem of deterministic task scheduling on the SIMD model with the following assumptions is NP-complete:

(1) $m = 2$;
(2) There exist precedence constraints among the requests;
(3) The optimization criterion is to minimize C_{max}.

Proof

Problem ϵ NP because a non-deterministic Turing machine can guess the sequence in polynomial time.

The problem can be reduced from a conventional two stage flow shop problem with a tree precedence graph and minimum C_{max}. The reduction of the problem is obvious and will not be presented here. Since the two stage flow shop problem with a tree precedence graph is NP-complete, it implies that the problem we are considering is NP-complete as well.

Q.E.D.

THEOREM 4.4

The problem of deterministic task scheduling on the SIMD model with the following assumptions is NP-complete:

(1) $m = 2$;
(2) The release dates of jobs may be $\geqq 0$, that is, not all jobs are available initially;
(3) The optimization criterion is to minimize C_{max}.

Proof

Problem ϵ NP because a non-deterministic Turing machine can guess the sequence in polynomial time.

The problem can be reduced from a conventional two stage flow shop problem with release dates ≥ 0 and minimum C_{max}. The reduction is obvious. Since the two stage flow shop problem with positive release dates is NP-complete, this implies that the problem we are considering is NP-complete.

Q.E.D.

THEOREM 4.5

The problem of deterministic task scheduling on the SIMD model with the following assumptions is NP-complete:

(1) $m = 2$;
(2) There are no buffers on the second stage, i.e. $buff(M_{b,0})$ $= buff(M_{b,1}) = 0$. Therefore, requests are not allowed to wait on the second stage;
(3) The optimization criterion is to minimize C_{max}.

Proof

Problem ϵ NP because a non-deterministic Turing machine can guess the sequence in polynomial time.

The problem is reducible from the Knapsack or the Partition problem. Let:

$$n = t + 2;$$

$$\forall\ i\epsilon T;\ P_i(M_a) = a_i;\ P_i(M_{b,0}) = 0;\ P_i(M_{b,1}) = 1;\ a_i \geqslant 1;$$

If A is even, then

$$P_{n-1}(M_a) = 1;\ P_{n-1}(M_{b,0}) = \frac{A}{2} + 1;\ P_{n-1}(M_{b,1}) = 0;$$

$$P_n(M_a) = 1;\ P_n(M_{b,0}) = \frac{A}{2} + 1;\ P_n(M_{b,1}) = 0;$$

$$y = A + 3;$$

If A is odd, then

$$P_{n-1}(M_a) = 2; \quad P_{n-1}(M_{b,0}) = \frac{A+3}{2}; \quad P_{n-1}(M_{b,1}) = 0;$$

$$P_n(M_a) = 2; \quad P_n(M_{b,0}) = \frac{A+3}{2}; \quad P_n(M_{b,1}) = 0;$$

$$y = A + 5.$$

If Knapsack (for A odd) or Partition (for A even) has a solution, then there exists a schedule with $\Sigma_{i\epsilon S}P_i(M_a) = A/2$ and $C_{\max} = y$ as illustrated in Figure 4.8. If Knapsack (Partition) has no solution, then $\Sigma_{i\epsilon S}{}^{a_i} - A/2 = c \neq 0$ for each $S \subset T$ and we have a processing order $(J_{n-1}; \{J_i : i\epsilon S\}; J_n; \{J_i : i\epsilon T{-}S\})$ such that for A even,

$$c > 0 \Longrightarrow C_{\max} \; = P_{n-1}(M_a) + \Sigma_{i\epsilon S} \, P_i(M_a) + P_n(M_a) + P_n(M_{b,0})$$

$$= 1 + \frac{A}{2} + c + 1 + \frac{A}{2} + 1$$

$$> y$$

$$c < 0 \Longrightarrow C_{\max} \; = P_{n-1}(M_a) + P_{n-1}(M_{b,0}) + \Sigma_{i\epsilon T-S} \, P_i(M_a) + 1$$

$$= 1 + \frac{A}{2} + 1 + \frac{A}{2} + c + 1$$

$$> y.$$

Note that in this case, although the jobs in S have finished, job n cannot be started until time $= 1 + A/2$ because there is no buffer available in $M_{b,0}$.

It follows that Knapsack has a solution iff this problem has a solution with $C_{\max} \leqq y$. Since the Knapsack problem is NP-complete, the problem we are considering is also NP-complete.

Q.E.D.

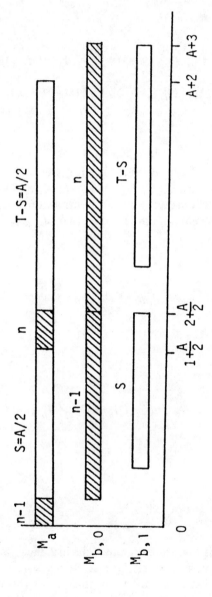

Figure 4.8. Timing Diagram for the Proof of Theorem 4.5 (*A* even)

We have therefore proved that the task scheduling problem on the SIMD model is NP-complete (with the assumptions stated in the theorems). To solve these problems, suitable heuristics can be designed. However, we delay this until section 4.5. In the next section, we show that by restricting the processing time on each machine, the task scheduling problem can be made polynomially solvable. The processing times of the tasks are restricted in a fashion such that $P_i(M_a) = 1$ and $P_i(M_{b,j}) = m$ (m = number of machines on the second stage) and each request needs the service of only one machine on the second stage. This particular model represents a model of an interleaved memory system.

4.4   The Restricted Model—An Optimal Algorithm for Scheduling Requests on an Interleaved Memory System

In this section, we evaluate two organizations of an interleaved primary memory system. We have designed a scheduling algorithm and have shown its optimality under the assumption of random independent requests. The random request assumption is tenable for multiprocessor systems with a large number of processors sharing a common memory and each processor making requests independent of others. For a lookahead processor such as a pipeline computer which executes directly from the primary memory (e.g. IBM 360/91), we have simulated the effects of the non-randomness of the accesses using execution traces, and have found that the algorithm performs well. Our study is useful in demonstrating that a polynomial time optimal average behavior algorithm can be found for the restricted model.

The restricted model is described in seven sub-sections. Section 4.4.1 presents the requirements in the design of an interleaved memory system. Section 4.4.2 describes the characteristics of the access sequence of pipelined processors. Section 4.4.3 presents a summary of the previous work in parallel memories; the deficiencies in these designs are pinpointed. Section 4.4.4 describes two organizations of the memory and shows that the second organization is equivalent to the first organization as far as average behavior is concerned. The optimal scheduling algorithm is also presented. Sections 4.4.5 to 4.4.7 evaluate the performance of the scheduling algorithm by proving that the algorithm has optimal average behavior for random requests, and by simulating with execution traces from actual programs and randomly generated requests.

4.4.1   Requirements for the Design of a Primary Memory

The requirements for the design of a primary memory are:

(1) Bandwidth

The bandwidth represents the average throughput of the memory system and is given in terms of bits returned per unit time. In a parallel memory system, the bandwidth is the sum of the bandwidths of all the modules

$$\text{Bandwidth} = \sum_{\text{module } k} \frac{[\text{word length of module } k] * [\text{average utilization of module } k]}{(\text{cycle time of module } k)}$$

where the average utilization of a module is the average fraction of time the module is busy. For the case of identical modules, the bandwidth can be written as:

$$\text{Bandwidth} = \frac{[\text{number of modules}] * [\text{word length}] * [\text{average utilization}]}{(\text{memory cycle time})}$$

$$\text{Bandwidth} = \frac{\text{constant} * [\text{average number of busy modules}]}{(\text{memory cycle time})} \qquad (4.1)$$

where the constant in Eq. 4.1 has a unit of bits. The organization of interleaved memories presented here assumes that all the modules are identical, that is, with the same memory cycle time, and that the word length of each module is kept constant. The objective of maximizing the bandwidth is, therefore, equivalent to maximizing the average utilization of the modules.

(2) Response time

The response time is the delay between the time a request is issued to the primary memory and the time the request is serviced, assuming that the datum resides in the primary memory. This is also called the waiting time of the requests.

(3) Size

This is the required memory size or capacity.

(4)   Cost

This is the maximum allowable cost of the resultant design that satisifes the above requirements.

The design of the memory must satisfy the above requirements. Moreover, the performance of the final system can be evaluated by using these parameters as evaluation criteria.

4.4.2   Characteristics of the Access Sequence of a Pipelined Processor

In order to utilize the parallel memories, there must be parallelism in the access sequence so that multiple accesses can be overlapped. In a conventional uni-processor system where there is a single access stream, an access cannot be issued until its predecessors have completed. There is no parallelism involved and at most one of the parallel memories is used at any time. The memory utilization is increased when multiple accesses can be issued and serviced in parallel. Architectures such as a multiprocessor system sharing a common primary memory or a pipelined computer would have the capability to issue multiple requests simultaneously.

In this description, a pipelined organization in the most general sense, instead of specially structured pipelined computers with different arithmetic units (e.g. CRAY I), applications (e.g. vector processing), additional memory support (e.g. cache), and interconnections (e.g. ILLIAC IV) are assumed. The processor is further assumed to be executing directly from the main memory. The scheduling algorithm developed is general enough to be applicable to the interleaved memories of all the specially structured pipelined computers. However, the exact performance is not found for each type of machine.

In a pipelined computer, the computational process (say an instruction) is segmented into several sub-processes which are executed by dedicated autonomous units (pipeline segments). Successive processes (instructions) can be carried out in an overlapped mode analogous to an industrial assembly line. The pipeline segments are able to generate memory requests independent of the others and, therefore, the dependencies in an access stream are bypassed.

Occasionally, there exist dependencies among the accesses. A dependency is a logical relationship between two accesses such that the second cannot be accessed until the first has been accessed. A memory access sequence generated by a pipelined processor has Class D dependencies as classified by Chang et al. [CHA77]. Anderson et al. have identified three main sources of dependencies: (a) register interlock, (b) branching, and (c) interrupts [AND67]. In this paper, we concentrate on analyzing the memory performance without taking into account the effects of dependencies. A subsequent paper estimates the performance degradation due to dependencies [RAM81b].

In addition to the effects of address dependencies, the order in which instructions and data are requested also affects the memory performance. For a pipelined processor, the request stream is a sequence of instruction-operand fetch pairs. However, not every instruction involves an operand fetch and if the bus is wide enough, two or more instructions can be fetched in one access. A notable characteristic in this access pattern is that instruction fetches are made in a sequence interlaced with operand accesses. The performance of the memory system may be improved by separating the memory modules into two sets, one for instructions and one for data. The effects on memory performance due to separation and no separation of instruction and data modules are compared in [RAM81a].

4.4.3 Previous Work on the Study of Interleaved Memories

One of the early successful implementations of interleaved memories is in the IBM 360/91 [BOL67]. In this computer, the storage system is made up of an interleaved set of memory modules and the degree of interleaving equals the number of memory modules. The memory can service a string of sequential requests by starting, or selecting, a storage unit every cycle until all are busy. In effect, the storage cycles are all staggered (Figure 4.9). By using a set of buffers called the request stack, conflicting requests which access the same module can be resolved by allowing only one of these requests to access the module and by storing the rest in the request stack to be issued in later cycles. Simulation results were shown for the average access time and the bandwidth with various degrees of interleaving.

The earliest attempt to model the performance of interleaved memories was done by Hellerman [HEL67]. A saturated request queue (a queue in which requests are never exhausted) with random requests is assumed, and no provision is made for the queueing of these requests on busy modules. The request queue is scanned until a repeated request is found. This constitutes a collision. Hellerman's results show that with m memory modules, the average number of requests scanned before a collision is approximately $m^{0.56}$ for m between 1 and 45. This is taken to be an indication of bandwidth. Knuth and Rao [KNU75] show an alternate, exact way to calculate the bandwidth. However, both of these results are pessimistic because they do not allow the queueing of conflicting requests to the same module.

Burnett et al. have developed a number of models on parallel memories. In two of these models, [BUR70, BUR73], they assume that the modules operate synchronously (all modules start and end their cycles simultaneously) and a scanner scans a saturated request queue and admits new requests to be serviced until it attempts to assign a request to a busy module. In two other models [COF71, BUR75], they further assume that a set of blockage buffers is present so that requests made to a busy module can be stored and issued in later cycles. The scanner continues to scan the request queue until all the modules have been allocated or until all the buffers are occupied. In effect, the maximum size of the request queue inspected by the scanner never exceeds $b+m$ where b is the number of buffers and m is the number of memory modules.

They have also studied a request model similar to Strecker's model [STR70] by assuming a probability α for the succeeding request to request the next module in sequence and a probability of $(1-\alpha)/(m-1)$ to request any other module. They have developed two algorithms that modified the request pattern in order to increase the bandwidth. The first one is called the instruction-data cycle structure, which divides the request queues into two sub-queues, the instruction queue and the data queue. These two sub-queues are inspected in alternate memory cycles. They found that there are improvements from –4% to 12% in bandwidth (the number of modules varies from 8 to 16) over a model with four blockage buffers and a single queue [BUR75]. The second algorithm, the group request structure, separates a memory cycle into two sub-cycles; the first sub-cycle is used for servicing the instruction queue, and the second sub-cycle is used for servicing the data queue. They found that there are 8% to 16% improvements over the same instruction-data cycle structure algorithm.

Terman [TER76] has made a trace driven simulation on the instruction-data cycle structure algorithm and found that the theoretical predictions of Burnett and Coffman fit well with the simulation results for instruction fetches, but their predictions do not fit well with the simulation results for data requests which are more random than instruction requests and are difficult to model accurately.

Many other researchers have studied models of parallel memories. These include Flores [FLO64], Skinner and Asher [SKI69], Ravi [RAV72], Bhandarkar [BHA75], Sastry and Kain [SAS75], Baskett and Smith [BAS76], Briggs and Davidson [BRI77], Chang, Kuck and Lawrie [CHA77], Smith [SMI77], and Hoogendoorn [HOO77], etc. These studies are directed toward multi-processor systems and we will not describe them here.

In the remainder of this section, the deficiencies found in the previous models are summarized.

(1) All the previous models assume that the memories operate synchronously. As Burnett and Coffman pointed out, simultaneous memory operations offer more opportunity to take advantage of program behavior in a particular memory system [BUR75]. However, with synchronous operations, there is the problem of returning the results of the accesses from the memory. Since the results from each module are available simultaneously, extra buses or queues are needed to return these data to the processor. Further, a pipelined processor usually makes requests in sequence rather than in batches. Therefore, it is desirable to study a model in which the memory modules operate out of phase. By out of phase, we mean either (a) the initiations of the modules are asynchronous, or (b) the initiations of the modules are timed by a clock and, during a clock interval, at most one module can be initiated. Because the operations of asynchronous modules are much more difficult to control, only case (b) is considered.

(2) Very few studies have been made to minimize the waiting time of a request to the memory. Flores [FLO64] has made a quantitative study relating the waiting time factor to the memory cycle time, the input/output time, and the worst case execution time for different numbers of memory banks. However, his study is directed toward the effect of interference from the input/output units and there is no queueing of requests. In other models, a saturated request queue is assumed, and the effects of waiting time are not considered. When the queue size is finite, it is possible to develop optimal algorithms which minimize the average waiting time of requests in the queue. In this discussion, the number of queued requests is assumed to be finite so that the effects on waiting time can be studied.

4.4.4   The Organizations of Primary Memory for a Pipelined Processor

We present in this section two different implementation alternatives of interleaved memories (Organizations I and II). The two organizations differ in the configurations of the memory request buffers. In Organization I, a single set of request buffers is assumed to be shared by all the modules while in Organization II, individual request buffers exist for each module. The general assumptions made are as follows:

(1) The request rate from the processor is assumed to be high enough so that any empty buffer in the memory system is filled up by an incoming request immediately. Buffers are assumed to exist at the processor end so that any additional requests generated by the processor can be queued there. The requests that can be served by the modules are those

that exist in the memory buffers only. The high request rate assumption, in essence, means that the request queue is always saturated and is made because we want to get an upper bound on the performance of the memory.

(2) Each request is assumed to be an integer from 0 to $m-1$, which is the module it requests, obtained as the residue of dividing the address by m.

(3) The service time of each module (the read time or the write time) for a request is assumed to be constant. This is a good model for semiconductor memories. We also assume that a memory module, once initiated to start a memory cycle, is not available until the end of the cycle.

(4) A memory cycle time is the time it takes for a memory module to service a request. Each memory cycle is assumed to consist of m equally spaced memory sub-cycles. It is further assumed that exactly one module can be initiated to service a request at the beginning of a memory sub-cycle and it takes m sub-cycles (1 memory cycle) to service any request, i.e., homogeneous service times. With this assumption, the problem of multiple data paths is resolved because at most one module finishes in each sub-cycle and the system is never confronted with returning results from more than one module simultaneously. The modules are, therefore, clocked by the memory sub-cycles.

(5) The waiting time of a request is the time between the initiation of request and the completion of service. A waiting cycle is defined similar to Flores [FLO64] as the ratio of the waiting time and the memory cycle time.

In Organization I (Figure 4.10), there are m memory modules; a single set of $b+1$ associative buffers, B_T, B_1, B_2, ..., B_b; and an intelligent scheduler which schedules a memory module to start a memory cycle. The modules operate out of phase in a fashion called staggered cycles. One example of a staggered cycle is shown in Fig. 4.9. The set of $b+1$ associative buffers is used to store incoming requests. A request queued on a specific module can be retrieved in one associative search operation. Whenever a request is taken out from a buffer, all the requests behind it are pushed one location up so that B_T is empty. The buffer B_T has an additional function, namely, to receive requests from the bus. Due to our assumption of high request rate, B_T is filled immediately whenever it is empty. The queueing discipline for those requests in the buffers which address the same module is essentially first-in-first-out (FIFO). Other queueing disciplines are not studied because only uni-processor systems are considered in this design.

The operation of the memory system is controlled by the intelligent scheduler. The scheduler, using a scheduling algorithm, decides at the

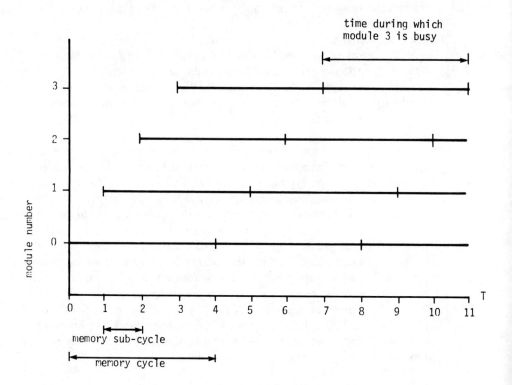

Figure 4.10. Organization I—An Interleaved Memory System with a Single Request Queue

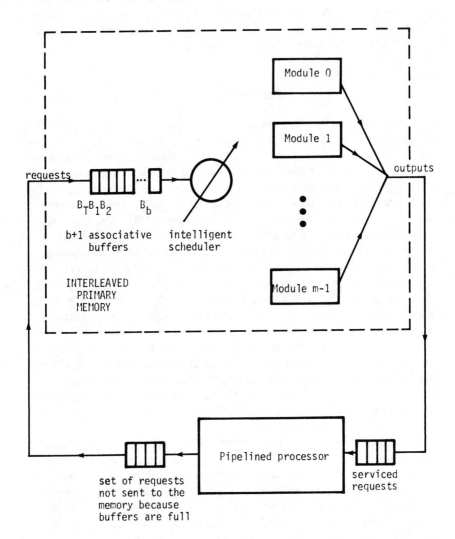

beginning of each memory sub-cycle whether to initiate a memory module and if so which module to initiate. The selection of a module to initiate is determined by the information about the requests in the associative buffers and by the knowledge about the status of the modules (free or busy). The optimal scheduling algorithm investigated is:

Algorithm 4.1 Maximum-Work-Free-Module-First
              (MWFMF) Algorithm

In this algorithm, a dynamic list of free modules is kept. Conceptually, at the beginning of a memory sub-cycle, the buffers are checked associatively to see if any requests are queued on the free modules. If there is none, no module is initiated. If there is at least one free module with a non-zero number of queued requests, an associative search is made on the buffers and the free module with the maximum number of requests queued on it is initiated. In case of ties, only the first one is initiated (Figure 4.11a)[2]. The implementation of this algorithm can be done by using an additional associative memory of size m in the scheduler (Figure 4.11b). Each word in this associative memory can function as a counter and is used to indicate the number of requests queued on the corresponding module. The corresponding word is incremented/decremented when a request enters/leaves the request buffers. The free module with the maximum number of requests can be obtained by performing a maximum search on those words in this associative memory corresponding to the free modules (a design for this is shown in Chapter 5, see also [RAM78]). The maximum search algorithm shown in [RAM78] is parallel by word and serial by bit and the time to perform a maximum search is proportional to the number of bits in the memory. The speed of this algorithm is, therefore, proportional to $\lceil \log_2(b+2) \rceil$, where $\lceil x \rceil$ is the smallest integer larger than or equal to x.

In addition to the overhead related to the execution of the scheduling algorithm, there is also the overhead of selecting the request from the associative buffers and sending it to the memory module. This overhead consists of matching the selected module number against all the requests in the buffers and selecting the first request if multiple responses occur in the match. Using a bit-serial word-parallel equality matching algorithm, e.g. [RAM78], and binary tree type multiple match resolution circuit, e.g.

---

2. Multiple requests can be initiated in a sub-cycle. But since the return bus can return at most one piece of datum in any sub-cycle, only one read (which generates return data) and multiple writes (which do not generate return data) can be initiated simultaneously. The effect due to this improvement, as seen later, is very small.

Figure 4.11a. MWFMF Scheduling Algorithm

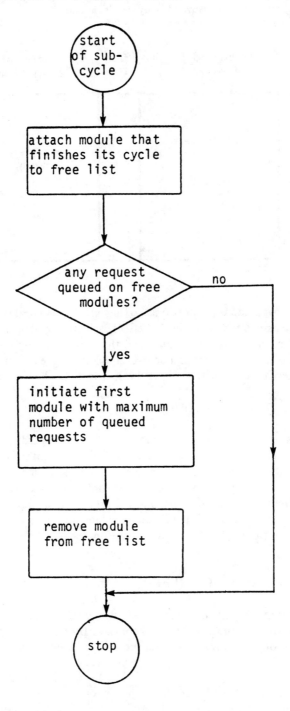

Figure 4.11b. Implementation of the MWFMF Scheduling Algorithm Using Associative Memory ($\lceil x \rceil$ is the smallest
integer larger than or equal to $\lceil x \rceil$)

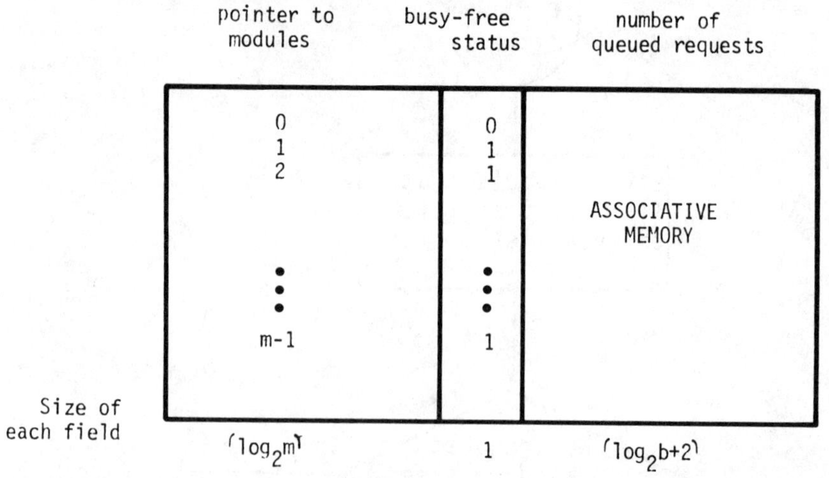

```
        pointer to          busy-free          number of
         modules              status        queued requests

              0                  0
              1                  1
              2                  1
                                                ASSOCIATIVE
              •                  •                 MEMORY
              •                  •
              •                  •
            m-1                  1

  Size of
each field   ⌈log₂m⌉              1              ⌈log₂b+2⌉
```

[FOS68], this overhead is proportional to $\lceil \log_2 m \rceil + \lceil \log_2(b+1) \rceil$. In general,
the overhead associated with the MWFMF scheduling algorithms is very
small, and the selection of a module and the corresponding request to be
initiated in the next sub-cycle can be overlapped with the current sub-cycle.

Two alternative algorithms have been investigated. They are:

Algorithm 4.2 Round-Robin (RR)

All the modules are initiated in a round-robin fashion regardless of whether
a request is queued on the module. The scheduler does not make use of any
information about the status of the system. The implementation of this
algorithm is very simple and the scheduler only has to know the current
module initiated. In Figure 4.9, the Gantt chart for the operation of a 4-way
interleaved memory with a RR scheduling algorithm is shown. This is the
scheduling algorithm that is implemented in most interleaved memory
systems today.

Algorithm 4.3 First-Free-First (FFF)

In this algorithm, only the information about the status of the modules (free
or busy) is utilized by the scheduler. There is a FIFO list of free modules. At
the beginning of a memory sub-cycle, the scheduler puts a busy module to

the end of the free list if this module finishes its cycle. It then initiates the module at the head of the free list if there are any requests queued on it, otherwise the module at the head is appended to the tail of the free list and no other module is examined in this sub-cycle. The scheduler may also check all the subsequent modules in the free list, but the time for this is proportional to the number of modules and is not feasible when this number is large.

In contrast, the MWFMF algorithm utilizes both the information about the status of the modules and the requests in the buffers and, therefore, is expected to perform better. The RR and FFF algorithms are inferior to the MWFMF algorithm under the assumption of random, independent requests because the MWFMF algorithm is shown to be optimal. The MWFMF algorithm is also seen to perform better under trace driven simulations. These are shown in section 4.4.7.

At the end of each memory sub-cycle, at most one request is serviced. The result is sent back to the processor. The necessary queue for storing these results is excluded from the memory organization.

The requests of the system come into the memory in a specific pattern. Two types of access patterns are considered in this design:

(1) *Random accesses with no address dependency*—The addresses are random and are independent of each other. Although this access pattern is not characteristic of pipeline computers, the random request assumption is useful as a lower bound for the performance when the accesses are correlated. It is also useful to model multiprocessor systems where the number of processors is much larger than the number of modules.

(2) *Accesses from the execution traces of a monoprogrammed pipelined computer*—The addresses in the execution traces are correlated and they represent a similar addressing behavior when the actual program is executed on a pipelined processor. We have used execution traces from a pipelined processor representing large scientific applications, the CDC 7600, in this study.

Organization II is similar to Organization I except that separate sets of buffers exist for each module (Figure 4.12). Requests from the processor are continuously moved into the buffers of each module via B_T until a request in B_T is directed toward a module whose buffers are already full. The request in B_T is blocked, and as a result, further requests are blocked from entering the memory. When the module responsible for this blocking has finished servicing its current request, one request from its buffers is serviced which results in an empty buffer. The blocking request in B_T is moved into this

Figure 4.12. Organization II—An Interleaved Memory System with
Multiple Request Queues

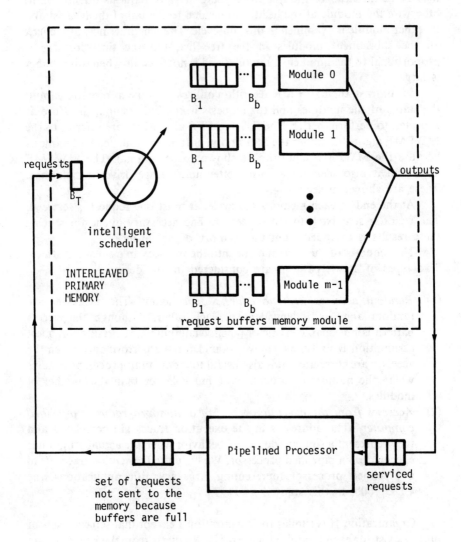

empty buffer. Because buffers for other modules may not be full before the blocking situation, one or more requests can then be accepted to the memory system until the previous blocking situation occurs with one of the modules. When $b=0$, there is only one buffer, B_T, in the system and this is exactly the same as Organization I with $b=0$. Therefore, Organization II degenerates into Organization I when $b=0$.

The buffers used in Organization II are simpler than that of Organization I. Associative search capabilities are not necessary for these buffers. The implementation of the scheduler is similar to that of Organization I. The advantage of this system is that the request buffers are simple shift registers and, therefore, are cheaper. However, in order for this organization to operate at full capacity, more than one request may have to be moved across the bus into the memory in a memory sub-cycle. Since we assume that a pipelined processor generates on the order of one request every memory sub-cycle, the blocking situation may not always occur and the memory is under-utilized. Further, it is necessary to build a faster bus so that multiple requests can be moved across the bus in a memory sub-cycle. Due to these reasons, the buffers in Organization II may be under-utilized and it is difficult to estimate its performance. However, if it is assumed that the bus is wide enough to transfer parallel requests into the memory in a sub-cycle and enough requests are generated so that blocking always occurs, the following shows that Organization II is equivalent to Organization I as far as the average behavior is concerned.

The two organizations discussed are operating in steady state. This means that the systems have been operating for a long time so that initial start up effects have diminished. Further, since the buffer size is limited and fixed and the request rate from the processor is assumed to be very high, the average arrival rate to the memory system must equal the average service rate. The average arrival rate and the average waiting time are finite and satisfy Little's formula [LIT61].
Let

m = number of memory modules;

b_I = number of buffers for the system in Organization I (not including B_T);

b_{II} = number of buffers for each module in Organization II (not including B_T);

$e_{B,i}$ = utilization of the buffers $B_1, \ldots, B_b$ in Organization i ($i =$ I, II; $e_{B,I} = 1$)

e_T = utilization of buffer B_T ($e_T = 1$ for both organizations);

B_I = number of buffers $B_1, \ldots, B_{b_I}$ in Organization I ($B_I = b_I$);

B_{II} = number of buffers $B_1, \ldots, B_{b_{II}}$ in Organization II ($B_{II} = m*b_{II}$);

$u_{m,b,i}$ = expected utilization of the modules in Organization i ($i=$I,II);

$w_{m,b,i}$ = expected waiting memory cycles of the requests in Organization i (i=I,II);

M_i = expected number of requests in Organization i (i=I,II);

λ_i = expected arrival rate per memory cycle in Organization i (i=I,II);

Then

$$M_i = (e_{B,i} * B_i + e_T) + u_{m,b,i} * m \qquad (4.2)$$

$$\lambda_i = m * u_{m,b,i} \qquad (4.3)$$

and they satisfy Little's formula,

$$M_i = \lambda_i * w_{m,b,i} \qquad (4.4)$$

The importance of Little's formula lies in the fact that the average module utilization, the average number of waiting cycles, and the average buffer utilization are related. Once two of them are obtained, the other can be calculated easily. Further, if $\lambda_I = \lambda_{II}$ and b_{II} is chosen to be $b_I/(e_{B,II}*m)$, then $M_I = M_{II}$ and $W_I = W_{II}$. That is, Organizations I and II are equivalent as far as the average behavior is concerned. The only difference lies in the buffer utilization which is less than 1 in Organization II whereas the buffers are fully utilized in Organization I. In the next section, we present our proofs for Organization I only because the two organizations are equivalent and the results are directly applicable. It is also implicit from now on that the subscript i ($i = I, II$) is omitted and Organization I is assumed unless otherwise stated.

4.4.5   Optimality of the MWFMF Scheduling Algorithm

So far, we have assumed that the request rate from the processor is very fast so that any empty buffers in the memory can be filled. If all the requests are available before the memory starts servicing them, this means that the request queue is infinitely long which is an unreasonable assumption. The request queue used in here means the queue of requests to be serviced by the memory whether or not they reside in the associative buffers.

In proving the optimality of the MWFMF algorithm, we assume that the requests in the request queue are independent, randomly generated, and of a finite size. The randomness assumption is made for mathematical tractability and is able to yield a lower bound in the memory utilization when the accesses are correlated. The size of the associative buffers may be greater than, equal to, or less than the number of requests in the request queue.

In a pipelined processor, memory requests can be generated continuously until a dependency occurs. At this point, the request stream is discontinued until the dependency has been resolved. The number of requests generated between two dependencies is finite and we can regard that they are available in the request queue after the first dependency has been resolved. Due to our high request rate assumption, the empty associative buffers in the memory are filled up immediately after the first dependency is resolved. Other requests in the request queue are also available, but they cannot be moved into the memory because there are no available buffers.

In a practical implementation, the pipelined processor is able to look ahead a fixed number of instructions and this is modelled by a fixed and finite number of associative buffers in the system (which may be greater than, less than, or equal to the size of the request queue). The intelligent scheduler is allowed to examine the associative buffers in making the scheduling decision. The objective of the scheduling algorithm is to complete the service of the requests in the request queue as fast as possible so that the throughput of the memory is maximized. The symbols used in the following theorems are:

$b =$ number of associative buffers $- 1$;

$m =$ number of memory modules

$N =$ total number of requests that have to be serviced between two dependencies;

$\{(l_0, i_0), (l_1, i_1), \ldots, (l_{m-1}, i_{m-1})\}_k =$ state of the memory system,

where

$(l_j, i_j) =$ state of module j;

$l_j =$ number of requests queued on module j in the buffers;

$$\Sigma_{j=0}^{m-1} l_j = b+1 \quad \text{and} \quad l_j \geqq 0 \quad j=0, 1, \ldots, m-1$$

$$i_j = \begin{cases} 0 & \text{if module } j \text{ is free} \\ n & 0 < n < m \text{ if module } j \text{ is busy} \end{cases}$$

In the case that module j is busy servicing a request, n is the number of sub-cycles that module j has serviced for this request. The number of sub-cycles remaining before the completion of service for the current request is $(m-n) \bmod m$.

$k =$ number of requests in the request queue not including those in the associative buffers, that have to be serviced; k is also used in the induction proof.

C_j = completion time for the jth request (the completion time is counted from the time that the system initially starts with an unserviced request queue to the time when the jth request has completed its service).

$C_{max}\{(l_0, i_0), (l_1, i_1), \ldots, (l_{m-1}, i_{m-1})\}_k$ = maximum completion time for processing all the requests in the associative buffers and the request queue given that the state is $\{(l_0, i_0), \ldots, (l_{m-1}, i_{m-1})\}_k$.

$EC_{max}\{(l_0, i_0), (l_1, i_1), \ldots, (l_{m-1}, i_{m-1})\}_k$ = expected maximum completion time for processing all the requests in the associative buffers and the request queue given that the state is $\{(l_0, i_0), \ldots, (l_{m-1}, i_{m-1})\}_k$.

Before the main theorem can be stated, the following three lemmas must first be proved. Lemma 4.1 establishes the need for executing the MWFMF scheduling algorithm at the beginning of each sub-cycle. Lemma 4.2 establishes a basis for the induction proof of the main theorem and it also shows the optimality of the MWFMF algorithm when the buffer size is very large so that all the requests in the request queue reside in the associative buffers. Lemma 4.3 augments Lemma 4.2 by further showing that algorithm MWFMF minimizes the sum of completion times of all the requests.

LEMMA 4.1

(1) In a period of m sub-cycles, every module can be initiated at most once.
(2) At the beginning of each sub-cycle, there exists at least one free module available for scheduling.

Proof

(1) Obvious, because each module takes a time of m sub-cycles to service a request.
(2) Consider a time interval of m sub-cycles. Since at most one module can be scheduled in each sub-cycle, the total number of modules scheduled in m sub-cycles is less than or equal to m. At the beginning of its current sub-cycle, if a module is scheduled m sub-cycles ago, then it will finish its service at the current sub-cycle and is available for scheduling. If a module is not scheduled m sub-cycles ago, then the total number of modules scheduled in the last m sub-cycles is less than m. Therefore, at least one module is available for scheduling at the beginning of a sub-cycle.

Q.E.D.

LEMMA 4.2

If all the requests in the request queue reside in the associative buffers (that is, the buffers are large enough to accommodate all these requests), then algorithm MWFMF minimizes the maximum completion time in Organization I.

Proof

The maximum completion time is determined by the module with the largest number of queued requests. Assume without loss of generality:

$$l_0 > l_1 > \ldots > l_{m-1} .$$

Case 1: $i_0 = 0$.

   MWFMF schedules module 0 first.

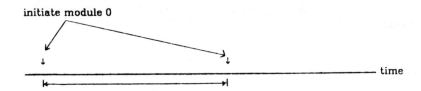

initiate module 0

time

All modules will be initiated at most once in here due to Lemma 4.1 (if number queued on it is non-zero) and all requests queued on every module except 0 can be initiated before the last request queued on module 0 is initiated.

$$C_{\max} = l_0{*}m \text{ sub-cycles} \quad \text{(initiate module 0 first).}$$

For another algorithm, if module $j \neq 0$ is initiated, then module 0 can only be initiated in the next sub-cycle after module j has been initiated:

$$\min C_{\max} = l_0{*}m+1 \text{ sub-cycles} \quad \text{(initiate module } j \neq 0 \text{ first).}$$

In this case, the minimum $C_{\max}$ is greater than the $C_{\max}$ of using the MWFMF scheduling algorithm.

Case 2: $i_0 > 0$.

Let module j be the module such that

$$i_j = 0 \text{ and } i_0 > 0, i_1 > 0, \ldots, i_{j-1} > 0.$$

Since $l_0 > l_1 > \ldots > l_{j-1} > l_j$, then module j is the free module with the largest number of queued requests. This will be the module scheduled by the algorithm MWFMF. In fact, the module scheduled at this point is unimportant because the maximum completion time is governed by module 0.

$$C_{max} = l_0 * m + (m - i_0) \text{ sub-cycles.}$$

In summary,

min $C_{max} = l_0 * m + (m - i_0) \bmod m$ sub-cycles.
Optimum algorithm: MWFMF.

On the other hand, if $l_0 = l_1 > \ldots > l_{m-1}$ and $i_0, i_1 = 0$, then the C_{max}'s are identical whether module 0 or 1 is scheduled first. A similar proof holds for the case $l_0 \geq l_1 \geq \ldots \geq l_{m-1}$.

Q.E.D.

LEMMA 4.3

If all the requests in the request queue reside in the associative buffers, then algorithm MWFMF minimizes ΣC_j in Organization 1 where C_j is the completion time for the jth request.

Proof

Assume without loss of generality:

$$l_0 > l_1 > \ldots > l_{m-1}.$$

Consider two modules a, b ($0 \leq a,b \leq m-1$) such that $i_a = 0$, $i_b = 0$ and $l_a > l_b$. Let $C_{a,b}(C_{b,a})$ be the sum of completion times of scheduling a before b (b before a) for modules a and b only. If b is scheduled before a, then

$$C_{b,a} = \Sigma_{i=1}^{l_b} im + \Sigma_{i=1}^{l_a} (im+1) = m/2 \quad [(l_a+1)l_a + (l_b+1)l_b] + l_a.$$

Comparing this with the case of scheduling a first, it is found that:

$$C_{a,b} = \sum_{i=1}^{l_a} im + \sum_{i=1}^{l_b} (im+1) = m/2 \quad [(l_a+1)l_a + (l_b+1)l_b] + l_b.$$

Since $l_a > l_b => C_{a,b} < C_{b,a}$, this implies that scheduling the module with a larger number of queued requests can reduce ΣC_j. By adjacent pairwise interchange[3], it is therefore better to schedule the module with the maximum number of queued requests if it is free. If this module is not available, scheduling the free module with the maximum number of queued requests is also optimum.

Q.E.D.

From the proofs of Lemmas 4.2 and 4.3, it is seen by using the MWFMF algorithm that:

(1) The throughput of the memory is at a maximum because the maximum time to complete a set of requests is minimized (Lemma 4.2).
(2) The average waiting time is minimized. This is because C_j, the completion time for the jth job equals the waiting time for the jth job, $W_j = C_j$ (all the jobs are available at $t = 0$). As a result, average waiting time $= \Sigma\, W_j/ M$ is also minimized (Lemma 4.3).

Lemmas 4.2 and 4.3 have also been proved with no assumption on the distribution and dependence of requests in the buffers. In proving Theorem 4.6, the assumption of independent, random requests must be made in order to calculate the expected maximum completion time.

THEOREM 4.6

If all the requests in the request queue do not reside in the associative buffers (that is, the buffers are not large enough to accommodate all the requests in the request queue), then algorithm MWFMF minimizes the expected maximum completion time for independent, random requests in Organization I.

---

3. Since a and b are any two modules such that $l_a > l_b$ and we discover that it is better to schedule module a than b, the same reasoning can be applied so that it is better to schedule module a' where $l_{a'} > l_a$. By propogating the same reasoning for every pair of modules, we see that the free module with the maximum number of queued requests should be scheduled.

Proof

In order to prove this theorem, the following two parts must be proven and the theorem follows from the result of part (a).

(a) Algorithm MWFMF minimizes the expected maximum completion time for independent, random requests.

(b) Let states

$$S_1 = \{\ldots, (l_a{}^1, i_a), (l_b{}^1, i_b), \ldots \}_k$$

$$S_2 = \{\ldots, (l_a{}^2, i_a), (l_b{}^2, i_b), \ldots \}_k$$

where "..." indicates that the remaining states are identical for S_1 and S_2. We assume that:

$$l_a{}^2 > l_a{}^1;$$
$$l_b{}^1 > l_b{}^2.$$

Since the states of other modules are identical,

$$l_a{}^1 + l_b{}^1 = l_a{}^2 + l_b{}^2;$$

and

$m > i_a > i_b > 0$ or $m > i_b > i_a > 0$ with equal probability.

If $l_a{}^2 > l_b{}^1$, then $EC_{\max}(S_1)_k \leqq EC_{\max}(S_2)_k$;

If $l_a{}^2 = l_b{}^1$, then $EC_{\max}(S_1)_k = EC_{\max}(S_2)_k$.

These two parts can be proved by induction. The truth is first established for $k = 0$, i.e. when all the requests reside in the buffers. These parts are then assumed to be true for any positive integer k and the proof will be complete by proving the case of $k + 1$.

(I) $k = 0$.

(a)   MWFMF is optimal. This is established by Lemma 4.2.

(b)   If there exists module z such that $l_z > l_a{}^2$, and since $l_a{}^2 \geqq l_b{}^1 > l_b{}^2$

and $l_a^2 > l_a^1$, then the maximum completion time for both S_1 and S_2 depends on l_z and are identical. Therefore,

$$EC_{max}(S_1)_0 = EC_{max}(S_2)_0.$$

If there does not exist module z such that $l_z > l_a^2$, then the maximum completion time of S_2 depends on module a. Let there be two modules, x in S_1 and y in S_2 such that $l_a^2 > l_x^1 > l_a^1$, $l_b^1 > l_y^2 > l_b^2$ and $i_x = i_y = 0$. The following three cases can be identified.

(1) $l_a^2 > l_b^1$, $i_b = 0$, $i_a < m$ at the beginning of a sub-cycle.

S_1 [b]   [x]   [a]   ...   [b] [a] [x]

———————————————————————————— time

S_2 [y] [b] [a]   ...   [b] [y]   [a]

      Starting Sequence   Ending Sequence

$$C_{max}(S_1)_0 = EC_{max}(S_1)_0 < C_{max}(S_2)_0 = EC_{max}(S_2)_0.$$

(2) $l_a^2 > l_b^1$, $i_a = 0$, $i_b < m$ at the beginning of a sub-cycle.

S_1 [x] [a] [b]   ...   [a] [x]   [b]

———————————————————————————— time

S_2 [a]   [y]   [b]   ...   [b]   [y]   [a]

      Starting Sequence   Ending Sequence

$$C_{max}(S_1)_0 = EC_{max}(S_1)_0 < C_{max}(S_2)_0 = EC_{max}(S_2)_0.$$

(3) $l_a^2 = l_b^1$, $i_b = 0$, $i_a < m$ at the beginning of a sub-cycle.

S_1 [b]   [x]   [a] ...   [a]   [x] [b]

———————————————————————————— time

S_2 [y] [b]   [a]   ...   [b] [y]   [a]

      Starting Sequence   Ending Sequence

$l_a^2 = l_b^1$, $i_a = 0$, $i_b < m$ at the beginning of a sub-cycle.

S_1 $\boxed{x}$ $\boxed{a}$ $\boxed{b}$ . . . $\boxed{a}$ $\boxed{x}$ $\boxed{b}$

_____ time

S_2 $\boxed{a}$ $\boxed{y}$ $\boxed{b}$ . . . $\boxed{b}$ $\boxed{y}$ $\boxed{a}$

Starting Sequence   Ending Sequence

Since $l_a{}^2 = l_b{}^1$, this implies that $l_a{}^1 = l_b{}^2$; therefore the states S_1 and S_2 are symmetric in the states of the modules a and b and the probability that $i_b = 0$, $i_a < m$ is equally likely as the probability that $i_a = 0$, $i_b < m$.

$$EC_{max}(S_1)_0 = C_{max}(S_1 \mid i_b = 0, i_a < m)_0 * Pr(i_b = 0, i_a < m)$$
$$+ C_{max}(S_2 \mid i_a = 0, i_b < m)_0 * Pr(i_a = 0, i_b < m)$$
$$= EC_{max}(S_2)_0;$$

(II)   Induction hypothesis:
Assume that the theorem is true for a positive integer k, that is,

(a)   MWFMF algorithm minimizes the expected maximum completion time for independent, random requests when the number of remaining requests in the request queue is k.

(b)   If $l_a{}^2 > l_b{}^1$, then $EC_{max}(S_1)_k \leq EC_{max}(S_2)_k$;

If $l_a{}^2 = l_b{}^1$, then $EC_{max}(S_1)_k = EC_{max}(S_2)_k$.

(III)   When the number of remaining inputs is $k+1$,

(a)   Without loss of generality, let modules 0, 1, ..., j be the set of free modules. Choose any two modules, say 0 and 1, so that $l_0 > l_1$ where $p \epsilon \{2,...,j\}$ does not exist such that $l_0 > l_p > l_1$. We want to compare the difference between scheduling modules 0 and 1.

(1)   Schedule module 0 at the beginning of this sub-cycle,

$$\{(l_0,0), (l_1,0), . . . , (l_{m-1}, i_{m-1})\}_{k+1}$$
$$=> \{(l_0-1,0), (l_1,0), . . . , (l_{m-1}, i_{m-1})\}_{k+1}.$$

A new input now enters the buffers; this input can be a request directed to any module in the set with equal probability $1/m$ (due to the assumption of independent random requests).

New states after scheduling module 0 and the current sub-cycle has ended:

$\quad$ 0 enters: $S^0 = \{(l_0,1), (l_1,0), \ldots, (l_{m-1}, (i_{m-1}+1) \bmod m)\}_k$

$\quad$ 1 enters: $S^1 = \{(l_0-1,1), (l_1+1,0), \ldots, (l_{m-1}, (i_{m-1}+1) \bmod m)\}_k$

$\quad$ - - -

$\quad$ $m-1$ enters: $S^{m-1} = \{(l_0-1,1), (l_1,0), \ldots, (l_{m-1}+1, (i_{m-1}+1) \bmod m)\}_k.$

(2)$\quad$ Schedule module 1 at the beginning of this sub-cycle.

$\quad$ $\{(l_0,0), (l_1,0), \ldots, (l_{m-1}, i_{m-1})\}_{k+1}$
$\quad$ $\Rightarrow \{(l_0,0), (l_1-1,0), \ldots, (l_{m-1}, i_{m-1})\}_{k+1}.$

New states after scheduling module 1 and the current sub-cycle has ended:

$\quad$ 0 enters: $\overline{S}^0 = \{(l_0+1,0), (l_1-1,1), \ldots, (l_{m-1}, (i_{m-1}+1) \bmod m)\}_k$

$\quad$ 1 enters: $\overline{S}^1 = \{(l_0,0), (l_1,1), \ldots, (l_{m-1}, (i_{m-1}+1) \bmod m)\}_k$

$\quad$ - - -

$\quad$ $m-1$ enters: $\overline{S}^{m-1} = \{(l_0,0), (l_1-1,1), \ldots, (l_{m-1}+1, (i_{m-1}+1) \bmod m)\}_k.$

It is seen that $EC_{\max}(S^0) = EC_{\max}(\overline{S}^1)$, $EC_{\max}(S^1) < EC_{\max}(\overline{S}^0)$ and $EC_{\max}(S^j) < EC_{\max}(\overline{S}^j)$ for $j \neq 0,1$. In proving $EC_{\max}(S^0) = EC_{\max}(\overline{S}^1)$, we can rename module 0 to be module 1 and vice versa in state S^0 and let $i_a=0$, $i_b=1$, $l_a^1=l_1$, $l_b^1=l_0$, $l_a^2=l_0$, $l_b^2=l_1$ in the induction hypothesis II(b). The other parts can similarly be proved. Since the expected $C_{\max}$ is a weighted sum of the expected $C_{\max}$ of all the corresponding states, it is, therefore, better to schedule module 0, the module with a longer queue, first. By using the adjacent pairwise interchange argument, the free module with the maximum number of queued requests should be scheduled first.

(b)$\quad$ In proving this part of the theorem, the following parts are identified.

(1) $l_a^2 > l_b^1$; Both modules a and b are not scheduled in the current sub-cycle. This can be due to (1) $i_a > 0$ and $i_b > 0$, i.e. both modules are busy; or (2) there exists a free module z such that l_z is greater than l_a^2 if $i_a = 0$ or l_b^1 if $i_b = 0$. Since it is assumed in the induction hypothesis II(a) that free modules with a longer queue should be scheduled, module z will therefore be scheduled in this case.

After module z is scheduled, a new input enters the buffers.
For state $S_1 \{\ldots, (l_a^1, i_a), (l_b^1, i_b), \ldots\}_{k+1}$

a enters and the current sub-cycle has ended:

$$S_1^a = \{\ldots, (l_a^1+1, (i_a+1) \bmod m), (l_b^1, (i_b+1) \bmod m), \ldots\}_k$$

b enters and the current sub-cycle has ended:

$$S_1^b = \{\ldots, (l_a^1, (i_a+1) \bmod m), (l_b^1+1, (i_b+1) \bmod m), \ldots\}_k$$

$j, j \neq a,b$ enters and the current sub-cycle has ended:

$$S_1^j = \{\ldots, (l_a^1, (i_a+1) \bmod m), (l_b^1, (i_b+1) \bmod m), \ldots\}_k$$

For state $S_2 \{\ldots, (l_a^2, i_a), (l_b^2, i_b), \ldots\}_{k+1}$

a enters and the current sub-cycle has ended:

$$S_2^a = \{\ldots, (l_a^2+1, (i_a+1) \bmod m), (l_b^2, (i_b+1) \bmod m), \ldots\}_k$$

b enters and the current sub-cycle has ended:

$$S_2^b = \{\ldots, (l_a^2, (i_a+1) \bmod m), (l_b^2+1, (i_b+1) \bmod m), \ldots\}_k$$

$j, j \neq a,b$ enters and the current sub-cycle has ended:

$$S_2^j = \{\ldots, (l_a^2, (i_a+1) \bmod m), (l_b^2, (i_b+1) \bmod m), \ldots\}_k.$$

By the induction hypothesis,

$$EC_{max}(S_1^a)_k < EC_{max}(S_2^a)_k$$

$$EC_{max}(S_1^b)_k < EC_{max}(S_2^b)_k \qquad \text{if } l_a^2 > l_b^1+1$$

$$EC_{max}(S_1^b)_k = EC_{max}(S_2^b)_k \qquad \text{if } l_a^2 = l_b^1+1$$

$$EC_{max}(S_1{}^j)_k < EC_{max}(S_2{}^j)_k \qquad \forall j \neq a,b.$$

Therefore,

$$EC_{max}(S_1)_{k+1} \leqq EC_{max}(S_2)_{k+1}.$$

(2) $l_a{}^2 > l_b{}^1$ and there exists a module x such that $i_x = 0$ and

$$l_a{}^2 > l_x > l_a{}^1 \qquad \text{if } i_a = 0 \text{ or}$$

$$l_b{}^1 > l_x > l_b{}^2 \qquad \text{if } i_b = 0.$$

Let us look at the first case:

$$S_1 = \{\ldots, (l_a{}^1,0), (l_b{}^1, i_b), \ldots, (l_x,0), \ldots\}_{k+1},$$

$$S_2 = \{\ldots, (l_a{}^2,0), (l_b{}^2, i_b), \ldots, (l_x,0), \ldots\}_{k+1}.$$

According to the MWFMF algorithm, module x should be scheduled in S_1 and module a should be scheduled in S_2. It is necessary to compare the expected C_{max} after these have been scheduled. Suppose module x is not scheduled in both states, from part III(b)(1), it is seen that $EC_{max}(S_1 | a \text{ scheduled})_k < EC_{max}(S_2 | a \text{ scheduled})_k$. However, due to the induction hypothesis, II(a), scheduling x in state S_1 would be better than scheduling a because $l_x > l_a{}^1$.

$$EC_{max}(S_1 | x \text{ scheduled})_k < EC_{max}(S_1 | a \text{ scheduled})_k.$$

Therefore:

$$EC_{max}(S_1 | x \text{ scheduled})_k < EC_{max}(S_2 | a \text{ scheduled})_k.$$

and

$$EC_{max}(S_1)_{k<+1} < EC_{max}(S_2)_{k+1}.$$

The other case, i.e. $l_b{}^1 > l_x > l_b{}^2$ and $i_b = 0$ can be similarly proved. For the remainder of the proof of this theorem, it is assumed that $l_a{}^2 \geqq l_b{}^1 > l_x$, for all $x \neq a,b$ and $i_x = 0$.

(3) $l_a{}^2 > l_b{}^1$, $0 < i_a < m$, $i_b = 0$.

Due to the induction hypothesis, module b should be scheduled in S_1 and S_2.

For state S_1, schedule module b in this sub-cycle.

$$\{\ldots, (l_a^1, i_a), (l_b^1, 0), \ldots\}_{k+1}$$

$$\Rightarrow \{\ldots, (l_a^1, i_a), (l_b^1 - 1, 0), \ldots\}_{k+1}$$

New input enters the buffer and the current sub-cycle has ended:

a enters: $S_1^a = \{\ldots, (l_a^1 + 1, (i_a+1) \bmod m), (l_b^1 - 1, 1), \ldots\}_k$

b enters: $S_1^b = \{\ldots, (l_a^1, (i_a+1) \bmod m), (l_b^1, 1), \ldots\}_k$

$j, j \neq a,b$ enters: $S_1^j = \{\ldots, (l_a^1, (i_a+1) \bmod m), (l_b^1 - 1, 1), \ldots\}_k.$

For state S_2, schedule module b in this sub-cycle:

$$\{\ldots, (l_a^2, i_a), (l_b^2, 0), \ldots\}_{k+1}$$

$$\Rightarrow \{\ldots, (l_a^2, i_a), (l_b^2 - 1, 0), \ldots\}_{k+1}$$

New input enters the buffer and the current sub-cycle has ended:

a enters: $S_2^a = \{\ldots, (l_a^2 + 1, (i_a+1) \bmod m), (l_b^2 - 1, 1), \ldots\}_k$

b enters: $S_2^b = \{\ldots, (l_a^2, (i_a+1) \bmod m), (l_b^2, 1), \ldots\}_k$

$j, j \neq a,b$ enters: $S_2^j = \{\ldots, (l_a^2, (i_a+1) \bmod m), (l_b^2 - 1, 1), \ldots\}_k.$

By the induction hypothesis:

$$EC_{\max}(S_1^a)_k < EC_{\max}(S_2^a)_k$$

$$EC_{\max}(S_1^b)_k < EC_{\max}(S_2^b)_k$$

$$EC_{\max}(S_1^j)_k < EC_{\max}(S_2^j)_k \qquad \forall j \neq a,b.$$

Therefore,

$$EC_{\max}(S_1)_{k+1} < EC_{\max}(S_2)_{k+1}.$$

(4) $l_a^2 > l_b^1$, $i_a = 0$, $0 < i_b < m$.

Due to the induction hypothesis, module a should be scheduled in S_1 and S_2.

For state S_1, schedule module a in this sub-cycle,

$$\{. \, . \, . \, , (l_a^1,0), (l_b^1, i_b), \, . \, . \, . \, \}_{k+1}$$

$$=> \{. \, . \, . \, , (l_a^1-1,0), (l_b^1, i_b), \, . \, . \, . \, \}_{k+1}$$

New input enters the buffer and the current sub-cycle has ended:

a enters: $S_1^a = \{. \, . \, . \, , (l_a^1,1), (l_b^1 \, (i_b+1) \bmod m), \, . \, . \, . \, \}_k$

b enters: $S_1^b = \{. \, . \, . \, , (l_a^1-1,1), (l_b^1+1, (i_b+1) \bmod m), \, . \, . \, . \, \}_k$

$j, j \neq a,b$ enters: $S_1^j = \{. \, . \, . \, , (l_a^1-1,1), (l_b^1, (i_b+1) \bmod m), \, . \, . \, . \, \}_k$.

For state S_2, schedule module a in this sub-cycle,

$$\{. \, . \, . \, , (l_a^2,0), (l_b^2, i_b), \, . \, . \, . \, \}_{k+1}$$

$$=> \{. \, . \, . \, , (l_a^2-1,0), (l_b^2, i_b), \, . \, . \, . \, \}_{k+1}$$

New input enters the buffer and the current sub-cycle has ended:

a enters: $S_2^a = \{. \, . \, . \, , (l_a^2,1), (l_b^2, (i_b+1) \bmod m), \, . \, . \, . \, \}_k$

b enters: $S_2^b = \{. \, . \, . \, , (l_a^2-1,1), (l_b^2+1, (i_b+1) \bmod m), \, . \, . \, . \, \}_k$

$j, j \neq a,b$ enters: $S_2^j = \{. \, . \, . \, , (l_a^2-1,1), (l_b^2, (i_b+1) \bmod m), \, . \, . \, . \, \}_k$.

By the induction hypothesis:

$EC_{\max}(S_1^a) \leqq EC_{\max}(S_2^b);$

$EC_{\max}(S_1^b) \leqq EC_{\max}(S_2^a);$

$EC_{\max}(S_1^j) \leqq EC_{\max}(S_2^j) \qquad \forall j \neq a,b.$

Therefore:

$EC_{\max}(S_1)_{k+1} \leqq EC_{\max}(S_2)_{k+1}.$

(5) $l_a^2 = l_b^1$ Both modules are not scheduled in the current sub-cycle. With the similar reasons as in III(b)(1), there exists a module z which is scheduled in the current sub-cycle. Due to the symmetry between the states of modules a and b and by the induction hypothesis II(b), we have,

$$EC_{\max}(S_1^a)_k = EC_{\max}(S_2^b)_k$$

$$EC_{\max}(S_1^b)_k = EC_{\max}(S_2^a)_k \text{ and}$$

$$EC_{\max}(S_1^j)_k = EC_{\max}(S_2^j)_k \qquad j \neq a,b.$$

Therefore:

$$EC_{\max}(S_1)_{k+1} = EC_{\max}(S_2)_{k+1}.$$

(6) $l_a^2 = l_b^1$ There exists a module x such that $i_x = 0$ and

$$l_a^2 > l_x > l_a^1 \quad \text{if } i_a = 0 \text{ or}$$

$$l_b^1 > l_x > l_b^2 \quad \text{if } i_b = 0.$$

For the first case,

$$S_1 = \{ \ldots, (l_a^1,0), (l_b^1, i_b), \ldots ,(l_x,0), \ldots \}_{k+1};$$

$$S_2 = \{ \ldots, (l_a^2,0), (l_b^2, i_b), \ldots ,(l_x,0), \ldots \}_{k+1}.$$

With a similar argument as in III(b)(2), suppose module x is not scheduled in both states and module a is scheduled. Due to the symmetry between the states of modules a and b, and by the induction hypothesis II(b),

$$EC_{\max}(S_1 \,|\, a \text{ scheduled})_k = EC_{\max}(S_2 \,|\, a \text{ scheduled})_k.$$

However, due to the induction hypothesis, II(a), scheduling x in state S_1 would be better than scheduling a because $l_x > l_a^1$.

$$EC_{\max}(S_1 \,|\, x \text{ scheduled})_k < EC_{\max}(S_1 \,|\, a \text{ scheduled}).$$

$$< EC_{\max}(S_2 \,|\, a \text{ scheduled})_k.$$

Therefore:

$$EC_{max}(S_1)_{k+1} < EC_{max}(S_2)_{k+1}.$$

The other case, i.e., $l_b{}^1 > l_x > l_b{}^2$ and $i_b = 0$ can be similarly proved.

(7) $l_a{}^2 = l_b{}^1,\ 0 = i_a < i_b < m$ or $0 = i_b < i_a < m$.

The proof is very similar to III(b)(3) and III(b)(4), except in this case, $l_a{}^2 = l_b{}^1$ and $l_a{}^1 = l_b{}^2$. Therefore, the states S_1 and S_2 are symmetric in the states of the modules a and b. By the same argument as in the proof of I(b)(3), the probability that $i_b = 0$, $i_a < m$ equals the probability that $i_a = 0$, $i_b < m$. This implies:

$$EC_{max}(S_1)_{k+1} = EC_{max}(S_2)_{k+1}.$$

From the above seven cases, it is seen that in all cases,

$$EC_{max}(S_1)_{k+1} \leqq EC_{max}(S_2)_{k+1}.$$

Therefore, by induction, part (b) of the theorem is proved. Because part (a) of the theorem utilizes the result of part (b) of the theorem, part (a) of the theorem is proved.

Q.E.D.

The above theorem has demonstrated that algorithm MWFMF is optimal in the sense that it minimizes the average completion time for a fixed set of random requests. Intuitively, algorithm MWFMF is better because it tries to keep all the modules as busy as possible. Suppose that some of the modules are requested more often than others. The requests to these more frequently requested modules become a bottleneck to the system whatever scheduling algorithms are used. However, a better scheduling algorithm should make use of the free cycles to schedule some requests for the less popular modules so that these requests would not accumulate after the processing of the more popular requests. This is the deficiency that occurs in other algorithms and is overcome by the MWFMF algorithm.

In addition to proving that the MWFMF algorithm has the best average case behavior, it may be necessary to show that the algorithm also possesses the best best-case-behavior and the best worst-case-behavior. However, in this case, the best-case and the worst-case-behavior are identical for all algorithms. The best-case-behavior occurs when all the requests are made in a sequential order, that is, $0, 1, \ldots, m-1, 0, 1, \ldots, m-1$, etc. No contention would occur and the throughput of the memory is maximized, that is, 1 request serviced every sub-cycle. On the other hand, the worst case behavior occurs when all the requests are directed to a single module. In this case, the bottleneck is at this module and the throughput of the memory is 1 request serviced every m sub-cycles. Algorithm MWFMF is better than other algorithms because it has a better average case behavior even though its best- and worst-case behavior are identical to the other algorithms.

Although the expected maximum completion time of the algorithm is minimized, it is not possible to make a conclusion similar to Lemma 4.2 that the expected throughput of the memory is maximized because in this case, there is no relationship between the expected maximum completion time and the expected throughput of the system. It is also difficult to prove a similar theorem for the ΣC_j case as in Lemma 4.3.

Although Theorem 4.6 establishes the fact that the MWFMF algorithm is optimal, no throughput values are obtained analytically. In the next two sections, the throughput of the system is evaluated by using two techniques, embedded Markov chains and simulations.

4.4.6   Embedded Markov Chain Technique

By assuming a saturated request rate, with inter-arrival time a constant multiple of the memory sub-cycle and a request queue with random requests, the two organizations can be analyzed by the embedded Markov chain technique [FEL50]. With a RR scheduling algorithm, a state of the system for Organization I is defined as $\{S_T, S_1, S_2, \ldots, S_b, S_m\}, 0 \leq S_T, S_1, S_2, \ldots, S_b, S_m \leq m-1$ where $S_T, S_1, S_2, \ldots, S_b$ are the states of the $b+1$ buffers and S_m is the memory module that is being initiated in the current memory sub-cycle. The state of a buffer is the module number that the request in it wants to access. The number of states is therefore finite. A similar state can be defined for Organization II. It is obvious that the conditional probability of any future event, given the past event and the present state, is independent of the past event, that is, it satisfies the Markovian property.

$$P\{X_{n+1} = i_{n+1} \mid X_0 = i_0, X_1 = i_1, \ldots, X_{n-1} = i_{n-1}, X_n = i_n\}$$

$$= P\{X_{n+1} = i_{n+1} \mid X_n = i_n\}$$

where $n = 0, 1, 2, \ldots,$

X_n = state of the system at the nth transition.

It is noticed that the Markovian property possessed by the two organizations is independent of n. Such a Markov chain is stationary. Let:

$$P_{i,j} = P\{X_{n+1} = i_{n+1} \mid X_n = i_n\}.$$

Further, the time between successive transitions is constant and equal to the duration of the memory sub-cycle. This is called an embedded Markov chain. The analysis of embedded Markov chains is similar to that of Markov chains.

For an irreducible, ergodic Markov chain [ROS76], there exists a unique stationary probability distribution $\pi = \{\pi_j, j = 1,2,\ldots,n\}$ such that:

$$\pi_j = \Sigma_{j=1}^n \pi_i P_{i,j}$$

and

$$\Sigma_{j=1}^n \pi_i = 1.$$

Using the matrix notation, it becomes

$$\pi = \pi P \tag{4.1}$$

where:

$\pi = \{\pi_1, \pi_2, \ldots, \pi_n\}$
$P = \{P_{i,j}\}$, the transition matrix
n = the number of states in the system.

The Markov chain used to model the interleaved memory system is irreducible and positive recurrent because the chain is finite and all states communicate with each other. However, this chain is not ergodic because the period of the chain equals m. In this case, some of the conditions of the ergodic Markov chains are weakened, but vector π still represents the unique fixed probability vector of P [KEM65]. Since the evaluation of the throughput only requires the use of the vector π, the technique for evaluating π in ergodic Markov chains can still be applied here. This technique is illustrated in the following two examples.

Example 1

Consider Organization I with the following attributes:

$m = 2$
$b = 1$
scheduling algorithm—RR
access pattern—random.

A state of the system is defined as $\{S_T, S_1, S_m\}$ where S_T is the state of B_T, S_1 is the state of B_1, and S_m is the current module that the system is initiating. The number of states can be reduced in half by considering only states in which $S_1 \leqq S_T$ and by treating states in which $S_T < S_1$ the same as states in which $S_1 \leqq S_T$. The transition matrix is defined as

$$P = \begin{array}{c} \\ \\ \\ \\ \\ \\ \\ \end{array} \begin{array}{cccccc} \{0,0,0\} & \{0,0,1\} & \{0,1,1\} & \{0,1,0\} & \{1,1,0\} & \{1,1,1\} \\ \begin{bmatrix} 0 & 0.5 & 0.5 & 0 & 0 & 0 \\ 1 & 0 & 0 & 0 & 0 & 0 \\ 0.5 & 0 & 0 & 0.5 & 0 & 0 \\ 0 & 0 & 0.5 & 0 & 0 & 0.5 \\ 0 & 0 & 0 & 0 & 0 & 1 \\ 0 & 0 & 0 & 0.5 & 0.5 & 0 \end{bmatrix} & \begin{array}{c} \{0,0,0\} \\ \{0,0,1\} \\ \{0,1,1\} \\ \{0,1,0\} \\ \{1,1,0\} \\ \{1,1,1\} \end{array} \end{array}$$

On the first row, only the transitions from state $\{0,0,0\}$ to states $\{0,0,1\}$ and $\{0,1,1\}$ have non-zero probabilities. The state $\{0,0,0\}$ means that currently module 0 is initiated and the requests in both buffers B_T and B_1 are requesting module 0. Therefore, the request in B_1 can be satisfied. The content of B_T is moved into B_1, and a new address is accepted into the memory. Since the access pattern is random, this new request can be directed to either module 0 or 1 which results in states $\{0,0,1\}$ or $\{0,1,1\}$. Note that S_m has changed from 0 to 1 because during the next memory sub-cycle, module 1 will be initiated. The other rows of the transition matrix can be interpreted similarly.

Solving the equation $\pi = \pi P$, we get:

$$\pi = \{0.2, 0.1, 0.2, 0.2, 0.1, 0.2\}.$$

The utilization of the memory can be found by defining a new random variable

$$e_{\{S_T, S_1, S_m\}} = \begin{cases} 1 & S_T = S_m \text{ or } S_1 = S_m \text{ or both} \\ 0 & \text{otherwise.} \end{cases}$$

$e_{\{S_T,S_1,S_m\}}$ equals 1 whenever during state $\{S_T,S_1,S_m\}$, one request is satisfied because there is a request in the buffers which requests a currently initiated module. For our example, the transpose of e is:

$$e^T = \{1 \ 0 \ 1 \ 1 \ 0 \ 1\}.$$

The utilization of the memory is $\pi.e = 4/5 = 0.8$. The bandwidth of the memory system is $0.8 * 2 = 1.6$ words/memory cycle.

Example 2

Consider again Organization I with the following attributes:

$m = 2$
$b = 1$
Scheduling algorithm—MWFMF
Access pattern—random.

The state space in this case is larger than the state space of the corresponding model with a RR scheduling algorithm because the next module to be initiated is determined dynamically and, therefore, the states of all modules must be known at all times.

The objective of introducing a more complex algorithm like MWFMF is to initiate any free module with queued requests without constraining on the order of initiation. However, in this case, with $m = 2$, improvement cannot be accomplished. Let us assume that module 0 is initiated during the current memory sub-cycle. In the next sub-cycle, module 0 cannot be initiated again because it has not finished its cycle. The only possibility is to initiate module 1. If all the requests in the buffers are requesting module 0, then no module is initiated in this sub-cycle and in the next sub-cycle, module 0 will be initiated again. The resulting sequence of initiation is the same as a model with an RR scheduling algorithm. Therefore, the utilization of the model is the same for both algorithms when $m = 2$. This happens because the maximum number of free modules is one in this special case. For $m \geqq 2$, the utilization for a MWFMF algorithm is higher because the maximum number of free modules is greater than one and the order of initiation is not necessarily the same as the RR algorithm.

Let us complete this example by setting up the state space of the model. We must know at the beginning of each memory sub-cycle which modules are in service and what are the remaining number of sub-cycles that these modules need. We must also know the contents of the buffers. A state of the system is defined as $\{M_0, M_1, B_1, B_T\}$. M_0 is the module number of a module that has been initiated 2 sub-cycles ago and has finished its service at this time. M_1 is the module number of a module that has been initiated 1 sub-cycle ago and still needs 1 more sub-cycle to finish its service. A value of 0 for M_0 or M_1 indicates that no module was initiated. B_1 and B_T are the states of the buffers and as in the last example, we consider only states with $B_1 \leq B_T$. We have the following ranges of values, $0 \leq M_0$, $M_1 \leq 2$; $0 \leq B_1$, $B_T \leq 1$. The total number of states is $3*3*2*2 = 36$. However, not all states are possible. For example, state $\{2,2,X,X\}$ is not possible because it indicates that module 1 was initiated twice and simultaneously in the last two cycles. Another example of an impossible state is $\{2,0,0,X\}$. This state indicates that no module was initiated in the last cycle ($M_1 = 0$), and the current contents of the buffers have a request for module 0. Since no new request was accepted in the last cycle, this request for module 0 must have existed in the previous cycle and, therefore, should have been initiated. By eliminating all these impossible states, we get a state space of 12 states: $\{0,1,0,0\}$, $\{0,1,0,1\}$, $\{1,0,0,0\}$, $\{1,2,0,0\}$, $\{1,2,0,1\}$, $\{1,2,1,1\}$, $\{0,2,1,1\}$, $\{0,2,0,1\}$, $\{2,0,1,1\}$, $\{2,1,1,1\}$, $\{2,1,0,1\}$, and $\{2,1,0,0\}$. Solving the equation $\pi = \pi P$, we get

$$\pi = \{\frac{1}{20}, \frac{1}{20}, \frac{1}{10}, \frac{1}{10}, \frac{3}{20}, \frac{1}{20}, \frac{1}{20}, \frac{1}{20}, \frac{1}{10}, \frac{1}{10}, \frac{3}{20}, \frac{1}{20}\}.$$

By defining e^T as

$$e^T = \{0, 0, 1, 1, 1, 1, 0, 0, 1, 1, 1, 1\}.$$

The utilization of the modules is $\pi . e = 0.8$.

The transition matrices P used in Eq. 4.1 are large sparse matrices. The memory space required to store P can be substantially less. However, the number of states is still very large. Although it can be reduced by eliminating duplicate or impossible states, the memory size and computer time required for solution is still beyond the present computers' capability. For example, with 16 degrees of interleaving and $b = 2$ (3 request buffers), the number of states for Organization I with a RR scheduling algorithm is 13056. This was calculated by treating permutations of the three buffers as equivalent states. With a RR scheduling algorithm, the module that the system currently initiates is sufficient to determine the next module to be initiated. With other scheduling algorithms, the number of states is larger because the next module to be initiated is determined dynamically, and, therefore, the states of all the modules (whether they are busy or free) must be known at all times. However, regardless of the scheduling algorithm, the number of equivalent states can be reduced by a factor of m by noting that if a constant is added (modulo m) to each state variable, the new state obtained must have the same stationary probability, and the corresponding transition probability must also be the same. For the RR example given above, the 13056 states would be reduced to 816.

Although the number of states is reduced, a solution using embedded Markov chains is still not practical. Approximation techniques can be employed to reduce the number of states. In [WAH76], an approximate embedded Markov chain solution for Organization I with a RR scheduling algorithm was presented. The approximation is achieved by combining some states of the transition matrix into a single state when their transition probabilities into another state are "approximately" equal for all the states in the group. However, the difference between the approximate and the exact solutions is sometimes large. Moreover, the time it takes to generate the approximate matrix is still exponentially large because the transition probabilities of a state must be generated first before it can be determined whether this state can be combined with another state. The analytical solution using embedded Markov chains is, therefore, not practical. In the next section, the evaluations by using simulations are presented.

4.4.7   Performance Evaluation by Simulations

4.4.7.1   Simulation results.   Due to the difficulties mentioned in the last section, our evaluations are based on simulations. The simulations are run on a CDC 6400 computer. The simulation program was written in FORTRAN and the total time to generate all the results took over 12 hours on the CDC 6400.

Table 4.1 shows the results of simulation runs on Organization I for the memory utilization and the average waiting cycles. Two types of request sequences are considered; one in which the requests are generated randomly, and one in which the requests are derived directly from the execution trace of a program. The traces used have a size of 500,000 and were obtained by running a scientific FORTRAN program derived from Ballistic Missile Defense applications on a CDC 7600; they personify program characteristics of scientific applications. Tables 4.1a-c show the results..

Table 4.1a. Simulation Results for Organization I with RR Scheduling Algorithm
(95% confidence interval shown assuming normal distribution)

m	b	Random Request Model		Trace Driven Model	
		E(Memory Utilization)	E(Waiting Cycles)	E(Memory Utilization)	E(Waiting Cycles)
2	0	0.668±0.0	1.75±0.0	0.727±0.003	1.69±0.0
	1	0.801±0.017	2.25±0.04	0.882±0.003	2.13±0.01
	2	0.858±0.001	2.75±0.0	0.928±0.003	2.62±0.33
	3	0.890±0.004	3.25±0.02	0.960±0.004	3.08±0.52
4	0	0.401±0.004	1.62±0.01	0.472±0.026	1.53±0.02
	1	0.565±0.015	1.89±0.02	0.636±0.043	1.79±0.07
	2	0.667±0.009	2.12±0.02	0.732±0.050	2.03±0.14
	3	0.726±0.007	2.38±0.02	0.825±0.059	2.21±0.23
8	0	0.222±0.002	1.56±0.0	0.276±0.026	1.45±0.06
	1	0.363±0.006	1.69±0.01	0.432±0.041	1.58±0.07
	2	0.461±0.005	1.81±0.01	0.525±0.049	1.72±0.10
	3	0.534±0.006	1.94±0.01	0.610±0.060	1.82±0.13
12	0	0.154±0.003	1.54±0.0	0.186±0.026	1.45±0.05
	1	0.266±0.005	1.63±0.01	0.306±0.042	1.55±0.10
	2	0.354±0.005	1.71±0.01	0.408±0.058	1.61±0.11
	3	0.423±0.008	1.79±0.01	0.484±0.070	1.69±0.10
16	0	0.117±0.002	1.53±0.01	0.157±0.015	1.40±0.05
	1	0.209±0.003	1.60±0.01	0.254±0.024	1.49±0.05
	2	0.285±0.003	1.66±0.01	0.345±0.033	1.54±0.06
	3	0.350±0.004	1.71±0.01	0.412±0.039	1.61±0.09

Table 4.1b. Simulation Results for Organization I with FFF Scheduling Algorithm
(95% confidence interval shown assuming normal distribution)

m	b	Random Request Model		Trace Driven Model	
		E(Memory Utilization)	E(Waiting Cycles)	E(Memory Utilization)	E(Waiting Cycles)
2	0	0.501±0.0	2.00±0.0	0.571±0.002	1.88±0.0
	1	0.668±0.014	2.50±0.05	0.789±0.003	2.27±0.11
	2	0.750±0.001	3.00±0.0	0.865±0.003	2.73±0.34
	3	0.802±0.003	3.50±0.02	0.924±0.003	3.17±0.53
4	0	0.289±0.003	1.86±0.01	0.316±0.018	1.79±0.04
	1	0.407±0.011	2.23±0.04	0.476±0.027	2.05±0.12
	2	0.489±0.007	2.53±0.04	0.600±0.041	2.25±0.25
	3	0.544±0.008	2.84±0.06	0.678±0.048	2.48±0.42
8	0	0.173±0.002	1.72±0.01	0.184±0.017	1.68±0.08
	1	0.264±0.004	1.95±0.02	0.304±0.029	1.82±0.12
	2	0.330±0.005	2.14±0.03	0.379±0.037	1.99±0.16
	3	0.378±0.003	2.32±0.03	0.441±0.043	2.13±0.20
12	0	0.126±0.002	1.66±0.01	0.147±0.023	1.57±0.06
	1	0.201±0.003	1.83±0.01	0.235±0.033	1.71±0.11
	2	0.258±0.002	1.97±0.02	0.305±0.042	1.82±0.13
	3	0.303±0.004	2.10±0.03	0.365±0.051	1.91±0.17
16	0	0.100±0.001	1.63±0.01	0.106±0.010	1.59±0.05
	1	0.163±0.002	1.77±0.01	0.187±0.017	1.67±0.08
	2	0.211±0.003	1.89±0.01	0.256±0.024	1.73±0.10
	3	0.252±0.003	1.99±0.02	0.314±0.030	1.80±0.13

Table 4.1c. Simulation Results for Organization I with MWFMF Scheduling Algorithm (95% confidence interval shown assuming normal distribution)

m	b	Random Request Model E(Memory Utilization)	Random Request Model E(Waiting Cycles)	Trace Driven Model E(Memory Utilization)	Trace Driven Model E(Waiting Cycles)
2	0	0.667±0.008	1.75±0.01	0.727±0.003	1.69±0.0
	1	0.800±0.0	2.25±0.0	0.882±0.003	2.13±0.11
	2	0.859±0.003	2.75±0.03	0.928±0.003	2.62±0.33
	3	0.888±0.001	3.25±0.02	0.960±0.003	3.08±0.04
4	0	0.479±0.003	1.52±0.0	0.515±0.029	1.49±0.02
	1	0.612±0.003	1.82±0.01	0.673±0.043	1.74±0.08
	2	0.691±0.004	2.09±0.02	0.776±0.053	1.97±0.18
	3	0.740±0.004	2.35±0.04	0.831±0.059	2.20±0.28
8	0	0.355±0.002	1.35±0.01	0.385±0.038	1.33±0.06
	1	0.466±0.002	1.54±0.01	0.533±0.052	1.47±0.08
	2	0.544±0.004	1.69±0.01	0.612±0.058	1.61±0.11
	3	0.597±0.005	1.84±0.02	0.686±0.068	1.73±0.16
12	0	0.295±0.002	1.28±0.0	0.330±0.052	1.23±0.05
	1	0.399±0.003	1.42±0.01	0.472±0.066	1.35±0.08
	2	0.475±0.003	1.53±0.01	0.533±0.079	1.45±0.10
	3	0.524±0.002	1.64±0.01	0.614±0.088	1.54±0.12
16	0	0.259±0.001	1.24±0.0	0.300±0.028	1.21±0.05
	1	0.357±0.003	1.35±0.01	0.416±0.040	1.30±0.07
	2	0.424±0.002	1.44±0.01	0.511±0.049	1.37±0.08
	3	0.476±0.002	1.53±0.01	0.570±0.055	1.44±0.10

fraction of instruction word fetches	0.597
fraction of data word fetches	0.336
fraction of data word stores	0.067
average number of operand accesses per inst. executed	0.600
number of instructions per instruction word	2.787
fraction of instructions that need data	0.242
fraction of instructions that are	
unconditional jumps	0.044
successful conditional jumps	0.030
unsuccessful conditional jumps	0.015
Average distance in terms of the number of instructions between the instruction setting the condition code and the jump instruction (unconditional or conditional) at the decode segment	0.890
Average distance in terms of the number of instructions between the instruction setting the condition code and the jump instruction (conditional) at the decode segment	1.693

number of instructions executed between

conditional jumps	mean	22.3
	st'd dev.	10.3
unconditional jumps	mean	22.8
	st'd dev.	24.7
successful conditional jumps	mean	33.9
	st'd dev.	19.2
all dependent events (cond. + uncond. jumps)	mean	11.4
	st'd dev.	10.1

In Table 4.2, the simulation results for Organization II are shown. Since the existence of multiple sets of buffers allows a request at B_T to be blocked by a set of full buffers in a module while buffers of other modules may be empty, a column has been included in Table 4.2 to show the buffer utilization (this excludes the buffer B_T). The queue utilization results shown in Table 4.2 are normalized with respect to the buffer size b.

4.4.7.2 Extrapolation by multiple linear regression. Using the results of the simulations and the assumption that the utilization is approximately 1 when $b \gg m$ (e.g. $b = 100$, $m = 4$), multiple linear regression is applied to fit a curve to the results [DRA66]. Based on the tail area of the partial F-value for testing the null hypothesis that a regression coefficient is zero, some of the terms in the polynomial have been eliminated. In Table 4.3, the coefficients for the regression analysis on the utilization and waiting cycles of the two organizations under MWFMF scheduling algorithm are shown. The errors in the estimation can be shown to be less than 4% in most cases except for a few cases with $b = 0$, where the error almost reaches 10%.

From the polynomial equation we have obtained, we can extrapolate our results beyond $b = 3$. The errors in extrapolating the values of utilization are small because the asymptotic value of utilization when b is large is known. However, the errors may be large when extrapolating the values of the waiting cycle because their asymptotic values are unknown. With Organization I, $e_B = 1$, and, therefore, the values of waiting cycles can be derived from the values of utilization by applying Little's formula. With Organization II, $e_B < 1$, and the values of $u_{m,b}$ and $w_{m,b}$ must be known in order to estimate e_B. Since asymptotic value of $w_{m,b}$ and e_B do not exist, the errors may be large.

In Figures 4.13 to 4.18, the performance of Organizations I and II is shown. The actual simulation results are used for $b \leqq 3$ while extrapolations are made for $b > 3$.

Some observations that can be made from these figures are:

(a) The memory utilization asymptotically approaches 1 as the buffer size is increased (Figure 4.13).

(b) The MWFMF algorithm gives the highest memory utilization and the smallest number of waiting cycles for both random request and trace driven simulations (Figures 4.13, 4.14).

(c) The trace driven simulation results show higher memory and buffer utilization and a smaller number of waiting cycles than the random request simulation results due to a higher correlation between consecutive requests. As a result, the requests are likely to be made in a consecutive order resulting in less contention in the system (Figures 4.13–4.18).

Table 4.2a. Simulation Results for Organization II with PR scheduling Algorithm
(95% confidence interval shown assuming normal distribution)

m	b	Random Request Model			Trace Driven Model		
		E(Memory Utilization)	E(Waiting Cycles)	E(Buffer Utilization)	E(Memory Utilization)	E(Waiting Cycles)	E(Buffer Utilization)
2	0	0.667±0.0	1.75±0.0	-	0.727±0.003	1.69±0.0	-
	1	0.801±0.004	2.50±0.02	0.700±0.006	0.882±0.003	2.43±0.18	0.760±0.049
	2	0.857±0.002	3.25±0.02	0.715±0.003	0.928±0.003	3.18±0.44	0.781±0.102
	3	0.890±0.003	4.00±0.01	0.732±0.004	0.960±0.003	3.92±0.61	0.768±0.142
4	0	0.401±0.004	1.62±0.01	-	0.472±0.026	1.53±0.02	-
	1	0.629±0.004	2.18±0.01	0.492±0.005	0.737±0.052	2.09±0.17	0.554±0.085
	2	0.731±0.005	2.75±0.03	0.515±0.009	0.847±0.058	2.70±0.36	0.597±0.136
	3	0.792±0.004	3.33±0.02	0.531±0.006	0.903±0.064	3.34±0.50	0.621±0.158
8	0	0.222±0.002	1.56±0.0	-	0.276±0.026	1.45±0.06	-
	1	0.487±0.006	1.97±0.01	0.347±0.006	0.586±0.055	1.87±0.11	0.384±0.063
	2	0.626±0.006	2.41±0.02	0.379±0.008	0.793±0.078	2.40±0.25	0.494±0.113
	3	0.705±0.004	2.86±0.04	0.397±0.006	0.862±0.085	2.95±0.45	0.518±0.148
12	0	0.154±0.003	1.54±0.0	-	0.186±0.026	1.45±0.05	-
	1	0.417±0.005	1.88±0.01	0.283±0.005	0.599±0.083	1.73±0.10	0.354±0.070
	2	0.569±0.007	2.26±0.02	0.318±0.007	0.733±0.105	2.22±0.28	0.404±0.125
	3	0.661±0.005	2.66±0.02	0.338±0.006	0.753±0.109	2.63±0.47	0.381±0.151
16	0	0.117±0.002	1.53±0.01	-	0.157±0.015	1.40±0.05	-
	1	0.379±0.005	1.82±0.01	0.249±0.004	0.502±0.048	1.73±0.09	0.303±0.049
	2	0.534±0.008	2.18±0.02	0.283±0.008	0.692±0.066	2.05±0.17	0.333±0.075
	3	0.626±0.004	2.54±0.08	0.300±0.005	0.745±0.072	2.23±0.32	0.284±0.094

Table 4.2b. Simulation Results for Organization II with FFF Scheduling Algorithm
(95% confidence interval shown assuming normal distribution)

		Random Request Model			Trace Driven Model		
m	b	E(Memory Utilization)	E(Waiting Cycles)	E(Buffer Utilization)	E(Memory Utilization)	E(Waiting Cycles)	E(Buffer Utilization)
2	0	0.501±0.0	2.00±0.0	-	0.571±0.002	1.88±0.0	-
	1	0.670±0.004	2.74±0.0	0.669±0.004	0.789±0.003	2.56±0.16	0.732±0.045
	2	0.751±0.003	3.50±0.02	0.688±0.010	0.865±0.003	3.30±0.48	0.743±0.097
	3	0.789±0.002	4.27±0.01	0.699±0.004	0.924±0.003	4.00±0.62	0.758±0.138
4	0	0.289±0.003	1.86±0.01	-	0.316±0.018	1.79±0.04	-
	1	0.458±0.005	2.54±0.01	0.454±0.007	0.557±0.042	2.38±0.22	0.519±0.095
	2	0.556±0.004	3.19±0.03	0.483±0.009	0.702±0.048	2.95±0.48	0.558±0.149
	3	0.628±0.003	3.80±0.04	0.503±0.007	0.801±0.057	3.54±0.72	0.596±0.184
8	0	0.173±0.002	1.72±0.01	-	0.184±0.017	1.68±0.06	-
	1	0.329±0.005	2.32±0.03	0.311±0.010	0.406±0.040	2.20±0.19	0.360±0.069
	2	0.436±0.002	2.88±0.02	0.348±0.004	0.604±0.060	2.73±0.36	0.461±0.121
	3	0.498±0.004	3.44±0.07	0.363±0.011	0.671±0.067	3.36±0.65	0.492±0.162
12	0	0.126±0.002	1.66±0.01	-	0.147±0.023	1.57±0.08	-
	1	0.278±0.004	2.20±0.03	0.250±0.007	0.396±0.055	2.03±0.18	0.325±0.080
	2	0.383±0.005	2.71±0.05	0.285±0.010	0.510±0.073	2.64±0.43	0.376±0.137
	3	0.457±0.004	3.22±0.05	0.310±0.009	0.529±0.085	3.19±0.55	0.358±0.752
16	0	0.100±0.001	1.63±0.01	-	0.106±0.010	1.59±0.05	-
	1	0.252±0.003	2.11±0.02	0.217±0.005	0.345±0.032	1.96±0.14	0.267±0.050
	2	0.349±0.003	2.61±0.03	0.250±0.005	0.478±0.046	2.33±0.30	0.286±0.082
	3	0.424±0.004	3.09±0.05	0.141±0.008	0.527±0.050	2.62±0.46	0.262±0.092

Table 4.2c. Simulation Results for Organization II with MWFMF Scheduling Algorithm
(95% confidence interval shown assuming normal distribution)

		Random Request Model			Trace Driven Model		
m	b	E(Memory Utilization)	E(Waiting Cycles)	E(Buffer Utilization)	E(Memory Utilization)	E(Waiting Cycles)	E(Buffer Utilization)
2	0	0.667±0.008	1.75±0.01	-	0.727±0.003	1.69±0.0	-
	1	0.799±0.003	2.50±0.01	0.700±0.005	0.882±0.003	2.43±0.16	0.760±0.049
	2	0.856±0.005	3.25±0.01	0.714±0.007	0.928±0.003	3.18±0.44	0.761±0.102
	3	0.890±0.020	4.00±0.02	0.724±0.006	0.960±0.003	3.92±0.61	0.768±0.142
4	0	0.419±0.003	1.52±0.0	-	0.515±0.029	1.49±0.02	-
	1	0.648±0.001	2.13±0.01	0.482±0.002	0.738±0.052	2.07±0.18	0.539±0.090
	2	0.743±0.003	2.72±0.01	0.515±0.005	0.838±0.059	2.70±0.36	0.588±0.135
	3	0.795±0.002	3.31±0.02	0.528±0.003	0.902±0.032	3.35±0.53	0.625±0.157
8	0	0.355±0.002	1.35±0.01	-	0.385±0.038	1.33±0.06	-
	1	0.534±0.005	1.85±0.01	0.328±0.007	0.624±0.062	1.84±0.13	0.398±0.077
	2	0.651±0.003	2.33±0.01	0.371±0.003	0.799±0.079	2.40±0.26	0.498±0.118
	3	0.717±0.003	2.81±0.02	0.391±0.004	0.849±0.083	2.95±0.44	0.510±0.144
12	0	0.295±0.002	1.28±0.0	-	0.365±0.052	1.23±0.05	-
	1	0.472±0.005	1.72±0.01	0.256±0.005	0.624±0.089	1.68±0.14	0.343±0.095
	2	0.602±0.004	2.16±0.01	0.308±0.004	0.735±0.106	2.19±0.29	0.395±0.135
	3	0.683±0.006	2.58±0.03	0.332±0.009	0.756±0.109	2.61±0.49	0.377±0.154
16	0	0.259±0.001	1.24±0.0	-	0.300±0.028	1.21±0.05	-
	1	0.439±0.006	1.64±0.01	0.217±0.007	0.565±0.054	1.62±0.10	0.289±0.061
	2	0.564±0.007	2.05±0.02	0.264±0.007	0.692±0.066	1.97±0.21	0.306±0.083
	3	0.647±0.003	2.44±0.02	0.290±0.004	0.745±0.072	2.17±0.34	0.271±0.096

Table 4.3. Coefficients of 3rd Order Polynomial Regression of Organization I and II under MWFMF Scheduling Algorithm (RRM—Random Request Model; TDM—Trace Driven Model)

Note: All other coefficients are set to zero.

Utilization

Model	m^2	m	$1/m$	$b^{1/3}$	$b^{1/2}$	$b^{1/4}$	$\dfrac{b^{1/3}}{m}$	$\dfrac{b^{1/2}}{m}$	const.
RRM-I	0.00050	-0.02011	0.58124	1.80176	-0.32495	-1.37185	0.27655	-0.21970	0.41273
TDM-I	0.00065	-0.02312	0.62805	2.29106	-0.45177	-1.89628	0.18115	-0.18268	0.45447
RRM-II	-0.00009	-0.00283	0.79465	3.04862	-0.64641	-2.17849	-0.22013	0.00866	0.26880
TDM-II	-0.00012	-0.00301	0.80863	2.72327	-0.61966	-1.80155	-0.44904	0.11118	0.33023

Waiting Cycles

Model	m^3	m^2	$m^2 b$	m	b	mb	const.
RRM-I	-0.00109	0.03312	0.00314	-0.31779	0.61021	-0.08138	2.30046
TDM-I	-0.00100	0.03038	0.00308	-0.29282	0.56690	-0.07881	2.19725
RRM-II	-0.00082	0.02570	0.00219	-0.26252	0.84230	-0.06200	2.19883
TDM-II	-0.00075	0.02432	0.00016	-0.25363	0.77708	0.03024	2.12700

Figure 4.13. The Improvement of Average Memory Utilization with
with Buffer Size for Organization I ($m=8$)

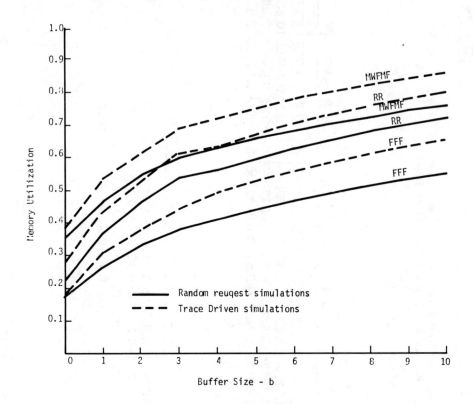

Figure 4.14. The Increase of Average Waiting Cycles with Buffer
Size for Organization I (m=8)

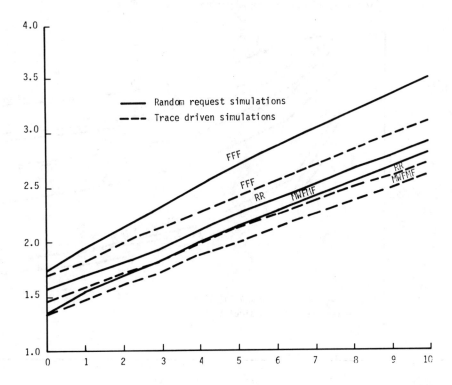

Figure 4.15. The Decrease of Average Memory Utilization with
respect to Degrees of Interleaving for Organization I
with MWFMF Scheduling Algorithm

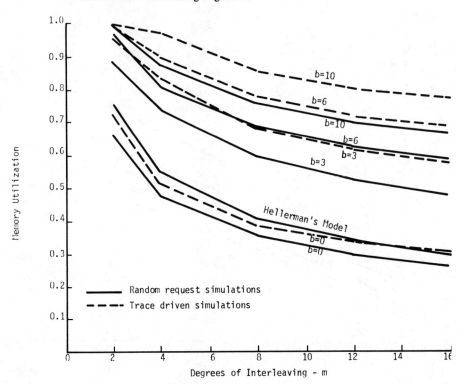

Figure 4.16. The Decrease of Waiting Cycles with respect to the
Degrees of Interleaving for Organization I with
MWFMF Scheduling Algorithm

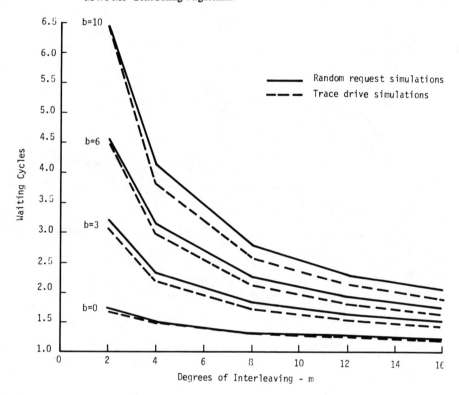

Figure 4.17. The Average Buffer Utilization for Organization II
$(m=8)$
(These do not include the utilization of B_T)

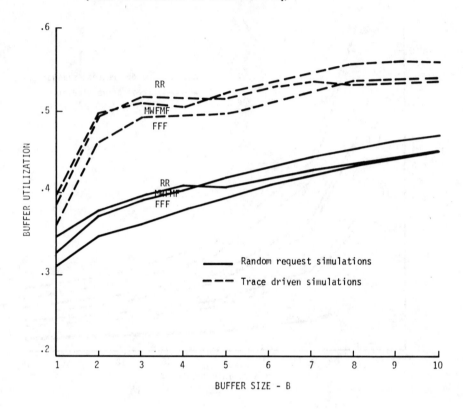

Figure 4.18. The Average Buffer Utilization vs. the Degrees of Inter-
leaving for Organization II with MWFMF Scheduling
Algorithm ($m=8$)
(These do not include the utilization of B_T)

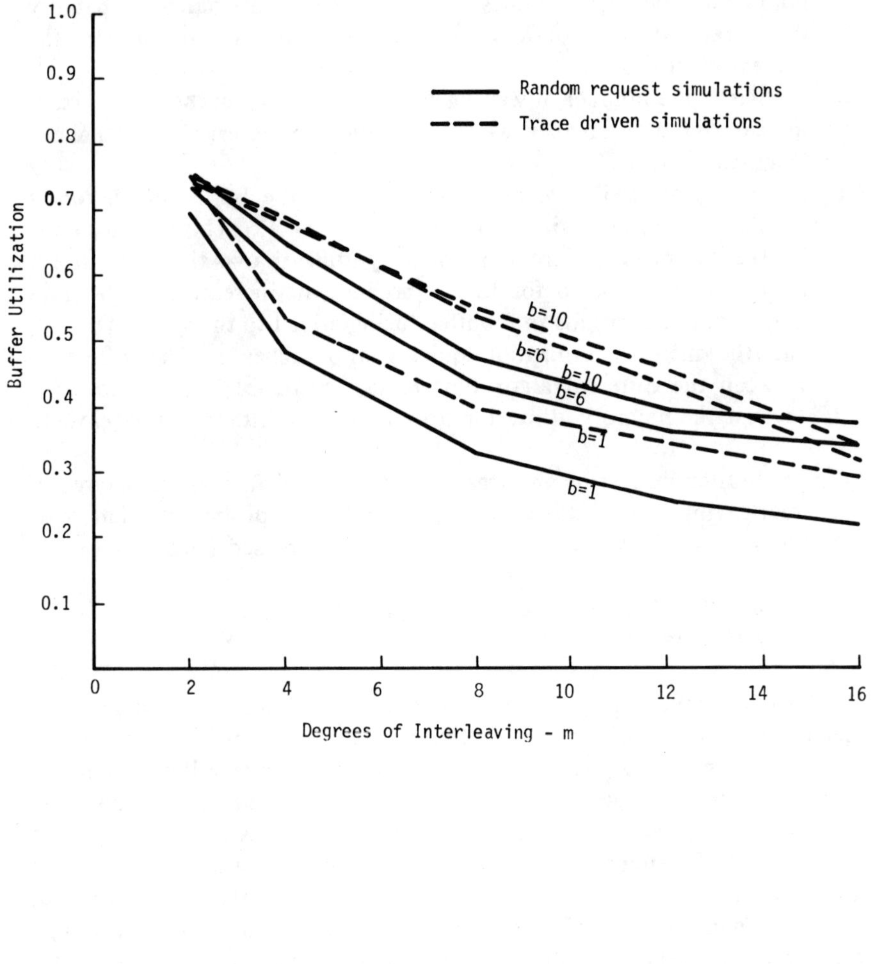

(d) The memory utilization is higher when the buffer size is increased but is smaller when the degree of interleaving increases (Figures 4.13, 4.15). A larger number of buffers results in a larger variety of requests and this accounts for the increased utilization. On the other hand, when the number of memory modules increases, there is a smaller probability that a request in the buffers can be serviced and this accounts for the decreased utilization.

(e) Similarly, the number of waiting cycles is larger when the buffer size is increased but is smaller when the degree of interleaving increases (Figures 4.14, 4.16).

(f) In Organization II, the rate of increase of the buffer utilization is smaller as the buffer size is increased (Figure 4.17). This also accounts for the diminishing increase in memory utilization as the buffer size is increased. The reason for this is because an increase in b by 1 in Organization II results in 8 buffers being added to the system ($m = 8$) and the memory utilization quickly approaches 1. The difference between the different algorithms is also small for large values of b because the memory utilization for all these algorithms is very close to 1.

(g) The buffer utilization in Organization II is smaller as the degree of interleaving increases because there is a higher probability that B_T is blocked when the number of modules is increased (Figure 4.18).

4.4.8 Some Final Remarks on the Design of Interleaved Memories

We have presented in this section two organizations of an interleaved memory system which utilizes a finite buffer space for the storage of requests. We have designed a scheduling algorithm which allows a finite set of requests to be processed in the minimum expected completion time. However, the performance of our system is obviously worse than the performance of systems with an infinite saturated request queue which is an unrealistic assumption. In Fig. 4.15, we have shown the performance of Hellerman's model [HEL67] together with our simulation results. Although Hellerman's model is a simple model and allows no queueing of requests, it is useful as a lower bound for comparing the performance with other systems. It is seen that with a random request queue, Hellerman's model is better than our Organization I with $b = 0$, but is worse for $b > 0$. Note that the performance curves all have the same shape. Since Organization II degenerates into Organization I for $b = 0$, it is worse than Hellerman's model for $b = 0$, but better for $b > 0$. The comparison with other models in the current literature is not meaningful because they differ significantly.

We can improve our design slightly by considering the following. The rationale behind the constraint that only one module may be initiated in any sub-cycle is because the return bus can return at most one piece of datum in any sub-cycle. But since reads generate return data while writes do not, we can initiate two or more modules in a sub-cycle provided that exactly one of the requests is a read. The improvement in utilization due to this is only about 2%. The improvement is not significant because the fraction of writes in our trace is less than 7% of all the accesses and its applicability is also limited by memory interference.

The MWFMF scheduling algorithm we have studied in this section is optimal in the sense that it minimizes the expected finish time for a finite sequence of random, independent requests. Although there exist restrictions and the performance of specially structured computers, e.g. CRAY I, ILLIAC IV, etc. is not found, our scheduling algorithm is applicable to machines which support vector-oriented computing, e.g. TIASC, and array type processors like ILLIAC IV. Related studies on the separation of the instruction and data modules and the effects of dependencies on the memory performance are shown in [RAM81a, RAM81b].

The organizations we have presented in this section can be extended to other levels of the memory hierarchy in which the modules can be disks and the requests can be disk requests instead of memory addresses. The service time distribution of a disk is not constant as in the case of a memory module. Some approximation can be made on the distribution (e.g. by an exponential distribution) and analysis techniques in queueing theory can be applied [BAS75]. In the next section, we return to the original task scheduling problem on the general model. We show a heuristic to schedule tasks and the heuristic is evaluated by simulations.

4.5 A Heuristic for the Scheduling of Tasks on the General Model

We have presented in detail in the last section the design of an interleaved memory which is a restricted case of the general model we have described in section 4.2. Although the task scheduling problem on the general model is NP-complete, an optimal average behavior algorithm can be designed when the model is sufficiently restricted.

We would like to return to the original task scheduling problem on the general model. Since the problem is NP-complete, a heuristic should be designed if it is not feasible to enumerate over all the possibilities in order to find the optimal sequence. We present in this section a heuristic for the task scheduling problem on the general model. This heuristic is extended from Johnson's optimal two stage flow shop algorithm [JOH54], and the performance of the heuristic is seen to perform reasonably well in a limited number of simulations.

The heuristic is designed for tasks with the following characteristics:

(1) Each request has the following precedence graph:

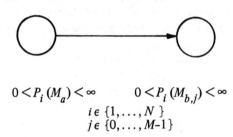

$$0 < P_i (M_a) < \infty \qquad 0 < P_i (M_{b,j}) < \infty$$
$$i \in \{1, \ldots, N\}$$
$$j \in \{0, \ldots, M-1\}$$

(2) There are no precedence constraints among requests.
(3) No preemption is allowed.
(4) *buff*(M_a) $= \infty$ and $r_i = 0$ (i $\in \{1, \ldots, N\}$).
     This says that the release times of jobs are 0 and the buffer size of M_a is very large, that is, all the requests are available initially for scheduling.
(5) $0 < buff\ (M_{b,0}) = \cdots = buff\ (M_{b,m-1}) < \infty.$
     That is, all the modules in the second stage have finite, non-zero amount of buffers.
(6) Permutation schedule is desired.

The heuristic for scheduling this class of jobs is:

Algorithm 4.4: Heuristic to Schedule Tasks on the General Model

1. Order jobs that require the service of $M_{b,j}$ ($j = 0, \ldots, m-1$) in increasing ratios of:

    $$P_i(M_{i,j}) - p^* P_i(M_a).$$

2. Merge the job sequences for different $M_{b,j}$'s into one stream using the MWFMF scheduling algorithm (Algorithm 4.1).
3. In the schedule obtained, for any continuous sequence of jobs that requires the same module on the second stage, reorder using Johnson's algorithm such that x should be scheduled before y if

    $$\min\ \{P_x(M_a),\ P_y(M_{b,j})\} \leq \min\ \{P_x(M_{b,j}),\ P_y(M_a)\}.$$

In step 1 of the algorithm, p is a constant to be selected. The rationale behind why the jobs have to be ordered in this fashion is because it is better to schedule jobs with smaller processing requirements on M_a first. This allows the processing on the second stage to be started earlier than if a job with a large processing requirement is started on M_a first. Even if two sequences finish at the same time, there is more leverage for adjustment in a sequence which starts the processing on the second stage earlier. Step 2 of the algorithm merges job sequences for different modules together. Since the MWFMF algorithm (Algorithm 4.1) is found to perform very well, it is also applied here. Lastly, the sequence obtained can still be improved if any two consecutive jobs in the sequence which require the service of the same module on the second stage are rearranged using Johnson's algorithm [JOH54]. Since Johnson's algorithm minimizes the finish time on a two stage flow shop, we hope that this can improve the completion time of the sequence.

Some simulations were done to determine the performance of this heuristic. This is shown in Figure 4.19. The results are plotted for 1000 samples of 7 randomly generated jobs. It is assumed that $m = 2$, $p = 2$ and four of these jobs require the service of $m_{b,0}$ and three require the service of $M_{b,1}$. Although the amount of simulations is limited, it is seen that the performance of the heuristic is very good. Approximately 67% of the simulations have no deviation from the optimal performance and only about 1% of the simulations deviate by 28% from the optimal performance. The exact worst-case and average-case performance are difficult to derive analytically.

4.6 Conclusion

In this chapter, we have studied the task scheduling problem on a DCS. This problem is related to the scheduling of tasks after the query has been decomposed and the files have been placed on the DCS. Because it is difficult to collect global information on the DCS, most of the scheduling decisions have to be made locally. We have, therefore, restricted the general task scheduling problem to the problem of scheduling tasks at each node independently. The model for such a system is the SIMD model proposed by Flynn [FLY66].

The contributions that we have made in this chapter are:

(1) We have proved the NP-completeness of the task scheduling problem on the SIMD model. These include the cases when the jobs have positive release dates, precedence constraints or no waiting space in the second stage. Therefore, it is unlikely that an optimal sequence can be obtained without exhaustive enumeration.

Figure 4.19. Simulation Results for Algorithm 4.4 using 1000
Samples of 7 Randomly Generated Jobs ($m=2$, $p=2$)

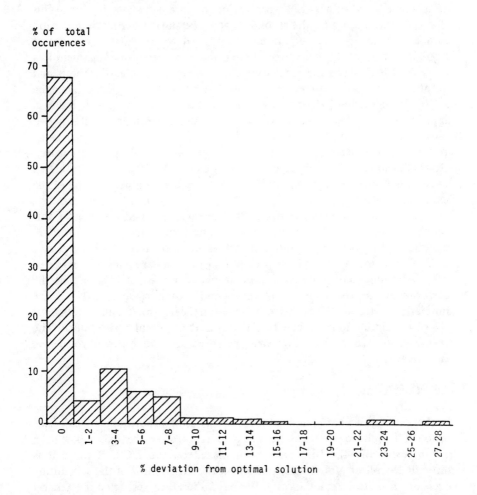

(2)   We have put additional constraints on the model so that the problem becomes polynomially solvable. We restrict the processing times of jobs so that they are constant and the ratio of processing times of the second stage to the first stage is m (where m is the number of modules on the second stage). We further assume that each job requires the service of one of the modules on the second stage. The resulting model is an organization of an interleaved memory system for a pipelined processor. We have evaluated several alternative scheduling algorithms and have proven that one of these algorithms minimizes the expected completion time for a finite set of random requests.

(3)   We have designed a heuristic for task scheduling on the general model. This heuristic is extended from Johnson's two stage flow shop algorithm [JOH54]. Although the algorithm is evaluated with a limited number of simulations, the performance is seen to be very good.

In the next chapter, we study some hardware support aspects for data management on a DCS. One particular hardware necessary is the associative memory which we have used in the design of interleaved memories (section 4.4). This associative memory is capable of performing equality, threshold, proximity and extremum searches. There are other hardware designs which are needed to support database operations such as simple retrievals and updates, selections and joins. A database machine, DIALOG, is proposed.

5

Hardware Support for Data Management
on Distributed Computer Systems

5.1 Introduction

In the past three chapters, we have discussed some logical solutions to data management on a DCS. Some of these solutions do not require specialized hardware support, e.g. query decomposition, file placement, and migration, while some others require dedicated hardware, e.g. request scheduling for an interleaved memory. In general, there is a tendency for increasing hardware support for data management functions on a DCS. The motivations for this tendency are:

(1) Parallelism

As the size of information processing grows, it becomes increasingly difficult to use a uni-processor to achieve the system's requirements. One alternative is to exploit the possibility of using multiple, less expensive, and less powerful processors to form a conglomerate of parallel processors which can usually achieve the system's requirements in a more cost-effective way.

(2) Communication overhead

Processing on large file systems are often I/O bound. Many of the file operations are quite simple and a significant communication overhead is incurred in transferring the file to a level of the memory hierarchy where the processor can process it. By distributing the intelligence to the different levels of the memory hierarchy, parallel processing can be performed with very little communication overhead.

(3) Hardware or firmware realization of database functions

The complexity of database system software is largely due to the processing of memory mapping operations. Memory mapping operations convert the file accesses by a query into actual memory addresses and must be highly optimized if they are to perform well. These operations often utilize complex data structures to achieve efficiency. Further, database software are divided into modules which perform specific tasks. For example, modules may exist for query parsing, directory access, directory processing, data retrieval and update, and data security. These modules usually have diverse capabilities, and bottlenecks may exist. The system performance is consequently degraded. Specialized database hardware solves the above two problems by eliminating the complex address mapping operations and utilizing hardware/firmware to replace the software. The query is transferred directly from the processor to the specialized hardware without address mapping.

As a result, there are many hardware designs proposed to speed up database processing. One of the earliest designs is the associative memory [SLA56] in which logic is distributed into each cell of the memory so that search operations can be performed associatively. Such a design is rather expensive because logic is duplicated for each bit in the memory.

A more recent design is the database machine [HSI77] which is a remedy to the costly associative memory by sharing one piece of the associative logic among a set of physically related data. A set of physically related data may be a track on a disk in which case the design is a logic per track disk; it may be a set of memory modules, in which case the design is a SIMD computer [FLY66]. Since the designer has the freedom to choose the degree of parallelism, there are a lot of issues related to database machine design. These issues will be addressed in section 5.3.

In this chapter, we present a design of an associative memory for ordered retrieval in section 5.2 and extend the design to a simple database machine in sections 5.3 and 5.4. In the associative memory design, we present some simple schemes for a variety of searches, each of which may be performed in one complete memory cycle using bit-memory logic primarily. The searches we study include the basic equality search, the threshold searches (both greater than and less than searches), the proximity search, and most importantly, the greatest value and the least value searches. For each kind of search, we present both the algorithm suitable for our needs and the logic circuit of the memory cell required by the algorithm. Based on the basic search schemes, an algorithm for ordered retrieval is developed. A comparison for ordered retrieval schemes is then made between the proposed scheme and the previous algorithms. It is found that this algorithm outperforms all the other algorithms compared, particularly in the resolution of multiple responses. Finally, issues relating to LSI implementation, manufacturing defects, and modular expansions are discussed.

In the database machine design, we investigate some problems that exist with the design and show that the design should be made as a combination of SIMD and MIMD computer models [FLY66]. A database machine— DIALOG—which uses distributed and associative processing and utilizes current memory technologies for implementation, is proposed. The physical storage device of a database system, such as a disk or a charge coupled device memory module is enhanced with additional processing logic for associative processing and join processing to form a data module. The associative memory proposed in section 5.2 is used as a sequential associative memory. The data modules are linked together through a fully connected network for conflict-free accesses. A particular link is established by a controller and since data in the system is piped, a link, once established, will continue to exist for a period of time. A hierarchical design is also proposed in which the data modules form clusters together in a similar fashion. The design utilizes current microprocessor and memory technologies, and can evolve as new technologies are available.

5.2 A Design of a Fast Cellular Associative Memory for Ordered Retrieval

5.2.1 Previous work

Content-addressable memories (CAMs), alternatively known as associative memories (AMs), have received much attention in the literature since they were first described in 1956 [SLA56]. The distinguishing feature of such memories is that stored words are accessed by matching some portion of their contents to a search word and selecting the first one that matches rather than accessing the data using its physical location in the memory as in standard random access memories (RAMs). It can be readily seen that CAMs must depend upon a high degree of parallelism in their search schemes in order to compete in memory access times with RAMs. Large speed improvements can be gained from this parallelism and this makes CAMs attractive to a wide variety of applications. A good survey of the current technology in CAMs can be found in [PAR73, FOS76, HAN66].

With the advent of large scale integration (LSI) technology, it becomes feasible to economically implement fast search algorithms in CAMs by incorporating much of the control logic into the memory plane. Several search algorithms for CAMs have been developed in the past two decades [FEN74, FRE61, SEE62, LEW62]. Some algorithms, such as [SEE62] and

[YAN66] have been based upon distributed logic design, but few have incorporated a high percentage of their search logic in the memory cell. An exception to this is found in a design by Kautz [KAU69] for a special purpose sorting array. His design is oriented towards ordering, rather than searching, of the memory, but does include associative capabilities as a by-product.

The trend in associative memory design is toward distributed logic. Previous designs have placed control logic outside the storage logic. These include comparison logic, propagation logic, multiple response resolution logic, arithmetic logic, etc. In a distributed logic design, the control logic and the storage logic are designed together. The controls are brought into the cells as part of the storage itself. The cells become more complex and have more control functions associated with them, but it also results in a more homogeneous and modular design. In this section, we propose the basic design of such a memory and present some searching and sorting schemes and the implementation of some basic searches using distributed cellular logic which is considerably faster than any of the previous sorting methods. The capabilities of the cells are actually a subset of the capabilities of Kautz's augmented CAM array [KAU71]. Further, the concept and the design of some of the searches have been investigated earlier [TUR72, RAM78a]. The searches that we examine include the basic equality search, the threshold searches (both greater than and less than searches), the proximity search, and most importantly, the greatest value search and the least value search.

5.2.2 Symbols Used in the Design

The following conventions are used throughout the design:

B_i	the value of the ith word of memory;
$B_{i,j}$	the value of the jth bit of the ith word of memory;
C	a priority circuit which is used to sequence response in W_2, W_3, W_4 or W_5;
D	a circuit used to detect reponses in W_2, W_3, W_4 or W_5;
$e_{i,j}$	the equality state signal for the jth bit of the ith word in the equality match between $B_{i,j}$ and R_j;
$E_{i,j}$	the equality enable signal for the jth bit of the ith word in the equality-inequality search mode and the least value search mode;
$E_{i,n+1}$	signal which can be gated to set (or reset) any one of the word control registers W_2, W_3, W_4 or W_5;
$F_{i,j}$	the enable signal for the jth bit of the ith word in the greatest value search;

$F_{i,n+1}$ signal which can be gated to set (or reset) any one of the word control registers W_2, W_3, W_4 or W_5;

G the associative memory search mode command (equality-inequality-proximity mode or the least value mode);

i an index for a word in the memory, $1 \leqq i \leqq m$;

I_j the value of the jth bit of the input/output register I;

j an index for a bit in the word, $1 \leqq j \leqq n$;

k a variable index, $1 \leqq k \leqq n$;

L_i the less than state signal for the ith word of memory; a signal which can be gated to set (or reset) any one of the word control registers W_2, W_3, W_4 or W_5;

LSB least significant bit;

m the number of words in the CAM;

M_j the value of the jth bit of the mask register M (used in the least value search, the equality search, the threshold searches and the proximity search);

M_j^* the value of the jth bit of the mast register M^* (used in the greatest value search);

MSB most significant bit;

MZ the set of all bit positions with $M_j = 0$;

n the number of bits in a word of the CAM;

P_j the synchronization bus signal for the jth bit-slice in the least value search;

Q_j the default-detection bus signal for the jth bit-slice in the least value search;

r an index in the word control logic, $1 \leqq r \leqq 5$;

R_j the signal for the jth bit-slice shared by the equality-inequality search, the proximity search and the least value search;

S the value of the search register S;

S_i the value of the jth bit of the search register S;

T_j the search-default feedback bus signal for the jth bit-slice in the greatest value search;

U_j the synchronization bus signal for the jth bit-slice in the greatest value search;

V_j the default-detection bus signal for the jth bit-slice in the greatest value search;

$w_{i,r}$ the ith flip-flop of the word control register W_r;

W_1 the word flags register with m flip-flops;

$W_2 - W_5$ result stores or temporary stores in the word control logic;

$X_{i,j}$ the proximity state signal for the ith word of the memory in the proximity search;

$X_{i,n+1}$ a signal which can be gated to set (or reset) any of the word control registers W_2, W_3, W_4 or W_5;

$\cup$ abbreviation for logical OR operation;

ϵ abbreviation for "an element of";

$\forall$ abbreviation for "for all";

$\exists$ abbreviation for "there exists".

5.2.3   Basic Associative Memory Organization

The associative memory organization shown in Fig. 5.1 is used to implement the search schemes to be presented. A bit-slice is a vertical slice through the memory as arranged in Fig. 5.1. The jth bit-slice is made up of the jth bit of every word in the memory. The search operations are parallel by word and serial by bit-slice. A minor cycle refers to the time needed to perform an operation on a single bit-slice and a major cycle refers to the time needed to complete an operation on all bit-slices of the memory. Hence, a major cycle for the present AM organization is composed of n minor cycles where n is the number of bits in a word. It is shown later that some searches will require a longer minor cycle than others, thereby lengthening the major cycle as well. A "basic" operation is an operation which may be performed in a single major cycle.

5.2.4   Definition of Search Operations

In each of the following search definitions, the set of words involved in the search are those where $w_{i,1} = 1$ and $i\epsilon\{1,2,\ldots,m\}$. The result of the search partitions this set of words into two sets, the set that satisfies the search condition and the set that does not. Let B_i be the content of the ith word in the memory, S the content of the search register, and M the content of the mask register. That is,

$$B_i = \Sigma_{j=1}^{n}\ 2^{n-j} \cdot B_{i,j},$$

$$S = \Sigma_{j=1}^{n}\ 2^{n-j} \cdot S_j$$

and

$$M = \Sigma_{j=1}^{n}\ 2^{n-j} \cdot M_j.$$

The search is performed only on that part of the search word which is not masked. In other words, only those S_j bits for which the corresponding M_j bits are 0's are included in the matching (comparison) process. Let MZ be

Figure 5.1. Cellular Logic Associative Memory Block Diagram

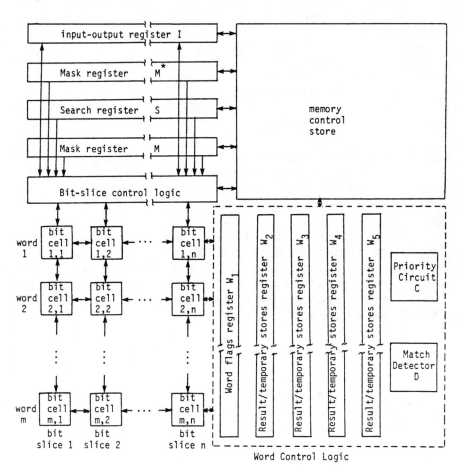

this set of bit positions. Other bit positions with $M_j = 1$ are bypassed. (Note that $j = 1$ for MSB and $j = n$ for LSB.) We define the various searches as follows:

A.   Equivalence Searches

1)   Equality Search:

$$B_{i,j} = S_j, \forall \; j\epsilon\{1, 2,\ldots, n\}.$$

2)   Inequality Search: $\exists \, k \; \epsilon \; MZ$ such that $B_{i,k} \neq S_k$.
3)   Similarity Search (Masked Equality Search): $B_{i,j} = S_j \; \forall \, j \, \epsilon \, MZ$.
4)   Proximity Search: There is exactly one $k \; \epsilon \; MZ$ such that $B_{i,k} \neq S_k$.

Note: The similarity search is also known as masked-equality search. It differs from the equality search in that the mask is effectively not used in the latter while it is used in the former search. In most cases, this distinction is so insignificant that the "equality search" is used to mean both the equality and the masked-equality searches. Unless specified otherwise, we will assume that all searches are masked.

B.   Threshold Searches

1)   Greater-Than Search: $B_i > S$.
2)   Less-Than Search: $B_i < S$.
3)   Greater-Than-or-Equal-To Search: $B_i \geq S$.
4)   Less-Than-or-Equal-To Search: $B_i \leq S$.

C.   Double-Limits Searches

1)   Between-Limits Searches: Let X and Y be the limits such that $X > Y$. Then B_i is

a) $< X$ and $> Y$,
b) $< X$ and $\geq Y$,
c) $\leq X$ and $> Y$,
d) $\leq X$ and $\geq Y$.

2)   Outside-Limits Searches: Let X and Y be the limits such that $X < Y$. Then B_i is

a) $< X$ or $> Y$,
b) $< X$ or $\geq Y$,
c) $\leq X$ or $> Y$,
d) $\leq X$ or $\geq Y$.

D. Extremum Searches

1) Least Value Search: $B_i \leq B_k$, $\forall k \neq i$ and $k\epsilon\{1,2,\ldots,m\}$.
2) Greatest Value Search: $B_i = B_k$, $\forall k \neq i$ and $k\epsilon\{1, 2,\ldots, m\}$.

E. Adjacency Searches

1) Nearest-Above Search: $\not\exists k \epsilon \{1,2,\ldots, m\}$ such that $B_i > B_k > S$.
2) Nearest-Below Search: $\not\exists k \epsilon \{1, 2,\ldots, m\}$ such that $B_i < B_k < S$.

There are other non-search operations that can be performed in associative memories. These include word addition, field addition, summation, counting, shifting, complementing, logical sum, logical product, etc. Devices that incorporate non-search operations may be referred to as associative processors [FOS76]. We will not investigate non-search operations any further in this chapter.

5.2.5 *Algorithms and Implementations of Basic Searches*

We define a basic search as one which can be completed in exactly one major cycle, assuming multiple response resolution as an operation separate from search operations. This definition applies only to the configuration of the CAM in Fig. 5.1. A multiple response is a situation when more than one word satisfies the given search condition. The multiple response resolution resolves this situation by means of a priority circuit [FOS68] or other schemes, e.g. [LAN77, HIL66a, WEI63], and outputs all the responders one at a time. Among the searches listed in the previous section, not all of them can be economically implemented as basic searches. Therefore, we choose to implement those searches which are most frequently used as basic searches while the rest can be performed in a series of the basic searches. As an example, the between-the-limits search ($Y \leq B_i < X$) can be generated by performing a less-than search ($<X$) followed by a greater-than-and-equal-to search ($\geq Y$) on the responders of the first search. In the implementation to be presented, the basic searches are the equality search, the similarity (masked equality) search, the proximity search, the four threshold searches, and the two extremum searches. Each of these basic searches can be

performed alone or a few combinations of them can be performed simultaneously. These searches are grouped into three groups called Mode A, Mode B, and Mode C operations. The mode groupings are as follows.

Mode A: The equality search, the similarity search, the proximity search, and the four threshold searches.

Mode B: The least value search.

Mode C: The greatest value search.

Searches in Mode A can be performed simultaneously. Furthermore, Mode A or Mode B operations can be performed simultaneously with Mode C operations. We will assume that positive logic is used throughout our designs. It should be noted that not all of these searches are required in a specific application. They are presented here for completeness.

5.2.5.1 Mode A: Equality-Threshold-Proximity-Search Mode. In the equality-threshold search, the CAM is partitioned according to the magnitude of the search word S into three sets, namely, words which are equal to S, words which are less than S, and words which are greater than S. The result of this search mode is stored in two of the word control registers, W_2 and W_3, and the interpretation is given in the algorithm to follow. Further, in the proximity search mode, the CAM is partitioned into two sets, words which are near to S, and words which are not. The results of this are gated into W_4. Note that if it is not necessary to perform the proximity search together with the threshold searches, the register W_5 can be eliminated from the design. This search mode is characterized by the signal $G = 0$, which gates the contents of the search register S to the search bus. That is, $R_j = S_j$ $\forall j \in \{1, 2, \ldots, n\}$. The basic searches performed in this mode are the equality search, the four threshold searches (namely, $>S$, $<S$, $\geq S$, and $\leq S$), and the proximity search. $M_j = 0$ means that S_j is not masked while $M_j = 1$ means S_j is masked.

The three query states are shown in the following table.

M_j	S_j	Query State
0	0	0
0	1	1
1	0	d
1	1	d

$$d = \text{don't care}$$

Algorithm 5.1—Mode A Search Operation

1) $\forall i \epsilon \{1, 2, \ldots, m\}$

   a) Initialization:

   $S \leftarrow$ Search word, $M \leftarrow$ Mask, $G = 0$, $j = 0$,

   $w_{i,1} = 1$, $w_{i,2} = 0$, $w_{i,3} = 0$, $w_{i,4} = 0$.

   b) Data Path Setting:

   Gate $X_{i,n+1}$ to $w_{i,4}$, $E_{i,n+1}$ to $w_{i,3}$, L_i to $w_{i,2}$, $w_{i,1}$ to $E_{i,1}$, $\overline{w}_{i,1}$ to $X_{i,1}$.

   These data paths and the control signal G are held until the completion of the major cycle.

2) Let $j \leftarrow j + 1$.

3) Compute $\forall i \epsilon \{1, 2, \ldots, m\}$ simultaneously

   a) $e_{i,j} = (M_j + B_{i,j} \cdot R_j + \overline{B}_{i,j} \cdot \overline{R}_j)$

   b) $E_{i,j+1} = E_{i,j} \cdot e_{i,j}$,

   c) $d_{i,j} = E_{i,j} \cdot \overline{B}_{i,j} \cdot \overline{e}_{i,j}$,[1]

   d) $L_i = \cup_{k=1}^{j} d_{i,k}$ (wired-OR),

   e) $X_{i,j+1} = X_{i,j} \cdot e_{i,j} + \overline{X}_{i,j} \cdot \overline{e}_{i,j} \cdot E_{i,j}$.

4) Is $j = n$?

   a) Yes—Proceed to step 5).
   b) No—Proceed to step 2).

---

1. $d_{i,j}$ will be sensitive to $\overline{B}_{i,j}$ and only to the first bit mismatch between B_i and S. A simpler design using $d_{i,j} = \overline{E}_{i,j+1} \cdot \overline{B}_{i,j}$ can be used. In this case, $d_{i,j}$ will be sensitive to all mismatches between B_i and S. Since L_i is obtained by wired-ORing $d_{i,j}$'s, the final output voltage of the wired-OR will depend on the number of mismatches. It will be more appropriate to eliminate this dependence by only taking the first mismatch as what is done here. We must confess that the exact design is highly technology-dependent.

5) Result Interpretation:

For those words i with $w_{i,1}=1$,

$w_{i,2}(=L_i)$	$w_{i,3}(=E_{i,n+1})$	Interpretation (Equality-Threshold search)
0	0	B_i is greater than search word.
0	1	B_i matches search word
1	0	B_i is less than search word
1	1	⌈does not occur⌉

$W_{i,4}(=X_{i,n+1})$	$W_{i,3}(=E_{i,n+1})$	Interpretation (Proximity search)
0	0	B_i is not near to search word
0	1	B_i matches search word
1	0	B_i is near to search word
1	1	⌈does not occur⌉

In this search algorithm, the minor cycle is composed of step 3) alone while the major cycle is composed of steps 2)–4). The result of this search mode is handled by the match detector D in the word control logic. Any multiple response is resolved by the priority circuit C. The bit-cell logic needed to implement this equality-threshold-proximity search mode is shown in Fig. 5.2. The delay in each minor cycle is one gate delay for the equality-threshold searches and three gate delays for the proximity search. The following example shows the state of L_i, $E_{i,j+1}$ and $X_{i,j+1}$ for a Mode A search of 6 words, each 5 bits long.

Example 5.1: "Mode A" Search Operation

Search Word—S 10110.
Mask Word—M 00100,
Effective Search Word—S' 10d10 (d = don't care).

	i	B_i	State of (L_i, $E_{i,j+1}$, $X_{i,j+1}$) lines at the end of the minor cycle					
			j=0	1	2	3	4	5
	1	10111	010	010	010	010	010	001
	2	11000	010	010	001	001	000	000
memory	3	10010	010	010	010	010	010	010
words	4	10110	010	010	010	010	010	010
	5	10101	010	010	010	010	101	100
	6	01101	010	101	100	100	101	100

Figure 5.2. Bit-cell with Equality, Greater-than, Less-than and
Proximity Capability for Mode A Operation

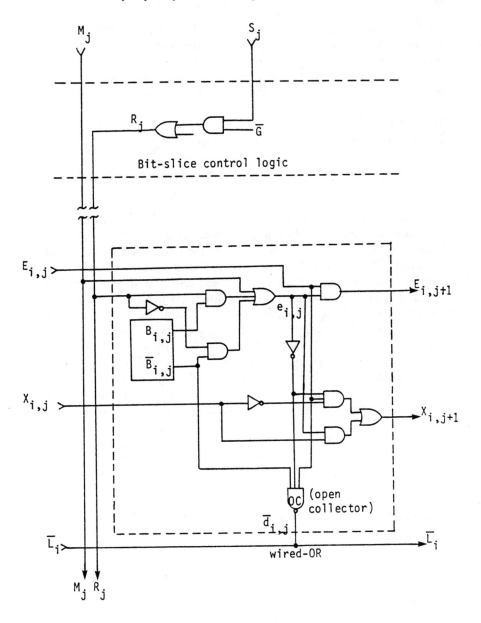

For interpretation of L_i, $E_{i,6}$, $X_{i,6}$ see step 5) of Algorithm 5.1 for Mode A search operations.

5.2.5.2   Mode B: Least value search mode.   In this mode, the search register is no longer needed because no search word is used. However, the minor cycle is more complicated than that in Mode A. It now consists of a comparison phase and a default phase. Consider the *j*th minor cycle. In the comparison phase, one of the three conditions is to be detected:

1)   that the bit-slice is masked,
2)   that the bit-slice is not masked and at least one enabled bit-cell contains a "0", and
3)   that the bit-slice is not masked and all enabled bit-cells contain "1"s.

In the first case, all the enable signals to this bit-slice are passed on to the next bit-slice on the right. In the second case, those enabled bit-cells containing "0"s pass their enable signal to the next bit-cells on the right. In both cases, the minor cycle is complete. The third case, however, is called the default case and the default phase is entered. The default condition is detected in the default-detection bus and the default signal Q_j is fed back to the bit-slice via R_j. R_j is connected to the default feedback circuitry ($R_j = P_j \cdot \bar{Q}_j \cdot G$) when this search mode is activated by setting $G = 1$. P_j is a synchronization signal and it also serves as the search signal in the comparison phase. After the default phase, all the enabled bit-cells pass their enable signals to the next bit-cells on the right, thus completing the minor cycle. The result of Mode B can be stored in one of the result/temporary store registers because Mode A does not operate simultaneously with Mode B.

The implementation of the Mode B search in bit-cell (i,j) is shown in Fig. 5.3. Note that this implementation shares much of the circuitry with that for Mode A and that at the beginning of the *j*th minor cycle, $R_j = 0$.

Algorithm 5.2—Mode B Search Operation—The Least
             Value Search Algorithm.

1) $\forall i \epsilon \{1, 2, \ldots, m\}$

   a)   Initialization:

      $G = 1$, $j = 0$, $w_{i,1} = 1$, $w_{i,2} = 0$,

Figure 5.3. Bit-cell with Least Value Search Logic for Mode B
Operation

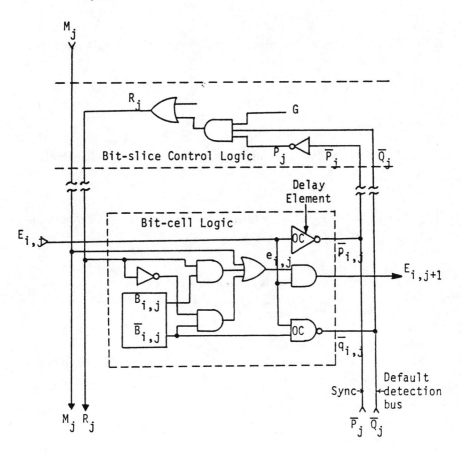

b) Data Path Setting:

Gate $E_{i,n+1}$ to $w_{i,2}$, $w_{i,1}$ to $E_{i,1}$,

The data paths and the control signal G are held until the completion of the major cycle.

2) Let $j \leftarrow j + 1$.

3) Minor Cycle:

a) Comparison Phase: Compute $\forall i \epsilon \{1, 2, \ldots, m\}$ simultaneously.

i) $E_{i,j+1} = E_{i,j} \cdot e_{i,j}$.

ii) $p_{i,j}(t) = E_{i,j}(t - 2)$ (delay element used to synchronize the feedback of Q_j via R_j).

iii) $q_{i,j} = E_{i,j} \cdot \bar{B}_{i,j}$,
$q_{i,j}=1$ means that $B_{i,j}$ is enabled and equals 0.

iv) $P_j = \cup_{i=1}^{m} p_{i,j}$ (wired—OR).

v) $Q_j = \cup_{i=1}^{m} q_{i,j}$ (wired—OR).
$Q_j = 1$ means at least one enabled bit in the jth column is 0.

vi) $R_j = P_j \cdot \bar{Q}_j \cdot G$.

b) Is $R_j = 1$?

i)   Yes—Default detected, proceed to step 3c).
ii) No—Default inhibited, proceed to step 4).

c) Default Phase: Compute $E_{i,j+1} = E_{i,j}$.

4) Is $j = n$?

a) Yes—Proceed to step 5).

b) No—Proceed to step 2).

5) Read out the words that are indicated by $w_{i,2} = 1$.

Example 5.2 shows an example search of Mode B operation on 5 words, each 10 bits long.

Example 5.2 "Mode B" Search Operation.

a) WORDS in which the least value is to be retrieved:

Word Number (i)	Bit Positions 1	2	3	4	5	6 (j)	7	8	9	10	Order of Retrieval
1	0	0	1	1	0	0	1	0	0	1	3
2	0	0	1	0	1	0	0	1	0	1	1
3	1	0	0	1	1	0	0	0	0	1	5
4	0	0	1	0	1	0	1	0	1	1	2
5	0	0	1	1	0	0	1	0	1	1	4

b) STATES of all enable lines $(E_{i,j+1})$ at the end of the major cycle:

Word Number (i)	0	1	2	3	4 (j)	5	6	7	8	9
1	1	1	1	1	0	0	0	0	0	0
2	1	1	1	1	1	1	1	1	1	1
3	1	0	0	0	0	0	0	0	0	0
4	1	1	1	1	1	1	1	0	0	0
5	1	1	1	1	0	0	0	0	0	0

Note: Minor cycles 3, 5, 8 and 10 go through the default phase.

c) Timing diagram for bit-slice 3 in the major cycle:

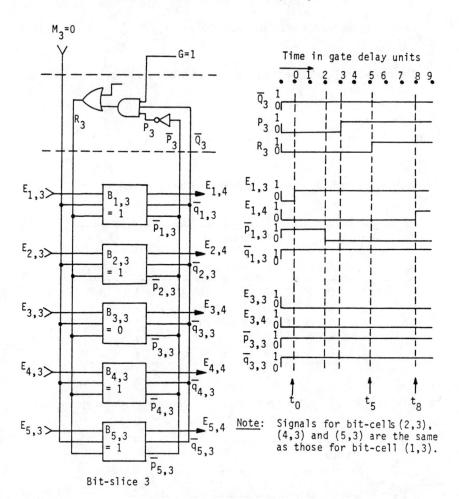

Bit-slice 3

Note: Signals for bit-cells (2,3), (4,3) and (5,3) are the same as those for bit-cell (1,3).

t_0:   Starting of minor cycle for bit-slice 3;
t_5:   Default condition detected;
t_8:   End of minor cycle for bit-slice 3;
FROM t_0 TO t_5:   Comparison phase of minor cycle;
FROM t_5 TO t_8:   Default phase of minor cycle.

d) Timing diagram for bit-slice 4 in the major cycle:

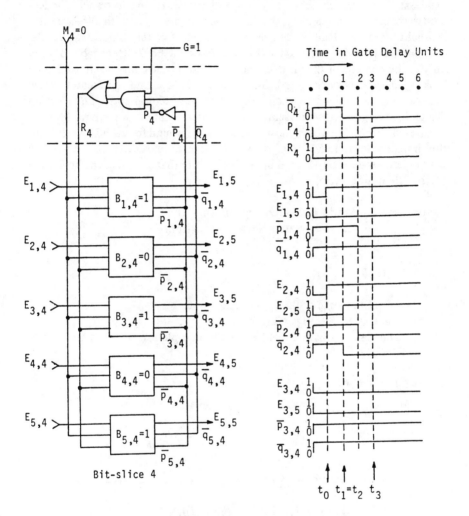

Bit-slice 4

Note: Signals for bit-cells (4,4) and (5,4) are the same as those for bit-cells (2,4) and (1,4) respectively.

t_0: Starting of minor cycle for bit-slice 4;

t_1: End of minor cycle for bit-slice 4;

t_2: Default-inhibit signal becomes stable;

t_3: Bit-slice control logic in stable state.

5.2.5.3 Mode C: Greatest value search mode.   In the implementation of
the least value search scheme, the speed for searching is traded for less
hardware in each bit-cell by sharing much of the logic with the equality-
inequality search. Had it not been required for the latter search, the
comparison time for the least value search could be shortened by looking
only at the content of the bit-cell, and the default time could be shortened by
looking at the feedback signal. Since the least value and the greatest value
searches are analogous to each other, we shall demonstrate the speed-up
design for the greatest value search. The implementation of the new design is
illustrated in Fig. 5.4 which shows the complete design for each bit-cell. With
this implementation, Mode C operations can be executed simultaneously
with either Mode A or Mode B operations. Note that $T_j = 0$ at the beginning
of the jth minor cycle.

Algorithm 5.3—Mode C Search Operation—The
Greatest Value Search Algorithm

1) $\forall i \in \{1, 2, \ldots, m\}$

   a)   Initialization: $j = 0$, $w_{i,1} = 1$, $w_{i,5} = 0$,
   b)   Data Path Setting: Gate $F_{i,n+1}$ to $w_{i,4}$, and $w_{i,1}$ to $F_{i,1}$,
        The data paths are held until the completion of the major cycle.

2)   Let $j \leftarrow j + 1$.

3)   Minor Cycle:

   a)   Comparison Phase: Compute $\forall i \in \{1, 2, \ldots, m\}$ simultaneously.

      i) $F_{i,j+1} = F_{i,j} \cdot (M_j^* + B_{i,j} + T_j)$,

      ii) $u_{i,j}(t) = F_{i,j}(t - 1)$ (delay element used to synchronize the
            feedback of V_j via T_j).

      iii) $v_{i,j} = F_{i,j} \cdot B_{i,j}$,
            $v_{i,j} = 1$ means that $B_{i,j}$ is enabled and equals 1.

      iv) $U_j = \bigcup_{i=1}^{m} u_{i,j}$ (wired—OR).

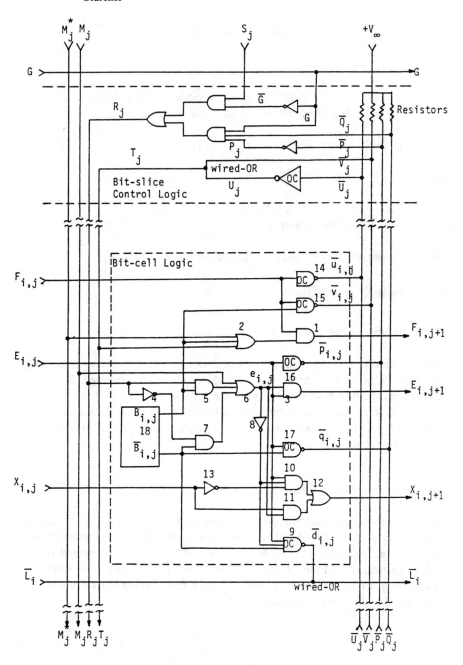

Figure 5.4. Bit-cell for Simultaneous Ascending Retrieval and
Descending Retrieval or Equality-Threshold-Proximity
Searches

    v) $V_j = \bigcup_{i=1}^{m} v_{i,j}$ (wired—OR).

          $V_j = 1$ means at least one enabled bit in the jth column is 1.

    vi) $T_j = U_j \bar{V}_j$ (wired—AND).

  b) Is $T_j = 1$?

      i)   Yes—Default detected, proceed to step 3c).
      ii) No—Default inhibited, proceed to step 4).

  c) Default Phase: Compute $F_{i,j+1} = F_{i,j}$.

4) Is $j = n$?

  a) Yes—Proceed to step 5).
  b) No—Proceed to step 2).

5) Read out the words that are indicated by $w_{i,5} = 1$.

5.2.6   Ordered Retrieval

A. Ascending Order Retrieval

The ascending order retrieval of a set of data can be achieved by performing the least value search repeatedly until all the data are retrieved. With the CAM organization that we have presented, a microprogram in the memory control store provides an economical and efficient implementation of such a retrieval algorithm. A flow chart for an ascending order retrieval algorithm is shown in Fig. 5.5.

B. Descending Order Retrieval

The algorithm described for the ascending order retrieval can be modified for descending order retrieval by substituting the greatest value search for the least value search. That is, Mode C search operation is executed in the CAM instead of Mode B search operation. Hence, the algorithm for descending order retrieval is to perform the greatest value search repeatedly until all the data are retrieved.

Figure 5.5. Flow Chart for Ascending Order Retrieval

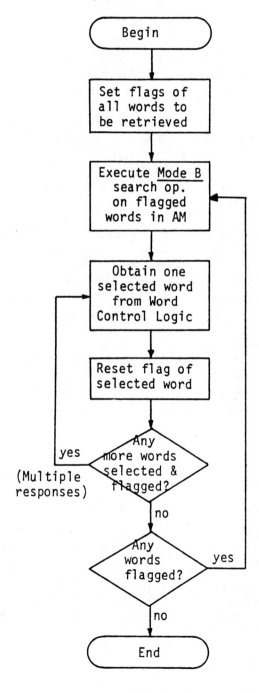

5.2.7   Some Speed-up Techniques

The design shown here has 1 to 3 gate delays per minor cycle in each of the mode A search operations.[2] The delay in Mode B operations ranges from 3 to 8 gate delays per minor cycle,[3] while for Mode C operations, it ranges from 1 to 4 gate delays per minor cycle. We now consider several techniques that can be used to reduce the search times. The four areas that bear investigation are lookahead techniques, external examination of retrieval process, implementation of additional basic operations, and modifications to the scheme involving greater parallelism in the search.

   In the first area, lookahead logic can be added to each word in the memory. The algorithms we have described previously are all bit-serial and word-parallel in nature. This means that the enable signals for each word propagate from bit to bit and operations for each word are performed in parallel. The speed of a search operation is, therefore, proportional to n where n is the number of bits in each word. We can increase the speed by adding some lookahead logic to each word. Each word is segmented into contiguous groups of bits of equal size k, and a lookahead circuit is added to each group (assuming k is a factor of n). Each lookahead circuit operates on all the bits in its group in parallel and passes the result onto the next group when it has finished. The speed of an equality-proximity search operation using this lookahead circuit will be proportional n/k, but for extremum searches, no improvement is found. This type of lookahead is essentially single-leveled or cascaded. This means that the signals still have to propagate from group to group instead of from bit to bit, and the lookahead circuits exist in a single level above the storage circuits of each word. The cellular

---

2.   Assuming that all the $e_{i,j}$ signals are available before the search begins, there is one gate delay per minor cycle in the equality-threshold search while there are 2 to 3 gate delays per minor cycle for the propagation of the $X_{i,j}$ signal.

3.   In the case of the least value search, the maximum and the minimum delays are actually shorter. The $e_{i,j}$ signal of each bit-slice can be assumed to be settled before the major cycle starts (see Fig. 5.4). This means that the M_j lines are enabled ahead long enough for the $e_{i,j}$ signal to settle. In this case, the minimum time to pass through each bit-slice is 1 gate delay. The maximum time to pass through each bit-slice is also shorter than 8 (the maximum gate delay count). When default occurs, $B_{i,j} = 1$ for all enabled words. Therefore, output from gate 7 is 0 and the feedback through R_j never has to go through gate 4. Hence, the maximum delay through a bit-slice is 7 gate delays.

property of the design is preserved because a group, instead of a bit in a word, can now be regarded as a cell. We will not investigate other types of lookahead circuits, e.g., tree-lookahead circuits, because they do not preserve the cellular property. We now illustrate the construction of these lookahead circuits for the equality-proximity and the Mode B and Mode C searches.

An examination of the equality-proximity search operation shows that each of the $E_{i,j+1}$ signals propagates from bit slice j to bit slice $j + 1$ in one gate delay where j ranges from 1 to n. Similarly, the $X_{i,j}$ signal propagates from bit-slice j to bit-slice $j + 1$ in 2 to 3 gate delays. Improvement can be achieved by grouping bits in each word and performing the comparisons in parallel. An example is shown in Fig. 5.6 where the necessary lookahead logic for grouping bits j and $j + 1$ of word i is shown. In the equality search, comparisons in each group are done in parallel. The results of comparison, $e_{i,j+1}$ and $e_{i,j+2}$, are ANDed together with $E_{i,j}$ to form $E_{i,j+2}$. The propagation time for these two bits is 1 gate delay instead of 2 in the usual bit serial operation. The speed of the equality search will therefore be proportional to $n/2$ gate delays. The number of gates for the propagation of the $E_{i,j}$ signal is also reduced from 2 to 1 for bit-slices j and $j + 1$. Similarly, in the proximity search, gates A and B of Figure 5.6 detect the condition when only one mismatch occurs in the group slice and gate C detects the condition when there is no mismatch in the group slice. The logic equation for $X_{x,j+2}$ is:

$$X_{i,j+2} = X_{i,j} \cdot (e_{i,j+1} \cdot e_{i,j+2})$$
$$+ \ \overline{X}_{i,j} \cdot E_{i,j} \cdot (e_{i,j+1} \cdot \overline{e}_{i,j+2} + \overline{e}_{i,j+1} \cdot e_{i,j+2})$$

which is similar to the $X_{i,j+1}$ equation in Algorithm 4.1. However, in this case, the propagation delay has been reduced to 3 instead of 6. The number of gates required is also reduced by a constant factor.

For Mode B and Mode C operations, lookahead requires more hardware. The existence of default cases has caused the increased complexity. Previously, without lookahead, default was detected for a bit-slice when certain conditions existed on all enabled words in that bit-slice. These conditions include 1) all enabled words which have 1's in this bit-slice for the least value search and 2) all enabled words which have 0's in this bit-slice for the greatest value search. The number of default feedback lines is 1 for each search mode. When a lookahead circuit is added to each word for a group of k bit-slices, the number of default feedback lines will be 2^k. These 2^k lines can be shared by both the least value search and the greatest value search.

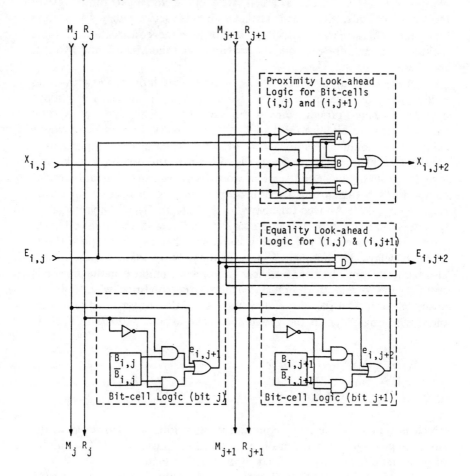

Figure 5.6. Bit-cells (i,j) and $(i,j+1)$ of Word i with equality-proximity search logic and Lookahead Logic

Consider a particular group; the following operations are to be carried out: a) The bits of each word in this group are decoded into 2^k lines. b) The corresponding lines from each word of this group are wired-ORed together to form default feedback lines 0 to $2^k - 1$; a particular feedback line p will be 1 when there exists an enabled word in this group whose decoded value equals p. c) In the group-slice control logic, if a Mode B operation exists, it will scan from feedback lines 0 to $2^k - 1$ until the first line with a 1 is found; similarly if a Mode C operation exists, it will scan from feedback lines $2^k - 1$ to 0; this line will represent the minimum/maximum of all the enabled words in this group. d) This line is encoded into k search bus signals to be fed back to each word in this group. e) In a particular word, the enabled line for the next group is enabled if the current group of this word is enabled and the value of this part of the word equals the search bus signal, i.e., it equals the minimum/maximum value found by the group slice control logic.

However, there are some disadvantages of using lookahead on Mode B and Mode C operations. The extensive amount of decoding requires an order of 2^k gates of fan-in k for each group in each word. For each group-slice, there are 2^k default feedback buses running across all the words and this can cause difficulty in integrated circuit implementation. The biggest difficulty, however, lies in the implementation of the scanning algorithm in the group-slice control logic. The algorithm of scanning across a set of lines until the first one is found is essentially a multiple match resolution problem. If a tree-type multiple match resolution circuit is used, e.g., [FOS68], a maximum delay of $\log_2 2^k = k$ will be observed. That is, the overall speed of a group of bit slices, with or without lookahead, is of the order of k. Unless a faster multiple match resolution circuit is used, and the cost of hardware is sufficiently low, lookahead for Mode B and Mode C searches is not cost-effective.

An examination of the example illustrated in the previous section points out another possible source of improvement, this time in the algorithm itself. In many cases the number of words still enabled at the end of a minor cycle rapidly drops to one within a few minor cycles. At this point the completion of the major cycle is a formality since the greatest (or the least) valued word must be the only remaining enabled word. Unfortunately, the detection of this condition, the only-one-respondent-left condition, is too complex to be performed at the end of every minor cycle, and would require extensive external wiring and logic.

We have implemented some of the search operations defined in section 5.2.4 as basic operations. Some other useful searches may be performed by combining two or more basic searches and possibly some nonsearch operations. An example is the between-the-limits search, which is generated by performing a less-than search followed by a greater-than search on words selected by the first search. In fact, all the searches described in section 5.2.4 can be performed as a basic search or a combination of the basic searches designed in this section. Speed improvement can of course be gained by implementing all of these search operations as basic searches, but the amount of logic circuits may be extensive. In most other cases, the more complicated searches, such as the case of ordered retrieval, are implemented as a combination of simple searches.

One modification to our ordered retrieval technique that yields positive results without compromising our cellular logic approach is to increase the parallelism of the algorithm itself. This can be done by simultaneously performing the greatest value search and the least value search on the same set of enabled words. The associative sort is complete when both searches select the same word, an easily detectable condition, or when no words are still enabled at the beginning of a major cycle, also an easily detectable condition. A small additional amount of external manipulation of the sorted file block is required by the non-associative processor controlling the sort to concatenate the two halves of the sorted block since one will be in the reverse of the desired order, but it is felt that this is a small price to pay for a speed-up factor of greater than 2. This technique is shown in Example 5.3 that follows.

The speed-up involved in this approach is greater than a factor of 2. To understand why it is greater than a factor of 2 instead of exactly equal to 2, we must consider the properties of the fields to be searched. Assuming an even distribution, there is on the average one more bit with the value "1" in the higher valued half of a sorted file than in the lower valued half of the same file. This can be verified in Example 5.3a. The greatest value search has a shorter minor cycle for bit positions with a value of "1" in the word with the greatest value than for bit positions with a "0" in the word with the greatest value. Likewise, the least value search has a shorter minor cycle time for bit positions with a value of "0" in the word with the least value than for bit positions with a "1" in the word with the least value. This provides for an average major cycle time five gate delays shorter than if all words were to be selected in an ordered retrieval by either search alone (assuming the delay for each minor cycle of both Mode B and Mode C search operations ranges from 3 to 7 gate delays). The design for this technique has been indicated in Fig. 5.4.

Example 5.3: "Mode B" and "Mode C" Parallel Operation.

a) WORDS to be retrieved:

Word Number	1	2	3	4	5	6	7	8	9	10	A = Number of 1's per Word	Ascending Order of Retrieval
					Bit Positions							
1	0	0	1	0	1	0	1	1	0	1	5	12
2	1	1	0	0	1	0	0	1	0	0	4	20
3	0	0	0	0	1	1	1	1	0	1	5	6
4	1	1	1	1	1	1	0	0	0	0	6	30
5	0	0	1	0	0	0	0	0	0	0	1	11
6	1	1	1	0	0	0	0	1	0	0	4	23
7	0	0	0	0	0	0	0	0	0	0	0	1
8	0	1	0	1	1	1	1	1	0	1	7	14
9	1	1	0	1	0	1	0	0	1	0	5	21
10	1	1	1	1	0	0	1	1	0	0	6	28
11	1	1	0	1	1	1	1	1	1	1	9	22
12	0	0	0	1	1	1	1	0	1	1	6	10
13	0	0	0	0	0	1	1	1	1	1	5	4
14	0	1	1	0	1	0	1	1	1	1	7	15
15	1	1	1	1	1	1	0	1	1	0	8	31
16	1	1	1	0	1	0	0	0	0	0	4	26
17	1	1	1	1	1	0	0	0	0	0	5	29
18	1	1	1	0	0	0	1	0	0	1	5	24
19	0	0	0	0	0	0	1	0	0	1	2	2
20	1	0	1	0	0	0	0	0	1	0	3	19
21	0	0	1	1	0	1	1	0	1	1	6	13
22	0	0	0	1	0	1	1	1	1	1	6	7
23	1	1	1	1	1	1	1	1	1	1	10	32
24	0	0	0	0	0	0	1	1	1	1	4	33
25	0	1	1	1	1	1	0	1	1	0	7	16
26	0	0	0	1	1	0	1	0	1	1	5	8
27	1	1	1	0	0	1	0	1	0	0	5	25
28	0	0	0	1	1	1	0	1	1	0	5	9
29	1	1	1	1	0	0	0	0	1	0	5	27
30	1	0	0	1	0	1	0	0	0	0	3	18
31	0	0	0	0	1	1	0	0	1	1	4	5
32	1	0	0	0	0	0	1	0	0	1	3	17

Number of 1's in memory: 160.
Number of bits in memory: 320.
Number of 1's per word in the smaller half of the ordered list = 4.69.
Number of 1's per word in the larger half of the ordered list = 5.31.

b)   ORDER of retrieval in parallel operation:

Let L_B and L_C be the lists of words retrieved by Mode B and Mode C search operations, respectively. Both lists are ordered with respect to time, in gate delay units, at which they are retrieved, and neglecting overhead time between major cycles. Assume that for the least value search, the gate delays for each minor cycle range from 1 to 7 and that for the greatest value search, they range from 1 to 4.

L_B	Time[a]	L_C	L_B	Time[a]	L_C	L_B	Time[a]	L_C
Start	0	Start	-	173	27	5	368	-
7	10	23	3	180	-	-	385	32
-	28	15	-	198	18	-	404	25
19	32	-	22	226	8	1	408	-
-	48	4	-	239	11	-	423	14
24	66	-	-	264	9	-	442	8
-	73	17	28	266	-	21	454	-
-	95	10	-	292	2	End of Retrieval		
13	106	-	28	306	-			
-	120	29	-	323	20			
31	140	-	12	352	-			
-	148	16	-	354	30			

[a]Time in gate delay units.

Throughput = 454 gate delays/(32 * 10) bits = 1.42 gate delays/bit.

5.2.8   *Issues and Limitations*

We have presented a design of an associative memory that can be used for fast ordered retrieval. From Example 5.3, neglecting the overhead in loading and unloading the memory, the sorting speed is 1.42 gate delays per bit. This design is therefore very attractive and can be used in many places where fast searching and sorting is required. However, there exist many issues that need to be carefully considered and resolved before successful operations can result. We discuss four of these issues here, namely, LSI implementation, manufacturing defects, modular expansion, and multiple match resolution. We do not contend that they exhaust all the issues in this design. New issues may come up during the implementation phase and will have to be resolved by the designer.

5.2.8.1   LSI implementation.   In Fig. 5.4, a complete design has been shown. Each bit cell requires 17 gates. There are extra logic associated with the registers and the controls. Consider a 32-bit word and a 32-word memory. This design needs over 17,000 gates for the logic in the bit-cells only, excluding all other registers, memory cells, and control logic. Therefore, the memory size that can be effectively implemented on an LSI chip is very limited. One solution is to reduce the number of functions in a cell when the application does not call for it. However, this is very much application dependent. Furthermore, the number of pins on the LSI package also limits the word size. In order to maintain fast response and high throughput, parallel reading and writing of bits of a word in the memory is necessary. The major portion of the pins of an LSI package is usually taken up for parallel reading and writing. For a 32-bit word memory, the pin requirement is 32 plus a few controls and selections. On the other hand, the pin limitation will set a maximum word size that can be implemented. It becomes obvious that modular expansion is necessary in order for this design to be practical. The issue of modular expansion is discussed later.

5.2.8.2 Manufacturing defects. After the LSI chip has been manufactured, tests are made to determine whether any cells are faulty. A faulty cell can be determined by injecting certain test patterns into the memory. If the number of defects are small and their locations can be determined up to the locality of certain gates in the cell, then these faults can be bypassed by utilizing some spare bit-slices designed into the memory. The difficulty in recovering an error in a faulty cell of the CAM is that the error may not only affect the word itself, but it may also affect other words because the value of the faulty bit is available to other words via the feedback circuitry. Therefore, it may be necessary to remove the current bit-slice or the current and all bit-slices to the right from operation when an error occurs in a cell.

We have assumed that only stuck-at faults can occur in the gates of memory cells and bit-slice control logic. Faults occurring in registers and control store are not considered since the logic there is only a small fraction of all the logic on the chip. By assuming that the jth bit of the ith word is faulty, we can identify three types of faults, one in which the jth bit-slice has to be removed from operation, one in which the ith word has to be removed from operation and one in which all the remaining bit-slices are rendered useless.

Referring to Fig. 5.4, for faults that occur in gates 14–17 and the bit-slice control logic, they only affect the feedback values but they do not affect the enable lines so long as the mask bit is 1, that is, the bit-slice is masked off. This can be done by setting a 1 permanently in the jth bit of the mask registers and shifting the external pin connection to the chip by 1 bit. For faults (stuck at 0 or stuck at 1) that occur at gates 2, 4–13 and the storage cell 18, and for stuck at 0 faults at gates 1 and 3, they do not affect the remaining words so long as the enable signals are set to 0, that is, the ith word is disabled. This can be done by setting a 0 permanently in the ith position of the word flag register W_1 and the result/temporary registers $W_2 - W_5$. For stuck at 1 faults that occur at gates 1 and 3, they affect the enable lines for the next bit-slice. If an enable line has a faulty value of 1, that is, the remaining bits of this word are enabled regardless of whether the current word or bit-slice are masked off, it may cause a faulty feedback to other bit-slices on the right. So unless all the remaining bit-slices are masked off, the fault that occurs in cell (i,j) will propagate to these bit-slices. A finer recovery procedure can be developed if we can identify the corresponding words to be disabled for a particular search operation.

From the above discussion, we see that recovery from manufacturing defects is easy and most of the faults are recoverable.

5.2.8.3 *Modular expansion.*

Our philosophy of the associative memory design is that we want to distribute the logic into the storage cells. In order for all the distributed logic to perform coherently, extra communication lines are needed to transfer enable and feedback signals from bit to bit. The number of these communication lines is usually large and this will eliminate the possibility of modular expansion which is easy in the case of RAMs.

Consider our design in Fig. 5.4; each cell has 4 enable lines to communicate with the cell on its right; and each bit-slice has 8 lines which are used for feedback, synchronization, and mask. These lines run across all words in the bit-slice (these exclude lines needed to read and write data into each bit). Suppose a memory chip of m words by n bits is available. To extend the word size of this memory, we can put two memory chips together side by side as shown in Fig. 5.7(a). However, this design needs $4m$ lines to pass the enable signals from the chip on the left to the one on the right. This is not feasible even for a small m. To extend the memory size, we can put two chips one over the other as shown in Fig. 5.7(b). This design needs $8n$ feedback lines to pass the feedback, synchronization, and mask signals between the two chips. Even for a small value of n, the number of interconnections is very large.

In order for our design to be practical, some other schemes of modular expansion are necessary. In Fig. 5.7(c), we show a scheme that allows us to extend the memory size by increasing the dimensions of the memory. A batch of m memory chips is put together in parallel. There is an extra dimension and is composed of a single memory chip running across the m parallel chips. A flow chart for an ascending order retrieval algorithm of m^2 words is shown in Fig. 5.8. The time needed to orderly retrieve m^2 words is $m^2 + m$ units of load time (time to store a word into the memory) and $m^2 + m$ units of search time (a search time includes the time to execute a Mode C operation and to read it out into the I/O register). The amount of search time can be reduced to $m^2 + 1$ units of search time when the Mode C

Figure 5.7. Modular Extension for Proposed Associative Memory

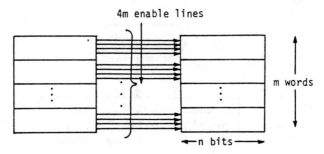

(a) Word Size Extension

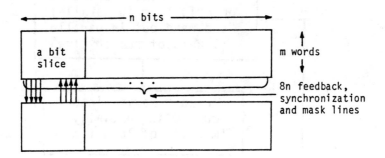

(b) Memory Size Extension

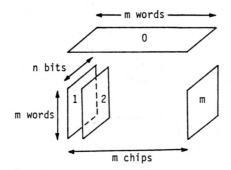

(c) 3-dimensional Associative Memory for Memory Size Extension

Figure 5.8. Flow Chart for Ascending Order Retrieval of m^2 words in a Three-dimensional Associative Memory (see Figure 5.7c)

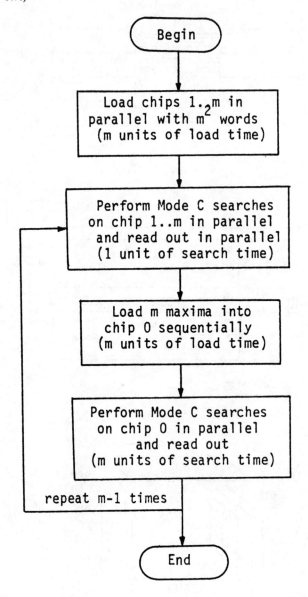

searches in chips $1, \ldots, m$ are performed in parallel with the Mode C searches in chip 0. In a single memory chip which can accommodate m^2 words, the time needed for this memory system is m^2 units of load and m^2 units of search time. Therefore the degradation in performance is minimal when m is large. For a memory size larger than m^2 words, extra dimensions are needed.

We conclude that our scheme on memory expansion has minimal degradation on performance. The difficulty still exists in word size expansion. The limitation is due to the pin requirements. However, we can trade performance for a smaller amount of external pin connections by loading bits of a word in groups instead of all in parallel. However, the degradation in performance due to this loading scheme is more pronounced than our memory size expansion scheme.

5.2.8.4 Multiple match resolution.   One of the most useful applications in our design is in the multiple response resolution. A tag field can be included in each word. Each tag is a distinguishable number. The size of each tag must be at least $\lceil \log_2 m \rceil$ for a memory size m. When there are multiple responses, each tag serves as a number for the ordered retrieval scheme. The words used in the ordered retrieval are those that respond. Only the bit-slices containing the tag are used in the search. The first cycle can retrieve two words, the one with the maximum tag, and the one with the minimum tag. Subsequent searches give two responses each time. The speed of this resolution scheme is $1/2$ memory cycle per word and is independent of the memory size.

There are two disadvantages in using tags for multiple match resolution. First, there are irregularities in implementation. Because each tag has a distinguishable value and if each tag is hardwired into the memory, it will involve a different design for each word and it will also be difficult to overcome the problem of manufacturing defects when a cell in the tag is bad. This problem can be solved by loading the tags from a PROM when the memory is first used. Second, when a cell in the tag becomes bad during operation, e.g., stuck at 0, then two of the words in the memory have identical tags and it is impossible to distinguish them.

We can also perform the multiple match resolution without using special fields as tags. This can be done by treating the contents of each word or part of the word as a tag itself. It requires all words under consideration in the memory to be different in order for unique responses to result.

5.2.9 Comparisons with Other Methods of Ordered Retrieval

We have presented in this section several of the search schemes, namely, the equality search, the threshold searches, the proximity search, and the extremum searches. The other searches defined in section 5.2.4 can be implemented as a combination of basic searches. Using the implementation in this section, we compute the maximum and the minimum search times for each search.

Search Type	Minimum Number of Gate Delays	Maximum Number of Gate Delays
Equality Search	$n + 5$	$n + 5$
Inequality Search	7	$n + 5$
Similarity Search	$n + 5$	$n + 5$
Greater-than Search	$n + 5$	$n + 5$
Less-than Search	7	$n + 5$
Greater-than-or-equal-to Search	$n + 5$	$n + 5$
Less-than-or-equal-to Search	$n + 5$	$n + 5$
Double-limit Search		
Between-limit Search, $X > Y$		
$< X \& > Y$	$n + 12$	$2n + 10$
$< X \& \geq Y$	$n + 12$	$2n + 10$
$\leq X \& > Y$	$2n + 10$	$2n + 10$
$\leq X \& \geq Y$	$2n + 10$	$2n + 10$
Outside-limit Search, $X < Y$		
$< X \& > Y$	7	$2n + 10$
$< X \& \geq Y$	7	$2n + 10$
$\leq X \& > Y$	$n + 5$	$2n + 10$
$\leq X \& \geq Y$	$n + 5$	$2n + 10$
Proximity Search	$2n + 4$	$3n + 6$
Extremum Search		
1) Least-Value Search	n	$7n$
2) Greatest-Value Search	n	$4n$
Adjacency Search		
1) Nearest-above Search	$2n + 5$	$8n + 5$
2) Nearest-below Search	$n + 7$	$5n + 5$

We see that the delay times in all these searches are proportional to n, the number of bits in a word, and is independent of the number of words in the memory.

Several methods of ordered retrieval and multiple response resolution have been proposed in the past. It would be of great value to evaluate the method of ordered retrieval presented in this section in terms of these other schemes. In particular, we compare this new algorithm with those of Frei and Goldberg [FRE61], Seeber and Lindquist [SEE62], Lewin [LEW62], Miiller [MII64], and Foster [FOS76]. In order to evaluate these various schemes, it is necessary to determine the significant characteristics that we wish to examine and to determine the comparable features of these diverse methods.

In order to facilitate these comparisons, the methods mentioned will be classified into two types, those with an algorithm to order the retrieval according to the contents of the stored words and those which use an external priority scheme, usually some form of priority tree, to order the retrieval according to the physical location in memory. Among schemes of the first type are those of Frei and Goldberg, Seeber and Lindquist, Miiller, and Lewin. Miiller's scheme uses the contents of the responding words to resolve multiple response conflicts but it does not necessarily order the selections in ascending or descending order. Among those schemes that use an external priority circuit to resolve conflicts are those of Weinstein [WEI63] and Foster. These schemes are not strictly comparable to the proposed algorithm since they cannot be used for sorting. Likewise, Miiller's scheme is not absolutely comparable to our proposed scheme but is similar enough that we will include it in the comparison.

The two main considerations for comparison are obviously the speed with which a method retrieves stored data and the cost in terms of amount of logic required. Rather than attempting an exhaustive analysis of the implementation cost for each of the various schemes, we shall look at the more readily available information as to the rate of cost increase for increasing memory size. In particular we are interested in the memory cost as a function of memory size.

We shall limit our discussion of speed comparisons to the number of search cycles required to retrieve each stored word. For several of the schemes under consideration, a significant parameter is the density of the flagged words, that is, the ratio of the number of words to be retrieved to the number of words addressable with the given tag field size. We will assume that the number of words addressable by the tag field is the same as the length of the memory.

The chart of Table 5.1 shows as direct a comparison as possible between the aforementioned searches and the search scheme proposed. The headings include relative speed (in terms of the number of cycles needed to retrieve each flagged word), comments upon dependencies of logic complexities to memory size, relative complexities of the hardware needed for implementation, and comments upon class of problems handled. Fig. 5.9 shows a plot of words to be retrieved for a memory with a five bit tag field in each word, corresponding to a memory size of 32 words. It is seen that our proposed scheme is equal to or better than all of the presented schemes in terms of speed, and in terms of the number of cycles needed to retrieve a word from memory. In terms of the absolute speed, the Foster method is somewhat

Table 5.1. A Comparison Table for Ordered Retrieval Schemes

Scheme	Speed - R (n,k) (Cycles per Retrieval of an n Bit Tag)	Memory Size Dependency	Relative Complexity of Hardware Required	Best Class of Problem
Frei and Goldberg	For n = 5 Best Case (k = 2^5): R = 2k Worst Case (k=1): R = 7k	Length of tag field (n) only	Basic CAM	High density of responders
Seeber and Lindquist	$t = 2^n$ $R(n,k) = \frac{1}{k}\{\{(t+k-1) +$ $\frac{t(t-1)^k}{t^k} - \frac{2t}{t^k}\sum_{i=1}^{n}(k(t-2^i)^{k-1} +$ $2^{-i}(t-2^{i^k})\}$	Length of tag field (n) only	Complex cryogenic logic at each bit (18 gates)	Density dependent
Lewin	$\frac{2k-1}{k}$ Exact	Independent	A registers plus 9 gates per bit slice	Independent

Miller	Best case : $\dfrac{k+1}{k}$ Worst case : $\dfrac{2k-1}{k}$	Independent	Basic CAM plus some additional control and storage	Multiple response resolution only
Foster	1 cycle per retrieval	External logic uses $3(2^{m-1})-1$ gates for 2^m words of memory	Tree Circuit external to CAM	Multiple response resolution only
Proposed	$\dfrac{1}{2}$ cycle per retrieval	Increases as $\log_2 m$ * for m words of memory	~ 17 gates per bit cell	Independent

* $\log_2 m$ is the size of a tag that must be used to uniquely identify each word for a memory size of m. This differs from the other schemes which do not use a specialized tag for ordered retrieval.

Figure 5.9. Comparison of Retrieval Speeds for a 5 bit Tag with k Words Flagged

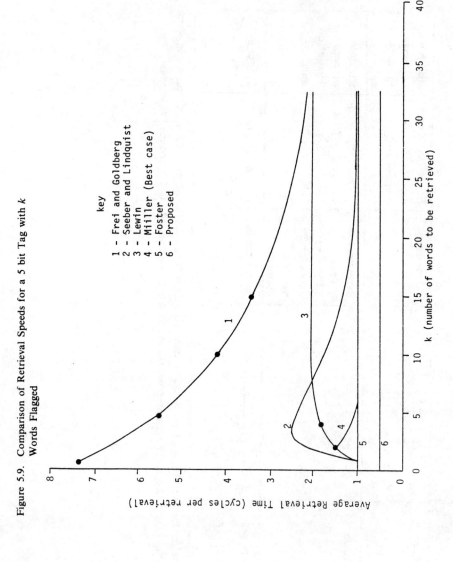

faster in terms of gate delays per retrieval since it uses an external priority logic tree. The Foster scheme, however, is not useful as a tool for ordered retrieval, but only for a multiple response resolution. At two retrievals per memory cycle, our proposed scheme is by far the fastest ordered retrieval scheme, even faster than the Miiller scheme which does not even produce ordering, only resolution. As far as the complexity of the hardware goes, our scheme is well within the realizable realm of LSI technology and in fact is no more complex than that used by Seeber and Lindquist or Yang and Yau [YAN66] in their implementation of Lewin's algorithm.

We conclude that the design we have proposed here may be a useful and realizable tool for associative processing in any applications where ordered retrieval is important. One of the applications is to use it as a multiple match resolver as we have described in section 5.2.8. Another application is to use it as a file processor in database applications. In the next section, we look at some of the requirements for offloading the processing onto a database machine and see how the associative memory proposed in this section can be extended to sequential memories.

5.3   Database Machines

5.3.1   Introduction

A Database Machine (DBM) is defined as an architectural approach which distributes processing power closer to the devices on which data are stored and offloads database processing functions from the main computer [LAN79]. There have been many DBM designs, among them data base computer (DBC) [BAU76, KER79, BAN79], context addressed segment sequential storage (CASSM) [LIP78, SU79], relational associative processor (RAP) [OZK77, SCH79], rotating associative memory for relational data base applications (RARES) [LIN76], datacomputer [MAR75], and list merging network [HOL79].

There have been many factors, both in the past and in the present, that pertain to the growth of DBMs. Apart from the growth of semi-conductor technologies and the rising need for larger databases (Figures 1.2, 1.3, 1.4, Table 1.1), the most important factor leading to the increasing hardware implementation of database functions is the growth in complexity and size of database management software. Because it is necessary to provide a high level view of the data to the users, it is essential to provide a complex translation from the physical data structure to the logical data view and vice versa. Conventionally, this has been done by the database management software. Depending on how complex the translation mechanism is, the amount of software to be developed and the amount of execution time needed is also different.

As an example, the INGRES database takes 350,000 machine instructions to process a simple transaction which can be a retrieval or an update of a simple record of data. Out of these 350,000 instructions, only 25,000 instructions are real work that perform the actual function of the query. The other part of the work (325,000 instructions) is purely overhead which includes 25,000 instructions for parsing, 75,000 instructions for validity checks, 125,000 instructions for task switches and pipes, and 100,000 instructions to interface with the users. Some of this overhead can be reduced. For example, the amount of validity checks can be reduced if the main memory is large enough to hold the system catalogue; the user interface can be made less complex; the query can be parsed at compile time in order to eliminate the run time interpreter overhead. Nonetheless, the overhead is still quite large. The execution of a simple transaction is, therefore, CPU bound.

On the other hand, in order to process a complex transaction in INGRES, which retrieves or updates multiple records, it takes about 25,000 machine instructions to process a 512 byte page and 20 msec. to fetch a page from the secondary storage. Out of these 25,000 instructions, only 6,000 are real work; the other part is overhead. The processing of a complex transaction can be speeded up by (i) compiling the query before execution; (ii) enlarging page size; (iii) developing better decomposition strategies; and (iv) building a one process real time system.

As a result of the overhead in processing a query, the use of a DBM, which executes the query in hardware outside the CPU, reduces the execution overhead of the CPU and the I/O overhead in transferring data into the main memory.

5.3.2 Issues in the Design of DBMs

Traditionally, the design of DBMs is plagued by many issues. Among them are:

(1) Parallelism—Kind and Degree.

The designer has to decide on the kind of functions that can be processed in parallel and the degree of parallelism. These functions include address mapping operators and the database functions as well.

(2) Technology dependence.

The designer of a DBM must take into account the available technology. Further, the design must be able to evolve as new technologies are made available.

(3) Interface, where and in what form.

The problem is to design a good interface between the DBM and the host processor. This interface may be implemented in hardware/firmware, software, or a combination of both. This interface translates queries from the host processor to database functions processable by the DBM. Important questions like where to put this interface and how much capability it should have, must be answered. Should it be a part of the host, or should it be a part of the DBM? Should the interface be able to access the memory hierarchy? How should the interconnection network be between the DBM and the storage sub-system? What type of language primitives should be used? These questions have to be considered carefully by the designer.

(4) Storage structure.

The kind of storage structure is very important. If keyed accesses, that is, accessing data via a key, are allowed, then additional hardware capabilities like associative memory or extra pointers are necessary to support it. Further, questions like whether the storage structure is dynamic should also be considered.

(5) Backend primitives.

The designer has to trade the availability of backend primitives (which include functions like sorting, file merging, etc.) with the cost and the difficulty of implementing it.

(6) Control algorithms.

Because the memories of a DBM are usually slow (of the order of 100 μsec access time), much overlap and parallelism are necessary in order to achieve a high throughput. Control algorithms like scheduling and file placement and migration are, therefore, very important.

The design of a DBM must consider all these issues together and make a judicious tradeoff in the design.

5.3.3   Classification of DBMs

The DBM proposed so far can be divided into two types, (1) backend systems using conventional mini-computers and (2) intelligent controllers which include cellular logic, associative memory, and MIMD architecture. We describe them briefly here.

(1)   Backend systems using conventional mini-computers
       (Figure 5.10)

Backend systems are generally added to a large CPU in order to enhance its database processing capabilities. The functions of the backend system include access validation, storage management, concurrency control, and I/O control. The advantages of such a system are the concurrent sharing of a single database and better security, integrity, and recovery measures. In such a system, network protocols are designed so that the CPU can offload the processing onto the backend machines. However, the system can only offload a fraction of the processing workload, e.g. validity checks cannot be offloaded, and the speed improvement is minimal. Further, there is an upper bound on the number of backend processors so that enough work can be offloaded onto these machines. Other disadvantages include costly software development and low reliability. The use of backend machines is only a temporary method to extend the processing power of a large CPU.

(2)   Intelligent controllers

The use of intelligent controllers is an extension on the concept of backend machines. In the case of backend machines, each machine can control a set of disks and can perform high level data manipulations on the stored data. In the case of the intelligent controllers, the logic is partitioned further down onto the stored data. The characteristics of this design are that simpler, less costly designs are used and each controller is dedicated to a smaller block of data. There may be a higher level controller which controls the intelligent controllers collectively. This design, therefore, approaches a multi-level control scheme. Basically, this design can be divided into three categories:

(a)   Cellular Logic (Figure 5.11)

The processors in this case are duplicated across each memory element which may be a track of a disk. They provide associative search for data in the memory and they access data directly by value. Most of the conventional designs follow this principle, e.g. TapeDRUM [HOL56], Slotnick's Logic

Figure 5.10. Backend Systems Using Conventional Mini-computers

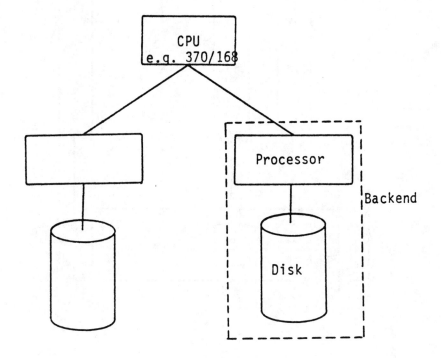

Figure 5.11. Intelligent Controllers—Cellular Logic

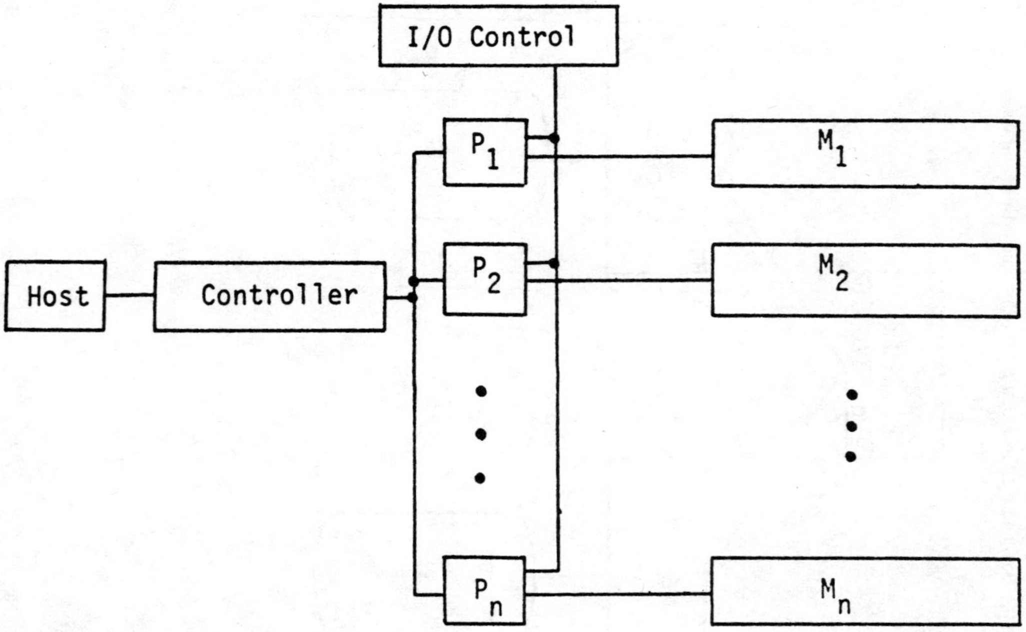

per Track Disk [SLO70], RAPID [PAR72], CASSM [LIP78, SU79], RAP [OZK77, SCH79], RARES [LIN76], DBC [BAU76, KER79, BAN79], Chang's Major/Minor Loop Machine [CHA78], etc.

Because the logics are distributed across the data, this design provides very fast searches and reduces the software overhead by performing content addressing. Further, the architecture is very suitable for a relational data model. A relation can be placed so that all the tuples can be searched associatively. Other data models can be modified to fit the architecture by adding additional data structures, e.g. CASSM.

However, there exist many disadvantages with this design: (i) Because of the large degree of replication, the logics are bound to be simple. Usually, only simple functions like equality match and maximum search are implemented and the designs are directed towards specialized applications. (ii) The database workload must be large ($>40\%$) in order to keep the parallel resources utilized. (iii) In a large database, the degree of replication may be large and the cost may become prohibitive. (iv) Because of the way that data is placed in the architecture, data types are limited to character strings and integers. More complex data structures would require more complicated external control. (v) If the database machine is built on a disk, the processors must be extremely fast because many fast signal translations are needed in order to perform real time processing and disk marking. (vi) Lastly, I/O is usually the bottleneck. Although the processing can be done in parallel, I/O is usually done serially. However, with the pre-processing of data using DBMs, it is hoped that a significant portion of the data transfer is eliminated.

(b)   Associative Memories (Figure 5.12)

In this design, an associative memory, such as STARAN [GOO75] or the proposed design in section 5.2 of this study, is used to provide associative search capabilities. The model in Figure 5.12 resembles a conventional memory hierarchy in which the fastest memory (the associative memory) is small and is interfaced to the slow mass storage through an intermediate buffer memory.

The advantages of this design are rapid search for array resident data and its suitability for the relational data model. However, associative memories are still relatively expensive and large associative memories are not feasible. This design therefore experiences the usual problems of a memory hierarchy, namely, the swapping of the data across various levels of the hierarchy. A high bandwidth bus is necessary to transfer data between the associative memory and the mass storage. In one such design [BER79], STARAN is used as the associative memory, and requires 1024 I/O lines

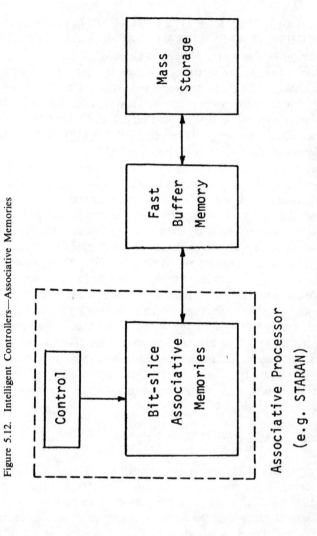

Figure 5.12. Intelligent Controllers—Associative Memories

with 300 to 450 nsec transfer time per bit slice to interconnect the associative memory and the buffer memory in order for the technique to be effective. This technique is unduly expensive in the associative memory and the I/O bus.

(c)   Multiple-Instruction-Multiple-Data-Stream (MIMD) Architecture (Figure 5.13)

In the MIMD architecture, the processors are interconnected with the memory elements through an interconnection network. This design offers more flexibility and better load balancing. Because of the fact that each processor can access multiple memory elements simultaneously, it is easier to perform database operations which require multiple files to be coupled, e.g. a multi-relation join. Further, expansion is easy and modular. However, this design suffers from the same disadvantages as the associative memory when the size of the memory is not large enough, in which case excessive swapping will occur. Again, since the processing logic is removed from the storage device, a large amount of unnecessary data is accessed and transferred. This design is exemplified by the DIRECT system [DEW79].

We note that the previous designs are built around a single type of storage device, e.g. disk, CCD, etc. Intra-module operations can be performed very efficiently because they do not utilize the I/O bus. However, inter-module operations often result in a bottleneck at the I/O bus. At any one instant, only one inter-module operation can be processed because the designs are essentially SIMD. In some designs, e.g. DIRECT, where the problem of the I/O bus has been solved by using a simple crossbar switch, the operations are expensive because data have to be transferred from the mass storage to the CCD storage modules. Only when a sizeable amount of operations are performed on the file transferred would the transfer be cost effective.

Since the DBM is a very special purpose hardware and requires a large degree of replication, it is important that unessential software not be placed in the DBM. In particular, software for protection, file system management, code swapping, task switches, pipes, or system calls should be eliminated from the DBM. These software modules can be shared at a higher level with no adverse effects on the system performance. On the other hand, the DBM should have a thin collection of utilities, the run time database management system and a self-managed buffer pool. The management of buffers is relatively easy here because the accesses are usually made in a sequential order.

In the next section, we propose a design of a backend database machine, DIALOG (DIstributed Associative LOGic database machine) which

Figure 5.13. Intelligent Controllers—MIMD Architecture

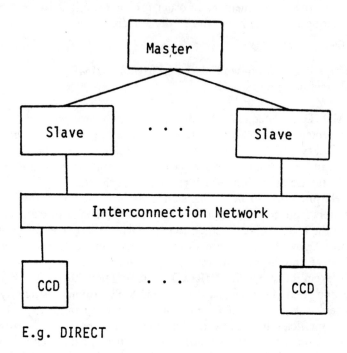

E.g. DIRECT

addresses some of the problems mentioned above. We want to design intelligent but simple processing logic so that they can be replicated on the storage modules. Algorithms such as select, project, and join will be implemented in hardware so that they can be processed very efficiently. These processors work directly on the storage devices, so that the amount of data transfer is kept at a minimum. A network is proposed which provides a uniform medium to connect heterogeneous memory devices together.

The next section is divided into six sub-sections. Section 5.4.1 presents the design objectives. Section 5.4.2 provides the overall architecture of the system. It also illustrates how an inter- or intra-module operation is performed. Section 5.4.3 describes the architecture of the data module. The functions to be performed in a module are partitioned into the select processor, the associative processor, the join processor and the communication processor. Section 5.4.4 presents an analysis on the buffer size required. Section 5.4.5 provides some discussions of this system and compares this system against other systems. Lastly, section 5.4.6 gives some concluding remarks.

5.4 DIALOG—A Distributed Processor Organization for Database Machine [WAH 80]

5.4.1 Design Objectives

The DIALOG database machine is designed with the following design goals in mind. First, the system should be extendable and able to support very large on-line databases in the future. Second, the design must have high performance and the cost should be low by replicating a few simple devices. Third, the system should use existing memory technologies in the design such that it can be implemented now, and the design should be able to evolve as new memory technologies are available in the future. Fourth, the system should accommodate heterogeneous storage devices such that files with different workload and sizes can be stored in the devices with appropriate speeds and sizes. Finally, the system should implement low level operations (such as select and join) and facilitate higher level query optimization.

5.4.2 System Architecture

The secondary storage, where the bulk of the database is stored, is usually made up of multiple types of storage devices like disks and tape drives. As the storage technology advances, devices such as CCD memories, bubble memories, EBAMs etc. could become part of the storage sub-system. Each of the these storage types has different capacities and speeds. Since many database operations require data stored in multiple files, it is often necessary to access these files simultaneously. One approach is to transfer all the required data for an operation to a uniform storage device such as CCD memories which are connected to a set of processors, before processing it. However, there is a significant overhead associated with this data transfer, especially when the original storage device has no selection capability. Further, if the intermediate device is not large enough to accommodate the entire file, costly multiple passes have to be made.

An alternative approach is to send the required data directly from the storage device on which the file is stored to a second storage device on which the file is to be processed. The time to stage these files to an intermediate storage device can be saved. If the storage devices are enhanced by sufficiently powerful processing elements, the results of database operations can be output at a very high speed. In order to facilitate the transfer of data, a communication network must be designed to connect the heterogeneous devices together.

In this section, we describe the general architecture for the latter approach to database machine design. The design of the network will be examined and the processing capability of the machine will be discussed.

A.   General Architecture

The general architecture of the system is shown in Figure 5.14. Data in the system are stored in the data modules. Each data module consists of a storage device and an associative processor. Data modules are connected together by an interconnection network. Only data can flow across this network. The cluster of data modules is connected directly with a backend controller which allows both data and control communication. The backend controller provides communciation between the cluster of data modules and the host computer. Queries expressed in a high level representation are sent from the host to the backend controller and query responses are returned to the host.

The major functions of the backend controller of a cluster include preprocessing and optimizing the queries, looking up system directory, establishing links between data modules, initiating and scheduling operations within each data module, receiving and buffering output from data modules, managing the sharing of resources, and initiating rollback and recovery as system components fail. All of the above functions will be implemented in software.

Depending on the number of data modules in the database machine, the interconnection network may become quite complex. It may be necessary to group data modules into multiple clusters. The backend controllers of these

Figure 5.14. System Architecture of a Cluster in DIALOG.

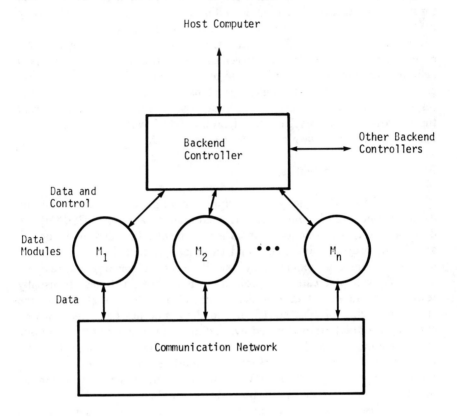

clusters are connected using a network of the same design as that developed for interconnecting the data modules within a cluster. A higher level backend controller is used to coordinate the controllers of all the clusters.

An example of this hierarchical network is shown in Figure 5.15. We note that the communication between data modules of different clusters is achieved by sending data through the backend controllers and a high level communication link. The highest level backend controller assumes the responsibility of communicating with the host computer. The operation of the network in each level of the hierarchy, which will be discussed later, behaves in the same fashion as the network in the lowest level.

B. Processing Capabilities

Although DIALOG is designed to support multiple data models, only the database operations defined on the relational data model [COD70] are discussed here. The relational operations currently included in the design are: select, project, join, union, and cartesian product.

Operations that require only one file, such as selecting records that satisfy a given predicate and projecting on certain attributes are usually resolved within one data module. Database operations that require the cross-referencing of files stored in two data modules (such as join and cartesian product) are performed by sending all the required records to one of the data modules and processing them there. In the case when the two files to be processed reside in the same data module, one of the files can be retrieved into the input buffer. The processing continues as if the file in the input buffer were received from a different module.

Database operations that access multiple files in several data modules are decomposed into a set of two-module operations which can be processed either in sequence or in parallel. The decomposition and scheduling of database operations and the routing of files are determined by the backend controller.

C. Network Design

The design of the interconnection network has an important implication on the throughput of the system. A ring network is the simplest form of a communication network, but it could cause a lot of contention. If the conflict is resolved by a centralized controller, the controller may become a bottleneck of the system. If the conflict is resolved in a distributed fashion, the software for the communication protocol may be complicated. It is, therefore, desirable to have a network that is conflict free and requires a small amount of software development.

Figure 5.15. An Example of the Hierarchical Network in DIALOG.

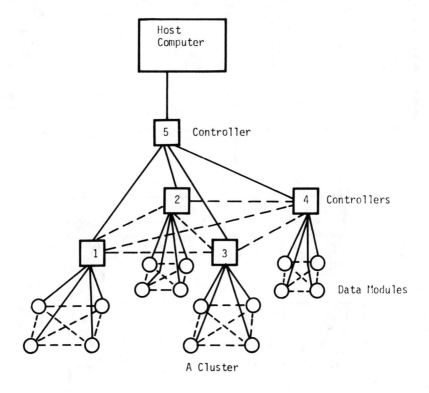

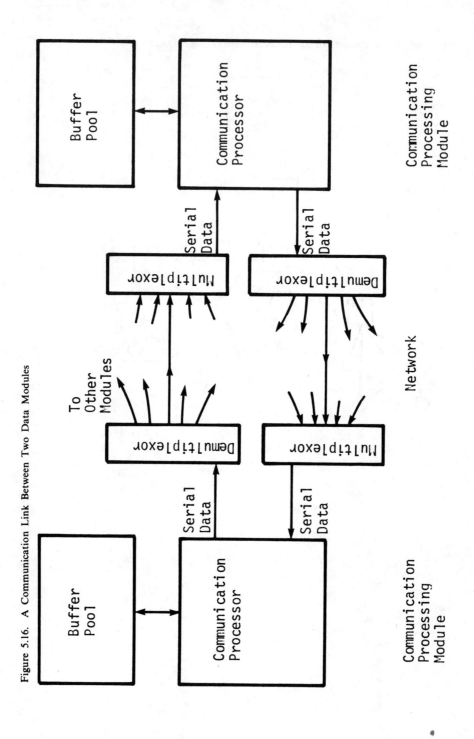

Figure 5.16. A Communication Link Between Two Data Modules

The simplest conflict-free network is the fully connected network. Although this network may seem very expensive because the number of links grows as n^2 where n is the number of data modules, these links are merely serial lines governed by a central clock, and their costs are minimal. An implementation of the link between two data modules is shown in Figure 5.16. The link can be established by the controller which sends a command to the communication processing modules of the two data modules. The communication processors at the two data modules then set the multiplexor and the demultiplexor and the link is established. The links can only be broken by a command from the controller. The communication processor is responsible for managing the buffer pool, detecting and correcting errors in the data, informing the controller if a non-recoverable error is detected, and signaling the source of a data transfer to stop when the buffer is full. Since the communication between two data modules is governed by a central clock, any type of memory device can be connected to the network. The design can also be modified to broadcast data to several modules simultaneously.

With this network design, global data transfer is very easy. Referring to Figure 5.15, suppose one of the data modules in cluster 1 wants to send data to a data module in cluster 3. Since there is no direct path of communication between these two data modules, data from cluster 1 will be sent first to its controller. Since there is a direct path of communication between controllers of clusters 1 and 3, this path is established by controller 5, the controller in one level higher than controllers 1 and 3. The file transfer can be carried out without the intervention of controller 5. Of course, this approach can result in excessive overhead for the lower level controllers when inter-cluster transfers are large. However, by carefully allocating the relations to the clusters so that the inter-cluster communciations are minimal, this technique is still a cost effective approach.

5.4.3 Data Module Design

In this section, we describe the internal design of a data module. The function of the data module is to store the data and to process relational queries directed on the stored data. The design should allow both inter- and intra-module queries to be performed efficiently. Furthermore, the design should be modular and functional so that current microprocessor and VLSI technologies can be used in the design.

A. General Data Module Architecture

The general architecture of a module is shown in Figure 5.17. There are five

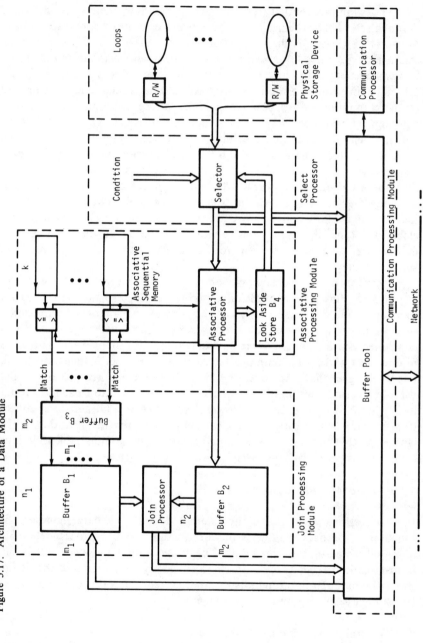

Figure 5.17. Architecture of a Data Module

basic sub-modules of the system, namely, the physical storage device which contains the database; the selection processing module which processes projection and selection operations; the associative processing module which compares the output from selection processing with the stored search keys and passes successful matches to the join processing module which then produces the join; and lastly, the communication processing module which manages the buffer pool and communicates with other data modules in the network. We describe each of these sub-modules here.

B. Data Allocation in the Physical Storage Device

The physical storage device is made up of multiple circulating loops of data with a single read/write head for each loop. The loops may be simple which can model devices like CCD memories. They may be more complicated, such as the major/minor loop of a bubble memory, the LARAM organization of the CCD memory, or a cylinder of a disk. The access time distribution for accessing a piece of data within the loop consists of two components; the time to switch to read/write a particular loop and the time to shift the data in the loop to the read/write mechanism. Different memory devices have different time delays for each component. In the case of a single loop, data can only be read out serially. However, in the case of a multi-loop organization, data may be read out one loop at a time with electronic switching between the loops. This is characterized by a cylinder of a disk or a LARAM organization of CCD memory. Data may also be read out serially from all the loops simultaneously. This type of memory is characterized by a multi-chip bubble or CCD memory and the parallel-transfer-disk [AMP78]. However, in some implementations, it may not be possible to synchronize all the parallel outputs on the device (e.g. a cell may be bad in one of the loops and unless all the corresponding cells in other loops are marked bad, the outputs will be out of synchronization). It is, therefore, not practical to organize the database such that a tuple of a relation is read out bit parallel but word serially.

The organization of the database in a multi-loop device is chosen to be bit-serial and word-parallel, that is, multiple tuples will be available simultaneously at the read heads. In this case, since we assume that the selection processing module can process one tuple at a time, a buffer is added between the physical storage device and the selection processing module so that all the parallel tuples are sequenced sequentially. Of course, the speeds of the other processing modules have to be increased correspondingly from a single loop model. With the use of a buffer, a multi-loop device behaves like a single loop device. We conclude that a single loop model is sufficient for our design.

C. Selection Processing

In selection processing, tuples are examined in the database one at a time and only those tuples satisfying a certain predicate will be output. This output can be sent to the buffer pool or it can be sent to the associative processing module. When the output is sent to the buffer pool, it may be sent to another data module in the system for join processing or it may be used to join with another relation in the same data module. Projection is a similar operation to selection. However, we assume that duplicates will not be removed in the data module because of the limited buffer capability.

D. Join Processing

In performing a join on this system, both the associative processing module and the join processing module will be used. The buffer data allocations are as follows (see Figure 5.17): Buffer B_1 contains m_1 tuples, each of n_1 bytes. The contents of B_1 are filled from the buffer pool and they represent part of the tuples of a relation coming from the same or a different data module in the system. These tuples are used to join with the tuples coming from the output of the selection processing module. The size n_1 is chosen so that it can accommodate the largest tuple used. The size of m_1 will be determined in section 5.4.4.

The associative sequential memory in the associative processing module is made up of m_1 circulating loops of size k. It contains the keys of the join domain of the corresponding tuples in buffer B_1. It is a one-to-one correspondence and the keys of the ith tuple in B_1 are contained in the ith loop of the associative sequential memory. The size k is chosen so that the loop can accommodate the largest key used. For smaller keys, multiple copies may be made in the same loop to allow faster access.

The associative processing module compares the serial output tuple from the selection processing module associatively against all the keys in the associative sequential memory. If at least one match occurs, it indicates that a join is possible between this tuple and the corresponding tuple in B_1. This tuple is put in buffer B_2 and it will be joined with the corresponding tuples in B_1 when all the previous joins are performed. B_2 contains a queue of m_2 tuples, each of n_2 bytes that can be used to join with keys in B_1. The size of n_2 is chosen so that it can accommodate the largest tuple used (n_1 and n_2 are probably chosen to be identical). The size of m_2 is determined in section 5.4.4.

As the match is done in the associative processor and a successfully matched tuple is added to B_2, a word is written into buffer B_3. B_3 is an m_1 by m_2 bit matrix. A column in B_3 represents the set of tuples in B_1 which match with the corresponding tuples in B_2, where a 1 indicates a match and a 0 indicates a no-match.

The example in Figure 5.18 illustrates the functions of B_1, B_2, B_3 and the associative sequential memory where m_1, m_2 are chosen to be 2 and n_1 and n_2 are chosen to be 12. In this example, suppose the following join is to be performed.

RETRIEVE (*A*.city, *B*.pname): A.*p#=B.p#*.

B_1 contains part of the tuples of relation A, and B_2 contains part of the tuples of relation B which are to be joined with the tuples in B_1. For the left column in B_3, it indicates that the first tuple in B_2 can be joined with the first tuple in B_1. Similarly, the right column in B_3 indicates that the second tuple in B_2 can be joined with the first tuple in B_1. The loops in the associative sequential memory contain the keys of the corresponding tuples in B_1. Note that in our example, the *p#* domains in B_1 and B_2 are never output from the join processor and they are not used by the join processor to determine which of the tuples in B_1 and B_2 are to be joined (because B_3 provides this information). These two domains, therefore, do not have to be included; however, they are shown here for illustration.

The join processor performs the join between the tuples in B_1 and B_2 by picking up the first tuple in B_2 and joining it with all the tuples with matched keys in B_1, before proceeding to the next tuple in B_2. The results of the join processor are routed to the buffer pool.

E. Associative Sequential Memory

The design of this associative sequential memory is based on the design discussed in section 5.2 [RAM 78]. The sequential memory is made up of multiple loops of circulating bits shifting in synchronism. It may be made up of CCD memory or bubble memory. In this design, m_1 keys are stored in the memory, with one key occupying each loop. The architecture of this design is shown in Figure 5.19. During a clock period, a bit-slice of these *m* is shifted out of the memory. This bit-slice is then processed by the associative logic and the enable signals are stored in temporary flip flops. Note that in the design presented earlier in section 5.2, the enable signals propogate from the MSB to the LSB and the data are stored in flip flops. In the case of a sequential memory, the enable signals are stored in temporary flip flops. As the bit-slice is shifted out, MSB first, the bit-slice, together with the stored enable signals, generate a new set of enable signals which are stored back into the flip flops. The exact design is shown in Figure 5.20.

There are three significant improvements in this design as compared

Figure 5.18. Example to Illustrate the Function of Buffers B_1, B_2, B_3 and the Associative Sequential Memory.

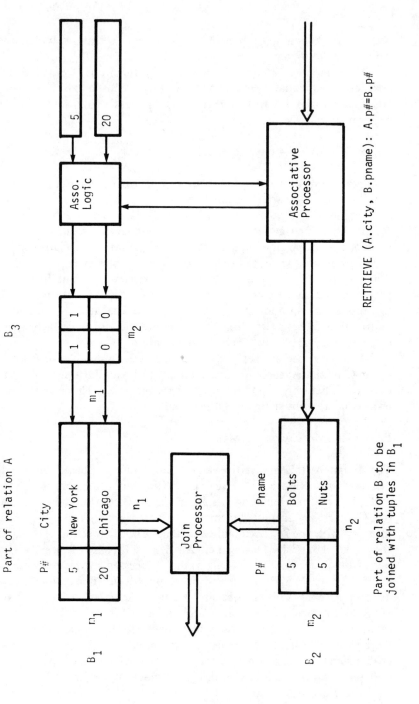

Figure 5.19.   Associative Sequential Memory

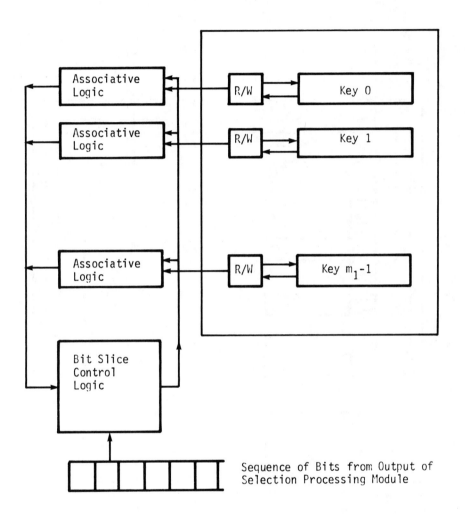

Figure 5.20. Associative Logic for Associative Sequential Memory

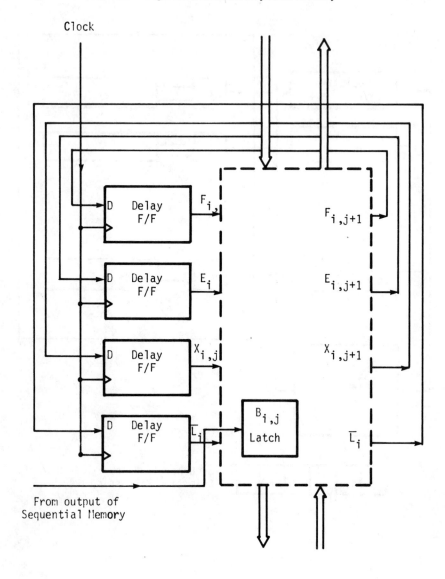

with a conventional logic-per-track device. First, the additional logic for each loop is very small and therefore the cost increase is minimal. Further, the cell logic is simple enough to be implemented on the same chip as the memory elements with only a minimal cost increase. Second, there are no communication lines between two adjacent loops and therefore the number of loops can be modularly expanded. Lastly, the number of loops is not governed by the number of read/write heads on the physical storage device. Previous database machine designs assume that the number of associative logic is replicated for each head of a disk which, therefore, limits the maximum degrees of parallelism. In our design, the number of heads on the disk is not a factor in the number of loops used in the associative sequential memory. The degree of parallelism can therefore be improved significantly.

One problem that exists with this design is to choose the loop size of the associative sequential memory so that the largest key can fit into the loop. However, if the loop size is too large and the time it takes for the loop to make one complete revolution is longer than the time it takes for a tuple to be shifted out, the associative sequential memory may not be able to catch up with the output rate of the selection processing module. In this case, one simple solution is to duplicate the keys in the loop so that the time to reach the key is always shorter than the time to shift out a tuple. Buffers may also be placed between the associative processing module and the selection processing module to smooth out the irregularities. Since the output of the associative processing module goes to the join processing module and there is a finite probability that B_2 is full, the associative processor may not be able to continue to process the tuples once B_2 is full. In this case, a look-aside buffer, B_4, is used to store the missed tuples. This buffer is a queue with each element being a tuple identifier. The size of B_4 is chosen so that it would accommodate all the missed tuple identifiers.

F. Join Processor

The join processor uses buffers B_1, B_2, and B_3 to produce the join outputs. One characteristic about B_2 and B_3 is that they are variable size queues. This feature may be implemented by a hardware or a software linked list. Further accesses to each column of B_3 must be made in parallel. The join processor uses one column of B_3 to find out which tuples in B_1 are to be joined with a tuple in B_2. This is a conventional multiple match resolution problem. We assume that a sequential search is made to find all the 1s in a column of B_3. However, tree circuits [FOS68] or associative memory (section 5.2.8.4) can be used to do the multiple match resolution.

Finally, when the tuples in B_1 have been matched with all the tuples in the physical storage device (e.g. a cylinder, a loop, etc.), the contents of B_1 and the associative sequential memory are switched to a new set. Since the size of B_1 is usually very small (see the analysis in section 5.4.4), the switching time is minimal. As data are moved into the buffers, they are also moved in parallel into buffers B_1 and the associative sequential memory. The processing of a join is, therefore, pipelined and the throughput of the system can be greatly enhanced. The throughput of the system is a function of the sizes of B_1, B_2, B_3, the tuple size, and the bit rate (the rate at which tuples are selected out from the physical storage device). We present in the next section an analysis for the sizes of B_1 and B_2 if the join outputs are to be made in disk transfer rate.

5.4.4   *Approximate Analysis of Buffer Size*

In this section, we perform an analysis on the size of the buffers. The sizes of B_1, B_2, and B_3 are critical factors in our design. We first establish an upper bound on the average queue length in B_2 and B_3 given the size of B_1 and the probability that a match occurs between the contents of B_1 and a tuple output from the selection processing module. We further assume that B_2 and B_3 are very large. Using the upper bound on the queue size of B_1, we can establish a size for B_2 and B_3 so that under most circumstances, B_2 and B_3 will not be full. The approximations are then compared with the simulation results.

Let:

$P=$ probability that a tuple of relation A in B_1 will be joined with a tuple of relation B;
$l_a=$ length of each tuple of relation A in B_1;
$l_b=$ length of each tuple of relation B in B_2;
$l'_a=$ length of each tuple of relation A after restriction;
$r=$ transfer rate of physical storage device;
$r_0=$ desired join output rate;
$s_1=$ number of tuples in B_1 ($=$ size of buffer B_1, m_1);
$s_2=$ number of tuples in B_2 (size of buffer B_2 is assumed to be very large);
$\overline{s_2}= E(S_2)$.

When the join processor picks up a tuple in B_2, there is at least one match with a tuple in B_1 (otherwise, the associative processor would not have passed this tuple to B_2). The time to produce all the corresponding joins depends on the number of matches in B_1. For i equal matches ($i=1, 2, \ldots, s_1$) with a probability of

$$\frac{\binom{s_1}{i} p^i (1-p)^{(s_1-i)}}{1-(1-p)^{s_1}}$$

the time to produce all the joins is $(l'_a + l_b) * i/r_0$. On the other hand, the inter-arrival time distribution is geometrically distributed, with a probability of $(1-p)^{s_1(i-1)} * (1-(1-p)^{s_1})$ for an inter-arrival time of $i*l_a/r$ $(i=1, 2, \ldots)$. This system is in effect a $GI/G/1$ queue. That queue is shown in Figure 5.21. We use Marshall's inequality [MAR68] to find the average delay time that a tuple spends in B_2, d.

$$d \leqslant \frac{\lambda(\sigma_a^2 + \sigma_g^2)}{2(1-\rho)} \qquad \text{(Marshall's inequality)}$$

where $1/\lambda$ and σ_a^2 are the mean and the variance of the inter-arrival time, $1/\mu$ and σ_g^2 are the mean and the variance of the service time and $\rho = \lambda/\mu$. After evaluating d, we can further apply Little's formula [LIT61] to find a bound on $\bar{s}_2$ $(\bar{s}_2 = \lambda d)$

$$\bar{s}_2 \leqslant \frac{\left[\bar{p} + \left(\frac{l'_a + l_b}{l_a} \right)^2 \left(\frac{r}{r_0} \right)^2 s_1 p(1-\bar{p}) \left[p(s_1 - 1) + 1 - \frac{s_1 p}{(1-\bar{p})} \right] \right]}{2 \left[1 - \frac{r}{r_0} \left(\frac{l'_a + l_b}{l_a} \right) s_1 p \right]}$$

where $\bar{p} = (1-p)^{s_1}$.

Assuming that $l_a = l_b = l'_a$, $r = r_0$, we have,

$$s_2 \leqslant \frac{\bar{p} + 4s_1 p(1-\bar{p}) \left[p(s_1 - 1) + 1 - \frac{s_1 p}{(1-\bar{p})} \right]}{2 [1 - 2s_1 p]}$$

Simulations are also carried out on the queue in Figure 5.21. The simulation program is written in ASPOL and is run with 2000 requests for each pair of p and s_1.

Table 5.2 shows the difference between the simulation results and the estimated bounds for a sample of values of s_2 for various values of s_1 and p. It is seen that the estimations, although not accurate, produce a close enough bound for s_2. We have also indicated in Table 5.2 a column that indicates the value of s_2 such that $\Pr(\text{queue size} < s_2) \leqq 0.95$. These values can be used to determine a fixed bound on s_2. For example, with $p = 0.01$, which means that there is a chance of 1% for a particular tuple in relation B to be joined with a tuple in relation A in B_1, s_1 and s_2 can be chosen to be 50 and 36, respectively. For these values of s_1 and s_2, the utilization of the server (join

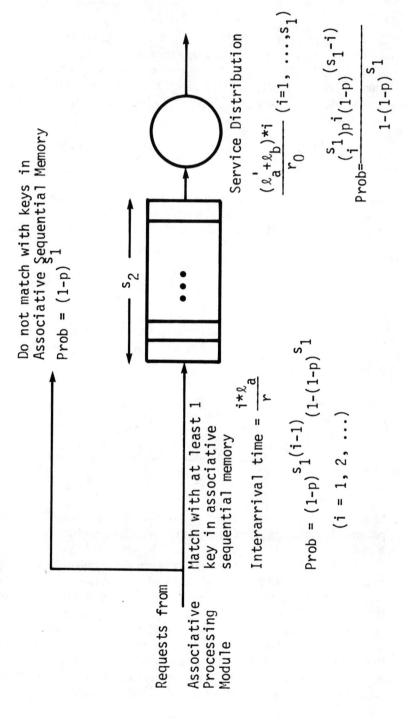

Figure 5.21. Queue to model operation of Associative Processing Module and Join Processing Module

Requests from

Associative Processing Module

Match with at least 1 key in associative sequential memory

Interarrival time $= \dfrac{i*\ell_a}{r}$

$\text{Prob} = (1-p)^{s_1(i-1)}(1-(1-p)^{s_1})$

$(i = 1, 2, \ldots)$

Do not match with keys in Associative Sequential Memory

$\text{Prob} = (1-p)^{s_1}$

s_2

Service Distribution

$\dfrac{(\ell_a^{'}+\ell_b)*i}{r_0} \quad (i=1, \ldots, s_1)$

$\text{Prob} = \dfrac{\binom{s_1}{i}p^i(1-p)^{(s_1-i)}}{1-(1-p)^{s_1}}$

processor) is 0.994, which means that the join output is indeed coming out at the disk transfer rate.

However, the choice of s_1 and s_2 is not arbitrary. If s_1 is set to be too large, the time to switch the contents of B_1 is large which induces large overheads on the system. On the other hand, if s_1 is too small, then there may not be enough requests in B_2 and, therefore, the join processor may be idle most of the time. It is important to choose s_1 as small as possible while giving a reasonably high utilization for the join processor. The choice is driven by the value of p which is dependent on the number of tuples in the relations and the number of distinct join keys in the two relations. For large relations, this is usually small. Table 5.2 shows some simulation results with p set to 0.001. It is seen that with s_1 set to 160, the utilization of the server (join processor) is 0.317 and s_2 can be set at 1. This means that the join processor will be idle 69% of the time and the output rate is 31% of the disk transfer rate. With s_1 set to be so large, there is a tremendous switching overhead in the system.

In order to remedy this, multiple sets of B_1 and associative sequential memories can be implemented in each data module. The join processing operations on one set of B_1 can be overlapped with the loading of another set of B_1. The switching overhead on B_1 is, therefore, overlapped with the join processing. This is feasible because the communication processor in each data module can be designed to send and receive from different data modules. As the join processor is producing outputs to be sent to one data module, the communication processor can be receiving tuples from another data module to load a different set of B_1.

A final problem occurs when p is extremely small. In this case, B_1 has to be chosen to be excessively large in order to attain a reasonable join output rate. It may be better to send different sets of tuples of relation A to a set of spare data modules, each with a small buffer memory. Relation B is then broadcast simultaneously to this set of spare data modules where the join can be performed in parallel. This approach provides a solution for an extremely small value of p without constraining on the size of B_1. Buffers B_1 can be kept relatively small at each data module. The use of spare data modules can also be applied for load balancing. This will be discussed in the next section.

5.4.5 Discussion

The database machine we have proposed uses both associative and distributed processing to enhance the system performance. Associative processing is used so that the data can be preprocessed and only the necessary data are selected. The associative processor designed is also very simple so that it can be implemented easily using VLSI technologies. On the other

Table 5.2. Sample of Values of s_2 for Various Values of s_1 and p

s_1	p	mean s_2	std. dev s_2	Pr(queue size<s_2) ≤ 0.95		Server Utilization	upper bound of $\overline{s_2}$
						Simulation	Estimation
5	0.01	0.003	0.055	0	(0.9970)	0.099	0.53
	0.05	0.152	0.445	0	(0.8737)	0.477	0.80
	0.10	10.538	7.784	24	(0.9440)	0.976	∞
	0.20	∞	∞	∞	(1.0)	1.0	∞
10	0.01	0.015	0.122	0	(0.9850)	0.191	0.57
	0.02	0.068	0.266	0	(0.9352)	0.377	0.68
	0.03	0.264	0.620	1	(0.9480)	0.570	0.97
	0.04	0.925	1.313	3	(0.9407)	0.773	1.89
	0.05	9.572	6.495	20	(0.9460)	0.978	∞
	0.07	∞	∞	∞	(1.0)	1.0	∞
15	0.01	0.032	0.183	0	(0.9698)	0.280	0.62
	0.02	0.252	0.550	1	(0.9570)	0.588	0.98
	0.03	3.066	3.484	10	(0.9588)	0.880	3.80
	0.04	∞	∞	∞	(1.0)	1.0	∞
25	0.01	0.177	0.523	0	(0.8641)	0.486	0.80
	0.02	29.993	12.346	46	(0.9534)	0.996	∞
	0.03	∞	∞	∞	(1.0)	1.0	∞
40	0.01	0.890	1.265	3	(0.9500)	0.770	1.91
	0.02	∞	∞	∞	(1.0)	1.0	∞
50	0.01	22.332	10.911	36	(0.9500)	0.994	∞
	0.02	∞	∞	∞	(1.0)	1.0	∞
75	0.001	0.007	0.082	0	(0.9933)	0.141	0.55
100	0.001	0.013	0.115	0	(0.9865)	0.192	0.57
120	0.001	0.019	0.136	0	(0.9816)	0.229	0.59
140	0.001	0.028	0.169	0	(0.9729)	0.278	0.61
160	0.001	0.046	0.225	0	(0.9578)	0.317	0.63

hand, distributed processing is used in the design of the system and, therefore, many useful techniques in distributed databases can be applied to enhance the performance. These techniques include query processing, file placement and migration, rollback and recovery, etc. We discuss several of these issues here.

A. Query Processing

Since the system functions as a distributed database, it is possible to optimize the sequence of processing of queries so that some optimization criteria, such as minimum total time, can be satisfied. There are many techniques developed, e.g. [WON76, WON77, EPS78, HEV79], which can be used to optimize the processing of queries here. The algorithm proposed in Chapter 2 can also be applied. The processing of queries using this kind of data flow analysis is new in this design. Previously, the intermediate result of a query usually had to be stored in a temporary file before it could be used, e.g. DIRECT. By allowing intermediate results to be piped to their destinations, higher throughput can be achieved.

B. File Placement and Migration

Because each data module can read only one file at a time, query processing will be sequentialized if all the queries access files on the same data module. By allocating the files on the system so that related files are allocated to the same cluster and files that need to be processed together are allocated to different data modules, conflicts can be kept to a minimum and maximum utilization of resources can be attained. The problem is easier to solve than the general file placement problem because duplicate copies are usually not needed in the system. Further, as the access characteristics change, the files can be reallocated dynamically.

C. Concurrency Control

Although there may exist multiple copies of a file on the system, we do not allow multiple copies to exist on the same type of memory device. Multiple copies of a file may exist in devices of different speeds and the copy on the fastest device is considered to be the primary copy. All the other copies are considered secondary copies and no write throughs are done during updates. With this restriction, the problem on concurrent updates is solved easily because the processor at each data module provides a secure gateway to the data on the device.

D. Load Balancing

Although our design does not require staging to transfer the files to a fast memory before the processing, it is not able to utilize multiple processors to process a join in parallel as is done in DIRECT. However, we can provide some spare data modules on the system, each of which has a small buffer memory. Instead of sending tuples directly from one data module to another, different sets of tuples of one relation are sent to the spare data modules. The tuples from the other relation are broadcast to the spare data modules and the join is performed in parallel in the spare data modules. In this sense, this resembles DIRECT's design. However, there are two significant differences. First, data sent to the spare modules have been reduced in size by the selection processing modules of the two data modules. Second, the distributed system approach allows queries to be processed very efficiently because data can continuously be piped to other data modules as they are produced.

The issues proposed in this section will be studied in the future.

5.4.6 Some Final Remarks

In this section, we have proposed a database machine design which facilitates query processing and parallel processing. Since the system is hierarchically designed, it can easily be extended to a very large database in the future. Communication at higher levels can be reduced by carefully allocating related files to individual clusters so that most of the communications are intra-cluster. The logic we have designed in the associative processing module is very simple and can be extended modularly. This is different from the conventional approach in which the degree of associative processing is limited by the number of read heads. Further, we have designed the system based on the assumption that current memory technologies are used, e.g. moveable arm disk, CCD, etc. This means that the system can be built now. However, we have made no restriction on the structure of the memory which is assumed to be a single loop of data. If in the future, data can be stored inexpensively in parallel transfer disks, the data can be assumed to be buffered so that a serial stream of access is always achieved. Since the network provides a homogeneous medium for data transfer, heterogeneous memory devices can always be connected together. This also facilitates future evolution of the system. Lastly, our design implements low level database operations and allows high level query optimization.

Our proposed design is given in a functional form. Although individual modules are separated, they do not have to be implemented in individual hardware. In fact, most of these functions can be built in either hardware or software. A detailed evaluation of the system will be done in the future.

5.5 Conclusion

We have presented in this chapter two hardware features to support data management on a distributed database. The first design is an associative memory which is capable of equality, threshold, proximity, and extremum searches. The design is completely asynchronous and is bit-serial and word-parallel, that is, the enable signals propagate from bit-slice to bit-slice, but all the processing within a bit-slice is done in parallel. The propagation time across a bit-slice is one to seven gate delays and each cell has a complexity of 17 gates. This design is by far the fastest in the literature. Although memory expansion presents a slight problem, by extending the dimensions of the memory, the memory can be expanded with only a slight degradation in performance.

The second hardware design presented is an extension of the associative memory to database machines. DIALOG—a database machine which uses distributed and associative processing and utilizes current memory technologies for implementation, is proposed. The physical storage device of a database system, such as a disk or a charge coupled device memory module is enhanced with additional processing logic for associative processing and join proccessing to form a data module. The associative memory designed is applied in the design of a sequential associative memory. The data modules are linked together through a fully connected network for conflict-free accesses. A particular link is established by a controller and since data in the system is piped, a link, once established, will continue to exist for a period of time. A hierarchical design is also proposed in which the data modules form clusters together in a similar fashion. The design utilizes current microprocessor and memory technologies and can evolve as new technologies are available. Lastly, issues related to the design of DIALOG are discussed.

6

Conclusion and Future Work

In this study, the issues on the resource management of data on a distributed database (DDB) system are studied. These issues are concerned with the management of data and files as resources so that they can be shared efficiently by the users. Four levels of the problem are investigated. These include the query level, the file level, the task level, and the hardware level.

(1) Query Decomposition on DDBs

A query is an access request made by a user or a program in which one or more files have to be accessed. When multiple files are accessed by the same query on a DDB, these files usually have to reside at a single location before the query can be processed. Substantial communication overhead may be involved if these files are geographically distributed. It is, therefore, necessary to decompose the query into sub-queries so that each sub-query accesses a single file. These sub-queries may then be processed in parallel at any location which has a copy of the required file.

In some cases, decomposition is impossible and some file transfers are still necessary. In order to avoid these extra transfers, two cost reduction methods have been designed to reduce the operational costs of a relational database. The first method reduces the retrieval cost but increases the update cost by adding redundant information to each domain of a relational database so that relational operations such as joins and aggregate functions can be performed without any file transfers. The second method reduces the update cost but increases the retrieval cost by partitioning the relations into segments so that they can be updated more readily. These two cost reduction methods can be combined together to further reduce the operational costs of a DDB. It is also shown that the optimization of placements of multiple relations under the use of these techniques can be achieved independently for each relation.

(2)   File Placement and Migration

This issue is related to the distribution and migration of database components, namely, schema, data, and control programs on a DDB with the objective of minimizing the overall storage, migration, updating, and operational costs on the system. In this study, the problem of selecting the times for migration under changing access frequencies has been proved to be NP-complete. Further, the isomorphism between the file placement problem and the facility location problem is shown. The implications of the last result are two fold. First, many results which have been derived in one problem can now be applied to solve the other problem. Second, some results obtained for one problem can be shown to be weaker than the corresponding results derived for the other problem. A file placement heuristic is also developed. While not necessarily yielding optimal design, the heuristic yields solutions of lower cost than those generated by other currently available heuristics.

(3)   Task Scheduling

In task scheduling, the requests on the nodal computer system and the distributed computer system are sequenced so that high parallelism and overlap can be achieved. The request may be a single word fetch or it may be a page or file access. A model for the scheduling of tasks on a distributed system has been developed. This model assumes that global control is infeasible and all the scheduling decisions have to be made locally at each node. It is shown that the scheduling of tasks in this model, when all the task processing times are deterministic, is NP-complete. A heuristic has been developed and the performance of this heuristic has been verified using simulations. A restricted model, which represents an organization or an interleaved memory system, is also proposed. Due to the restrictions imposed on the model, it is proved that the optimal scheduling problem is polynomially solvable. The performance of the scheduling algorithm is verified using simulations.

(4)   Hardware Support

Beyond the problem of resource management studied here, the hardware support for the database system has also been investigated. In particular, an associative memory which is capable of equality, threshold, and extremum searches in a time independent of the number of words in the memory has been designed. The complexity of the design is 17 gates/cell. The design is asynchronous and utilizes a word-parallel and bit-serial algorithm. The delay is one to four gate delays across each bit-slice. This design can be applied to the resolution of multiple responses. Further, such a design can be extended to the design of database machines. DIALOG—A database machine which uses distributed and associative processing and utilizes current memory technologies for implementation, is proposed. An interconnection network for conflict-free accesses is also presented.

Although in this study, four general areas of the management of data on a DDB have been defined and several of the important issues have been studied, many related problems are still open for research. We discuss in the rest of this chapter, the future issues to be studied.

A.   Integration of Query Processing Techniques into a Real Database

In the two techniques discussed in chapter 2 for query processing, it is assumed that a methodology exists for introducing redundant information and partitioning a relation in a database. This methodology still remains to be designed and it must by integrated into the design of a database. We plan to examine with a prototype database, the effectiveness of these two techniques.

B.   Logical Design of a DDB

The research of DDBs has generally concentrated on the extension of centralized database systems to a DDB and the study of related problems on file placement, concurrency control, etc. One significant difference between the centralized and distributed database systems lies in the distribution of the queries. In a centralized database system, the query characteristics and the relationships of the data entities are enough to define a single external schema to represent the database. On the other hand, in a DDB system the queries are distributed and queries of different characteristics may originate from different geographical regions. An external schema may be defined similarly and is valid for non-redundant data. When redundant copies exist on the system, only queries originating in the locality of a copy would access this copy of the file. The external schema defined upon the global query characteristics and the data relationships is invalid for this copy. A different external schema may have to be defined for each redundant copy in order to tailor it to the characteristics of the local queries. However, this approach causes undue non-uniformity and complexity to the users and it would be difficult for a user to transfer his processing to a different node on the DCS.

This motivates us to study the design of an intermediate data model that would serve as a mapping between a uniform external data model and the internal data representation. The need for different external schemas is shifted to the need for different intermediate schemas, and it becomes the responsibility of the system, rather than the users, to maintain the intermediate schemas. Since the strategies for processing a query and the placement of redundant copies of a file must be taken into account in the design of this intermediate schema, our studies will integrate the studies of file placement, query processing, and logical design together.

C. Data Compression on Database

The amount of data sent across two levels of a memory hierarchy or two nodes of a DDB is usually huge. Data compression is a viable technique which can be applied to reduce the size of information transfer. We wish to study the effects of data compression in two major areas:

(i) The efficient utilization of shared data: This concerns the identification and reduction of data redundancy, and the improvement and measurement of processing efficiency with data compression.

(ii) The reliability of the data management system and the integrity of data in the presence of data compression schemes: The related issues are the feasibility of microprocessor-based hardware realization of data compression and the detection and correction of data errors while updates are present.

D. File Migration on DDB

In chapter 3, we have presented several conditions under which migration should be carried out. Research is still needed in the design of file migration heuristics. The problem of file migration is related to the conventional database restructuring problem in which the data in a centralized database is restructured to fit the access characteristics of the users. Techniques developed in database restructuring can be extended to this study.

E. Restructuring of Memory Words for Interleaved Memory

In chapter 4, we have presented an optimal scheduling algorithm for an interleaved memory system. This algorithm assumes that program and data are allocated in the interleaved memories as they are generated by the compiler. The utilization of the interleaved memories is less than one because there exists a contention of accesses. By restructuring the allocation of storage in an interleaved memory system, the contention on memory modules can be reduced. By restructuring, we mean the rearrangement of the allocation of instructions and data in the interleaved memory so that the next memory access made by the processor will have a high probability of falling in the subsequent memory module.

This research will be conducted in four different phases:
(i) We will study the characteristics of access sequence and the tradeoffs that need to be made among the design of the instruction set, the CPU architecture, and the memory architecture. We can then generalize this to make a probabilistic assumption about the access characteristics.
(ii) Using a precedence graph, we will develop efficient heuristics to allocate the instructions and data into the memory modules.
(iii) Using trace-driven simulation, we will compare the bandwidth of memory with and without restructuring. This will then indicate the improvement in performance due to restructuring.
(iv) The last phase is to implement a code generator front-end for a compiler.

F.   General Task Scheduling on Distributed
      Computer Systems

In chapter 4, a simple model for scheduling tasks has been developed and an efficient heuristic is presented. This heuristic has to be extended so that additional system parameters are taken into account. These parameters include the tolerable delay time in communication, the communication protocol, the reliability requirements, and the job characteristics. The techniques that can be used to analyze this model are a combination of Petri nets and queueing theory.

G.   The Design of a Parallel Computer Architecture
      to solve NP-complete Problems

Most of the problems for data management are NP-complete. Since the processing time for solving these problems is exponential, the common approach is to solve optimally for small problems and to solve sub-optimally using heuristics for large problems. The most general technique that can be used to solve a wide variety of these problems, optimally or sub-optimally, is the branch and bound algorithm [LAW66].
    Conventionally, the branch and bound algorithm has generally been studied with respect to limited memory space, the selection and bounding criteria, the theoretical behavior, and the adaptation to a single computer system. What little work that has gone on from the viewpoint of parallelism has been directed toward a general purpose computer network. The problem of the necessary parallel computer architecture and its associated operating

system, which provides an execution environment for a branch and bound algorithm, has been little studied or less understood. The significance of this study, therefore, lies in two aspects. First, it can result in the design of a special purpose VLSI parallel computer system to execute the parallel branch and bound algorithm. The number of computers can be designed to fit the need of the applications. Second, a better understanding of the parallel branch and bound algorithm will enable it to be designed into existing computer networks and distributed computer systems.

Although we have identified a few of the issues to be studied in the future, the study of data management on DDBs is by no means complete. New issues will be discovered in the process of solving the old issues. Our discussion in this study has, therefore, served to define and initiate future research on data management. We believe that our objective has been achieved.

Appendix A

The Isomorphism Between Stone's Process Allocation Problem and the Single Commodity Quadratic Assignment Problem

Stone's process allocation problem studies the allocation of processes to computers [STO77a, STO77b, STO78a, STO78b, STO79]. The amount of communication between two processes is defined and this in turn defines the cost to be incurred if these two processes run on different computers. There is also a cost of executing a process on a computer. The problem is to place the processes so that the total cost of the system is minimal.

On the other hand, the single commodity quadratic assignment problem studies the allocation of plants to plant sites. There are certain fixed quantities of the single type of commodity that are to be shipped between the plants and these define an overhead cost to the system if these plants are located in different plant sites. There are also fixed costs of locating a plant at a plant site. The problem is to locate the plants so that the total cost is minimal.

We can now prove the following theorem.

THEOREM A-1

Stone's process allocation problem is isomorphic to the single commodity quadratic assignment problem.

Proof

The theorem can be proved by associating the variables of Stone's problem with the variables of the single commodity quadratic assignment problem. This association is shown in Table A-1.

Table A-1. Mapping between Stone's Process Allocation Problem and the Single Commodity
Quadratic Assignment Problem

Stone's Process Allocation Problem	Single Commodity Quadratic Assignment Problem
Locations of computers	Possible plant sites
Process	Plant
Communications between two processes	Commodity to be shipped between two plants
Cost of communication between two computers	Cost to ship commodity between two plant sites
Fixed cost of executing a process on a computer	Fixed cost of locating a plant at a plant site

Q.E.D.

Appendix B

The Linear Programming Lower Bound
of a Candidate Problem [EFR66]

Efroymson and Ray's formulation of the linear programming lower bound is based on the optimization problem of Eq. 3.1, with an exception that $\Sigma_{k=1}^n X_{j,k} S_{j,k}$ is not evaluated to be $\min_{k\in I} S_{j,k}$ where $X_{j,k}$ is the fraction of Q_j that is directed towards node k. The optimization problem that Efroymson and Ray considered is (using the notations defined in this study):

$$\min\ C(I) = \Sigma_{j,k}\ Q_j\ S_{j,k}\ X_{j,k} + \Sigma_k\ G_k\ Y_k \qquad \text{(B-1)}$$

such that

$$1 = \Sigma_{k=1}^n X_{j,k} \qquad (j = 1, \ldots, n)$$

$$0 \leq X_{j,k} \leq Y_k \leq 1 \qquad (i,j = 1, \ldots, n)$$

$$Y_k = 0,1.$$

By defining the following notations,

N_j = set of indexes of those nodes that can be accessed by user j;
P_k = set of indexes of those users that can access node k;
n_k = number of elements in P_k.

The objective function can be rewritten as:

min

$$C(I) = \Sigma_{j,k}\ Q_j\ S_{j,k}\ X_{j,k} + \Sigma_k\ G_k\ Y_k \qquad \text{(B-2)}$$

such that

$$1 = \Sigma_{k \in N_j} \, X_{j,k} \qquad (j = 1, \ldots, n)$$

$$0 \leq \Sigma_{j \in P_k} \, X_{j,k} \leq n_k Y_k \qquad (k = 1, \ldots, n)$$

$$Y_k = 0, 1.$$

Recall that,

$$K_0 = \{k \colon Y_k = 0\};$$
$$K_1 = \{k \colon Y_k = 1\};$$
$$K_2 = \{k \colon Y_k = \text{unassigned}\}.$$

The linear programming solution to the above optimization problem, neglecting the integrality constraint of Y_k, is,

$$X_{j,k} = \begin{cases} 1 & \text{if } S_{j,k} + \dfrac{g_k}{n_k} = \min_{l \in K_1 \cup K_2} \left[S_{j,l} + \dfrac{g_l}{n_l} \right] \\ 0 & \text{otherwise} \end{cases} \tag{B-3}$$

$$Y_k = \left\lceil \frac{1}{n_k} \right\rceil \Sigma_{j \in P_k} \, X_{j,k} \tag{B-4}$$

where

$$g_k = \begin{cases} G_k & k \in K_2 \\ 0 & k \in K_1. \end{cases}$$

This is the optimal solution because for $k \in K_2$,

$$\Sigma_{j \in P_k} \, X_{j,k} \leq n_k Y_k$$

which implies that in the optimal solution, the equality sign will hold, i.e.,

$$\Sigma_{j \in P_k} \, X_{j,k} = n_k Y_k$$

or

$$\frac{1}{n_k} \Sigma_{j \in P_k} \, X_{j,k} = Y_k.$$

Substituting this value for Y_k, $k \epsilon K_2$ into the objective function, the linear program becomes,

$$\min \ C(I) = \Sigma_{k \epsilon K_1} \ G_k + \min \ \{\Sigma_{k \epsilon K_1} \ Q_j \ S_{j,k} \ X_{j,k}$$

$$+ \ \Sigma_{k \epsilon K_2} \ [Q_j \ S_{j,k} \ + G_k / n_k] \ X_{j,k}\}$$

such that,

$$1 = \Sigma_{k \epsilon N_j} \ X_{j,k} \qquad (j = 1, \ldots, n).$$

This leads to the optimal solution.

Appendix C

The Expected Value of a
Candidate Problem

Recall that,

$$K_0 = \{j: \ Y_j = 0\}$$
$$K_1 = \{j: \ Y_j = 1\}$$
$$K_2 = \{j: \ Y_j = \text{unassigned}\}.$$

We can rewrite the objective function (Eq. 3.1) on conditions K_0 and K_1.

$$C(I) = \Sigma_{i \epsilon K_1} \ G_i$$

$$+ \ \Sigma_{i \epsilon K_0} \ Q_i \ * \ \min_{j \epsilon I} \ S_{i,j}$$

$$+ \ \Sigma_{i \epsilon K_2} \ Q_i \ * \ \min_{j \epsilon I} \ S_{i,j} + \Sigma_{i \epsilon K_2} \ G_i \ Y_i$$

$$C(I) = \Sigma_{i \epsilon K_1} \ G_i + \Sigma_{i \epsilon K_0 \cup K_2} \ Q_i \ * \ \min_{j \epsilon I} \ S_{i,j} + \Sigma_{i \epsilon K_2} \ G_i \ Y_i \qquad \text{(C-1)}$$

where G_i is defined in Eq. 3.2.

Let

$$Z_1 = \Sigma_{i \epsilon K_0 \cup K_2} \ Q_i \ * \ \min_{j \epsilon I} \ S_{i,j} \qquad \text{(C-2)}$$

$$Z_2 = \Sigma_{i \epsilon K_2} \ G_i \ Y_i \ . \qquad \text{(C-3)}$$

So

$$C(I) = \Sigma_{i \epsilon K_1} G_i + Z_1 + Z_2. \tag{C-4}$$

Assuming that each of the combinations of Y_j for $j \epsilon K_2$ can be assigned uniformly, we would like to find the expected value of $C(I)$. We first define some notations:

For each row i of matrix S, we define a mapping μ_i such that

$$\mu_i: j \to k \quad j,k \epsilon \{1,\ldots,n\} \text{ such that } S_{i,\mu_i^{-1}(k)} \leqslant S_{i,\mu_i^{-1}(k+1)}.$$

The mapping μ_i maps the original set of nodes onto a new set such that the costs of access from node i in the mapped matrix are in increasing order.

$$S_{i,t} = \min_{j \epsilon K_1} S_{i,j}$$

$t \epsilon K_1$ is the node which has the minimum cost of access from node i.

$|\overline{K}_2| = |K_0 \cup K_1|$ (cardinality of $\overline{K}_2$).

$K = K_0 \cup K_1 \cup K_2.$

$$C(K) = \begin{cases} 2^{n-|\overline{K}_2|} - 1 & \text{if } |K_1| = 0 \\ 2^{n-|\overline{K}_2|} & \text{if } |K_1| > 0. \end{cases}$$

$$K_{2iq} = \{x: x \epsilon K_2 \text{ and } \mu_i(x) \geqslant \mu_i(q)\}.$$

Now

$$E(Z) = \Sigma_{i \epsilon K_1} G_i + E(Z_1) + E(Z_2)$$

$$E(Z_1) = E\left(\Sigma_{i \epsilon K_0 \cup K_2} Q_i * \min_{j \epsilon I} S_{i,j}\right)$$

$$= \Sigma_{i \epsilon K_0 \cup K_2} Q_i * E\left(\min_{j \epsilon I} S_{i,j}\right)$$

$$E \left(\min_{j \in I} S_{i,j} \right) = \frac{\left[\sum_{\substack{q \in K_2 \\ \mu_i(q) < \mu_i(t)}} S_{i,q} 2^{(|K_{2iq}|-1)} + S_{i,t} 2^{|K_{2it}|} \right]}{C(K)}$$

$$E(Z_2) = E \left(\sum_{j \in K_2} G_j Y_j \right)$$

$$= \sum_{j \in K_2} G_j E(Y_j)$$

$$E(Y_i) = \frac{2^{(n-|\bar{K}_2|-1)}}{C(K)}$$

$$E(Z) = \sum_{i \in K_1} G_i$$

$$+ \frac{1}{C(K)} \sum_{i \in K_0 \cup K_2} Q_i * \left[\sum_{\substack{q \in K_2 \\ \mu_i(q) < \mu_i(t)}} S_{i,q} 2^{(|K_{2iq}|-1)} + S_{i,t} 2^{|K_{2it}|} \right]$$

$$+ \left(\sum_{i \in K_2} G_i \right) \frac{2^{(n-|\bar{K}_2|-1)}}{C(K)} \tag{C-5}$$

Bibliography

[AKI77]   Akinc, U., and Khumawala, B., "An Efficient Branch and Bound Algorithm for the Capacitated Warehouse Location Problem", *Management Science*, Vol. 23, No. 6, Feb. 1977, pp. 585–594.

[ALC76]   Alcouffe, A., and Muratet, G., "Optimum Location of Plants", *Management Science*, Vol. 23, No. 3, Nov. 1976, pp. 267–274.

[AND67]   Anderson, D. W., Sparacio, F. J. and Tomasulo, R. M., "The IBM System 360 Model 91: Machine Philosophy and Instruction Handling, *IBM J. of Research and Develop.*, Jan. 1967, pp. 8–24.

[AND75]   Anderson, G. A. and Jensen, E. D., "Computer Interconnection Structures: Taxonomy, Characteristics and Examples", *Computing Surveys*, Vol. 7, No. 4, December, 1975.

[ARM63]   Armour, G. C., and Buffa, E. S., "A Heuristic Algorithm and Simulation Approach to Relative Location of Facilities", *Management Science*, Vol. 9, No. 2, Jan. 1963, pp. 294–309.

[ASC74]   Aschim, F., "Data-Base Networks—An Overview", *Management Information*, Vol. 3, No. 1, 1974.

[BAC75]   Bachman, C., "Trends in Data Base Management", *Proc. of AFIPS National Computer Conference, 1975*, Vol. 44, AFIPS Press, Montvale, N.J. 1975, pp. 569–576.

[BAD78]   Badal, D. Z., "Data Base System Integrity", *Digest of Papers*, Compcon Sp. 78, pp. 356–359.

[BAN79]   Banerjee, J., Hsiao, D. K., and Kannon, K., "DBC—A Data Base Computer for Very Large Data Bases", *IEEE Trans. on Computers*, Vol. C-28, No. 6, June 1979, pp. 414–429.

[BAS70]   Baskett, F., Browne, J. C., and Raike, W. M., "The Management of a Multi-level Non-paged Memory System", *Spring Joint Computer Conference*, 1970, pp. 459–465.

[BAS75]   Baskett, F., Chandy, K. M., Muntz, R. R., and Palacios, F. G., "Open, Closed, and Mixed Networks of Queues with Different Classes of Customers", *JACM*, Vol. 22, No. 2, April, 1975, pp. 248–260.

[BAS76]   Baskett, F., and Smith, A. J., "Interference in Multiprocessor Computer Systems with Interleaved Memory", *CACM*, Vol. 19, No. 6, June 1976, pp. 327–334.

[BAU58]   Baumol, W. J., and Wolfe, P., "A Warehouse Location Problem", *Operations Research*, Vol. 6, March-April, 1958, pp. 252–263.

[BAU76]   Baum, R. I., and Hsiao, D. K., "Data Base Computers—A Step Towards Data Utilities", *IEEE Trans. on Comp.*, Vol. C-25, No. 12, Dec. 1976.

[BEL77]   Belady, L. A., and Lehman, M. M., *The Characteristics of Large Systems*, IBM Research Report, RC6785, Sept. 1977.

[BEN77]   Bentley, J. L., and Shamos, M. I., *Divide and Conquer for Linear Expected Time*, Dept. of Computer Science and Mathematics Report, Carnegie-Mellon University, 1977.

[BER79]   Berra, P. B., and Oliver, E., "The Role of Associative Array Processors in Data Base Machine Architecture", *IEEE Computer*, March 1979, pp. 53–61.

[BHA75]   Bhandarkar, D. P., "Analysis of Interference in Multiprocessors", *IEEE Trans. on Computers*, vol. C-24, No. 9, Sept. 1975, pp. 897–908.

[BOB71]   Bobeck, A. H., and Scovil, H. E. D., "Magnetic Bubbles", *Scientific American*, Vol. 224, No. 6, pp. 78–90, June 1971.

[BOL67]   Boland, L. J., Granito, G. D., Marcotte, A. V., Messina, B. V., and Smith, J. W., "The IBM System 1360 Model 91: Storage Systems", *IBM J. of Res. and Dev.*, Jan. 1967, pp. 54–68.

[BON64]   Bonner, R. E., "On some Clustering Techniques", *IBM J. of Research and Development*, Vol. 8, No. 1, Jan. 1964, pp. 22–32.

[BOO76]   Booth, G. M., "Distributed Data Bases—Their Structure and Use", *Infotech State of the Art Report on Distributed Systems*, 1976.

[BRA76]   Bray, O. H., "Distributed Data Base Design Considerations", *Trends and Applications, Computer Networks*, 1976.

[BRI77]   Briggs, F. A. and Davidson, E. S., "Organization of Semiconductor Memories for Parallel—Pipelined Processors", *IEEE Trans. on Comp.*, Vol. C-26, No. 2, Feb. 1977, pp. 162–169.

[BUR70]   Burnett, G. J., and Coffman, Jr. E. G., "A Study of Interleaved Memory Systems", *Proc. AFIPS 1970 SJCC*, Vol. 36, pp. 467–474, AFIPS Press, Montvale, N.J.

[BUR73]   Burnett, G. J., and Coffman, Jr. E. G., "A Combinational Problem Related to Interleaved Memory Systems", *JACM*, 20, 1, Jan. 1973, pp. 39–45.

[BUR75]   Burnett, G. J., and Coffman, Jr. E. G., "Analysis of Interleaved Memory Systems Using Blockage Buffers", *CACM*, Vol. 18, No. 2, Feb. 1975, pp. 91–95.

[CAS72]   Casey, R. G., "Allocation of Copies of a File in an Information Network", *AFIPS, SJCC*, 1972, pp. 617–625.

[CHA75]   Chandy, K. M. and Herzog, U., and Woo, L., "Approximate Analysis of General Queueing Networks", *IBM J. of Research and Development*, Jan 1975, pp. 43–49.

[CHA77]   Chang, D. Y., Kuck, D. J., and Lawrie D. H., "On the Effective Bandwidth of Parallel Memories", *IEEE Trans. on Comp.*, May 1977, pp. 480–490.

[CHA78]   Chang, H., "On Bubble Memories and Relational Data Base", *4th Int'l Conf. on Very large Data Bases*, Berlin, Sept. 13–15, 1978, pp. 207–229.

[CHU69]   Chu, W. W., "Multiple File Allocation in a Multiple Computer System", *IEEE Trans. on Comp.*, Vol. C-18, No. 10, Oct. 1969, pp. 885–889.

[CHU76]   Chu, K. C., *Decentralized Dynamic Allocation Scheme for Large Congested Networks*, IBM Research Report, RC6337, 1976.

[COD70]   Codd, E. F., "A Relational Model of Data for Large Shared Data Bases", *CACM*, Vol. 13, No. 6, June 1970.

[COF71]   Coffman, Jr., E. G., Burnett, G. J., and Snowdon, R. A., "On the Performance of Interleaved Memories with Multiple Word Bandwidths", *IEEE Trans. Comput.*, C-20, 12, Dec. 1971, pp. 1570-1573.

[COR77]   Cornuejols, G., Fisher, M. L., and Nemhauser, G. L., "Location of Bank Accounts to Optimize Float: An Analytic Study of Exact and Approximate Algorithms", *Management Science*, Vol. 23, No. 8, April 1977, pp. 789–810.

[DAN51]   Dantzig, G. B., "Application of the Simplex Method to a Transportation Problem", Ch. 23 of *Activity Analysis of Production and Allocation*, T. C. Koopmans Ed., Cowles Commission Monograph, No. 13, John Wiley and Sons, 1951.

[DAT77]   Date, C. J., *An Introduction to Data Base Systems*, 2nd Edition, Addison-Wesley, 1977.

[DDP78]   Distributed Data Processing Workshop, Stanford University, Feb. 15-17, 1978.

[DEN70]   Denning, P. J., "Virtual Memory", *Computing Surveys*, Vol. 2, No. 3, Sept. 1970, pp. 62-97.

[DEW79]   DeWitt, D. J., "DIRECT—A Multi-processor Organization for Supporting Relational Data Base Management Systems", *IEEE Trans. on Computers*, Vol. C-28, No. 6, June 1979, pp. 395-406.

[DOW77]   Downs, D., and Popek, G. J., "A Kernel Design for a Secure Data Base Management System", *Proc. Very Large Data Base*, Oct. 1977, pp. 507-514.

[DRA66]   Draper, N. R. and Smith, H., *Applied Regression Analysis*, John Wiley and Sons, New York, 1966.

[EFR66]   Efroymson, M. A., and Ray, T. C., "A Branch and Bound Algorithm for Plant Location", *Operations Research*, May-June 1966, pp. 361-368.

[EPS78]   Epstein, et. al., *Distributed Query Processing in a Relational Data Base System*, Report No. UCB/ERL M78/18, Electronics Research Laboratory, University of California, Berkeley, 1978.

[ERL74]   Erlenkotter, D., "Dynamic Facility Location and Simple Network Models", *Management Science Notes*, Vol. 26, No. 9, May 1974, pp. 1131.

[ERL78]   Erlenkotter, D., "A Dual-Based Procedure for Uncapacitated Facility Location", *Operations Research*, Vol. 26, No. 6, Nov.-Dec. 1978, pp. 992-1009.

[ESW74]   Eswaran, K. P., "Placement of Records in a File and File Allocation in a Computer Network", *Information Processing, 74*, IFIPS, North Holland Publishing Co., 1974.

[ESW76]   Eswaran, K. P. et al., "The Notions of Consistency and Predicate Locks in a Data Base System", *CACM*, Vol. 19, No. 11, Nov. 1976, pp. 624-633.

[FEL50]   Feller, W., *An Introduction to Probability Theory and its Applications*, Vol. I, John Wiley & Son Inc. 3rd ed. 1950.

[FEL66]   Feldman, E., Lehner, F. A., and Ray, T. L., "Warehouse Location under Continuous Economies of Scale", *Management Science*, Vol. 12, No. 9, May 1966, pp. 670-684.

[FEN74]   Feng, T., "Data Manipulating Functions in Parallel Processor and Their Implementations", *IEEE Trans. Comput.*, Vol. C-23, pp. 309-318, Mar. 1974.

[FET76]   Feth, G. C., "Memories: Smaller, Faster, and Cheaper", *IEEE Spectrum*, June, 1976, pp. 36-43.

[FLO64]   Flores, I., "Derivation of a Waiting-Time Factor for a Multiple Bank Memory", *JACM*, Vol. 11, No. 3, July 1964, pp. 265-282.

[FLY66]   Flynn, M. J., "Very High Speed Computing Systems", *Proc. of the IEEE*, Vol. 54, pp. 1901-1909.

[FOS68]   Foster, C. C., "Determination of Priority in Associative Memories", *IEEE Trans. Electron. Comput.*, Vol. EC-17, pp. 788-789, Aug. 1968.

[FOS76]   Foster, C. C., *Content Addressable Parallel Processors*, New York: Van Nostrand Reinhold, 1976.

[FOS77]   Foster, D. V., Dowdy, L. W., Ames, J. E. IV, "File Assignment in Star Network", *Proc. of the 1977 Sigmetrics/CMG VIII Conf. on Comp Perf.: Modelling, Measurement and Management*, Washington, D.C., Nov. 1977, pp. 247-254.

[FRA63]   Francis, R. L., "A Note on the Optimum Location of New Machines in existing Plant Layouts", *The Journal of Industrial Engineering*, Jan-Feb 1963.

[FRE61]   Frei, E. H. and Goldberg, J., "A Method for Resolving Multiple Responses in a Parallel Search File", *IEEE Trans. Electron. Comput.*, Vol. EC-10, p. 718, Dec. 1961.

[FRY76]   Fry, J. P. and Sibley, E. H., "Evolution of Data Base Management Systems", *Computing Surveys*, Vol. 8, No. 1, March 1976, pp. 7–42.

[GIG73]   Giglio, R. J., "A Note on the Deterministic Capacity Problem", *Management Science Notes*, Vol. 19, No. 12, Aug. 1973, pp. 1096–1099.

[GEO72]   Geoffrion, A. M. and Marsten, R. E., "Integer Programming: A Framework and State-of-the-Art Survey", *Management Science*, Vol. 18, No. 9, May, 1972, pp. 465–491.

[GHO76]   Ghosh, S. P., "Distributing A Data Base with Logical Associations on a Computer Network for Parallel Searching", *IEEE Trans. on Software Engr.*, vol. SE-2, No. 2, June, 1976, pp. 106–113.

[GIL70]   Gilmore, P. C., "Optimal and Sub-optimal Algorithms for the Quadratic Assignment Problem", *Journal of the Society for Industrial and Applied Mathematics*, Vol. 10, No. 2, June, 1962, pp. 305–313.

[GOO75]   Goodyear Aerospace Corporation, *STARAN Reference Manual*, Revision 2, GER-15636B, Akron, Ohio, June 1975.

[GRA70]   Graves, G. W., and Whinston, A. B., "An Algorithm for the Quadratic Assignment Problem", *Management Science*, Vol. 16, No. 7, March 1970, pp. 453–471.

[GRA77a]   Graham, R. L., Lawler, E. L., Lenstra, J. K., and Rinnooy Kan, A. H. G., "Optimization and Approximation in Deterministic Sequencing and Scheduling: A Survey", *Proc. of Discrete Optimization, 1977*, Vancouver, Canada, Aug. 8–12, 1977.

[GRA77b]   Grapa, E., Belford, G. G., "Some Theorems to Aid in Solving the File Allocation Problem", *CACM*, Vol. 20, No. 11, Nov. 1977, pp. 878–882.

[HAN66]   Hanlon, A. G., "Content-Addressable and Associative Memory Systems: A Survey", *IEEE Trans. Electron. Comput.*, Vol. EC-15, pp. 509–521, Aug. 1966.

[HEL67]   Hellerman, H., *Digital System Principles*, McGraw Hill, New York, 1967, pp. 228–229.

[HEV79]   Hevner, A. R., and Yao, S. B., "Query Processing in Distributed Data Bases", *IEEE Trans. on Software Engineering*, Vol. SE-5, No. 3, May 1979, pp. 177–187.

[HIL66a]   Hilberg, W., "Simultaneous Multiple Response in Associative Memories and Readout of the Detector Matrix", *IEEE Trans. Electron. Comput.*, Vol. EC-15, pp. 117–118, Feb. 1966.

[HIL66b]   Hiller, F. S., and Connors, M. M., "Quadratic Assignment Problem Algorithms and the Location of Indivisible Facilities", *Management Science*, Vol. 13, No. 1, Sept. 1966, pp. 42–57.

[HOF78]   Hofri, M., and Jenny, C. J., *On the Allocation of Processes in Distributed Computer Systems*, IBM Research Report, RZ905, 1978.

[HOL56]   Hollander, G. L., "Quasi-Random Access Memory Systems", *AFIPS Conf. Proc. EJCC*, 1956, pp. 128–135.

[HOL79]   Hollar, L. A., "A Design for a List Merging Network", *IEEE Trans. on Computers*, Vol. C-28, No. 6, June 1979, pp. 406–413.

[HOO77]   Hoogendoorn, C. H., "A General Model for Memory Interference in Multi-processors", *IEEE Trans. on Comp.*, Vol. C-26, No. 10, Oct. 1977, pp. 998–1005.

[HSI77]   Hsiao, D. K., and Madnick, S. E., "Database Machine Architecture in the Context of Information Technology Evolution", *Proc. Very Large Data Base*, Oct. 1977, pp. 63–84.

[HUG75]   Hughes, W. C., et. al., "A Semiconductor Nonvolatile Electron Beam Accessed Mass Memory", *Proc. IEEE*, Vol. 63, No. 8, Aug. 1975, pp. 1230–1240.

[JAR71]   Jardine, N. and Van Rijsbergen, C. J., "The Use of Hierarchical Clustering In Information Retrieval", *Information Storage and Retrieval*, Vol. 7, 1971, pp. 225–239.

[JEN77]   Jenny, C. J., *Process Partitioning in Distributed Systems*, IBM Research Report, RZ873, 1977.

[JOH54]   Johnson, S. M., "Optimal Two- and Three-Stage Production Schedule with Setup Times Included", *Naval Research Logistics Quarterly*, Vol. 1, pp. 61–68.

[KAR72]   Karp, R. M., "Reducibility among Combinatorial Problems", *Complexity of Computer Computations*, R. E. Miller and J. W. Thatcher, eds., Plenum Press, New York, 1972, pp. 85–104.

[KAU69]   Kautz, W. H., "Cellular Logic in Memory Arrays", *IEEE Trans. Electron. Comput.*, Vol. EC-18, pp. 719–727, Aug. 1969.

[KAU71]   ———, "An Augmented Context-Addressed Memory Array for Implementation with Large-scale Integration", *JACM*, Vol. 18, pp. 19–33, Jan. 1971.

[KEM65]   Kemeny, J. G. and Snell, J. L., *Finite Markov Chains*, D. Van Nostrand Company, Inc., 1965.

[KER79]   Kerr, D. S., "Data Base Machine with Large Content-Addressable Blocks and Structural Information Processes", *Computer*, Vol. 12, No. 3, March 1979, pp. 64–79.

[KHU72]   Khumawala, B. M., "An Efficient Branch and Bound Algorithm for the Warehouse Location Problem", *Management Science*, Vol. 18, No. 12, Aug. 1972, pp. B718–B731.

[KLI74]   Klimov, G. F., "Time Sharing Service Systems I", *Theory of Probability and its Applications*, Vol. 19, 1974, pp. 532–551.

[KNU75]   Knuth, D. E., and Rao, G. S., "Activity in an Interleaved Memory", *IEEE Trans. On Comp.*, Vol. C-24, No. 9, Sept. 1975, pp. 943–944.

[KON68]   Kongeim, A. G., "A Note on Time Sharing with Preferred Customers", *Z. Warsch, Verw, Geb.* 9, 1968, pp. 112–130.

[KOO57]   Koopmans, T. C. and Beckmann, M., "Assignment Problems and the Location of Economic Activities", *Econometrica*, Vol. 25, No. 1, Jan. 1957, pp. 53–76.

[KRI78]   Krishnarao, T., *A Systematic Design and Analysis of Reconfigurable Distributed Computer Systems*, Ph.D. Dissertation, University of California, Berkeley, June 1978.

[KUE63]   Kuehn, A. A., and Hamburger, M. J., "A Heuristic Program for Locating Warehouses", *Management Science*, Vol. 9, No. 4, July 1963, pp. 643–666.

[LAN77]   Landis, D., "Multiples-response Resolution in Associative Systems", *IEEE Trans. Comput.*, Vol. C-26, pp. 230–235, Mar. 1977.

[LAN79]   Langdon, Jr., G. G., "Data Base Machine, An Introduction", *IEEE Transactions on Computers*, Vol. C-28, No. 6, June 1979, pp. 381–383.

[LAW63]   Lawler, E. L., "The Quadratic Assignment Problem", *Management Science*, Vol. 9, No. 4, July 1963, pp. 586–599.

[LAW66]   Lawler, E. L., and Wood, D. W., "Branch and Bound Methods: A Survey," *Operations Research*, Vol. 14, pp. 699–719, 1966.

[LEH76]   Lehman, M. M., and Parr, F. N., "Program Evolution and its Impact on Software Engineering", *Proc. of the 2nd International Conference in Software Engineering*, Oct. 1976.

[LEN77]   Lenstra, J. K., Rinnooy Kan, A. H. G. and Brucker, P., "Complexity of Machine Scheduling Problems", *Annals of Discrete Mathematics*, Vol. 1, North Holland Publishing Co., 1977, pp. 343–362.

[LEV74]   Levin, K. D., *Organizing Distributed Data Bases in Computer Networks*, Ph.D. Dissertation, University of Pennsylvania, 1974.

[LEV75]   Levin, K. D., Morgan, H. L., "Optimizing Distributed Data Bases—A Framework for Research", *Proc. NCC*, 1975, pp. 473–478.

[LEW62]   Lewin, M. H., "Retrieval of Ordered Lists from a Content-addressed Memory", *RCA Rev.*, Vol. 23, pp. 215–229, June 1962.

[LIN76]   Lin, C. S., et al., "The Design of a Rotating Associative Memory for Relational Data Base Applications", *ACM Trans. on Data Base Systems*, Vol. 1, No. 1, March, 1976.

[LIP78]   Lipovski, G. J., "Architectural Features of CASSM: A Context Addressed Segment Sequential Memory", *Proc. 5th Ann. Symp. on Comp. Arch.*, ACM-SIGARCH, pp. 31–38.

[LIT61]   Little, J. D. C., "A Proof of the Queuing Formula L=λW", *Operations Research*, Vol. 9, pp. 383–387, 1961.

[LOO75]   Loomis, M. E. S., *Data Base Design: Object Distributions and Resource Constrained Task Scheduling*, Ph.D. Dissertation, Comp. Sci. Dept., UCLA, 1975.

[LOO76]   Loomis, M. E. S., and Popek, G. J., "A Model for Data Base Distribution", *Comp. Networks: Trends and Applications, 1976*, IEEE, pp. 162–169.

[MAH76]   Mahmoud, S., Riordon, J. S., "Optimal Allocation of Resources in Distributed Information Networks", *ACM Trans. on Data Base Systems*, Vol. 1, No. 1, March 1976, pp. 66–78.

[MAN64]   Manne, A. S., "Plant Location Under Economies of Scale Decentralization and Computation", *Management Science*, Vol. 11, No. 2, Nov. 1964, pp. 213–235.

[MAR68]   Marshall, K. T., "Some Relationships between the Distributions of Waiting Time, Idle Time and Input/Output Time in the GI/G/I Queue", *SIAM Journal of App. Math.*, 16, 1968.

[MAR75]   Marill, T., and Stern, D., "The Datacomputer—A Network Data Utility", *AFIPS Conference Proceedings*, 44, 1975, pp. 389–395.

[MEI77]   Meilijson, I., and Weiss, G., "Multiple Feedback at a Single Server Station", *Stochastic Processes and their Applications*, North Holland Publishing Co., Vol. 5, 1977, pp. 195–205.

[MII64]   Miiller, H. S., "Resolving Multiple Responses in an Associative Memory", *IEEE Trans. Electron. Comput.* Vol. EC-13, Short Notes, pp. 614–616, Oct. 1964.

[MOE78]   Moeller, A., "Fabrication Technology and Physical Fundmentals of Components used for Semiconductor Memories", *Digital Memory and Storage*, W. E. Proebster Ed., Braunschweig: Vieweg, 1978.

[MOR77]   Morgan, H. L., and Levin, K. D., "Optimal Program and Data Locations in Computer Networks", *CACM*, Vol. 20, No. 5, May, 1977, pp. 315–322.

[MUN74]   Muntz, R. R., et al., "Stack Replacement Algorithms for Two Level Directly Addressable Paged Memories", *SIAM J. on Computing*, Vol. 3, No. 1, March, 1974, pp. 11–22.

[NUT77]   Nutt, G. J., "Memory and Bus Conflict in an Array Processor", *IEEE Trans. on Comp.*, Vol. C-26, No. 6, June 1977, pp. 514–521.

[OZK77]   Ozkarahan, E. A., et al., "Performance Evaluation of a Relational Associative Processor", *ACM Trans. on Data Base Systems*, Vol. 2, No. 2, June 1977, pp. 175–195.

[PAR72]   Parhami, B., "A Highly Parallel Computing System for Information Retrieval", *AFIPS Conf. Proc., 1972, FJCC*, Vol. 41, Part II, pp. 681–690.

[PAR73]   ———, "Associative Memories and Processors: An Overview and Selected Bibliography", *Proc. IEEE*, Vol. 61, pp. 722–730, June 1973.

[POH75]   Pohm, A. V., "Cost/Performance Perspectives of Paging with Electronic and Electro-mechanical Backing Stores", *Proc. of the IEEE*, Vol. 63, No. 8, Aug. 1975, pp. 1123–1128.

[RAM70]   Ramamoorthy, C. V., and Chandy, K. M., "Optimization of Memory Hierarchies in Multi-programmed Systems", *JACM*, Vol. 17, No. 3, July, 1970, pp. 426–445.

[RAM76]   Ramamoorthy, C. V., and Krishnarao, T., "The Design Issues in Distributed Computer Systems", *Infotech State of the Art Report on Distributed Systems, 1976*, pp. 375–400.

[RAM78a]   Ramamoorthy, C. V., Turner, J. C., and Wah, B. W., "A Design of a Cellular Associative Memory for Ordered Retrieval", *IEEE Trans. on Comp.*, Vol. C-27, No. 9, Sept. 1978.

[RAM78b]   Ramamoorthy C. V., and Ho, G. S., "A Design Methodology for User Oriented Computer Systems", *Proc. National Computer Conference*, AFIPS Press, 1978, pp. 953–966.

[RAM79a]   Ramamoorthy, C. V., and Wah, B. W., "Data Management in Distributed Data Bases", *Proc. National Computer Conference*, AFIPS Press, 1979, pp. 667–679.

[RAM79b]   Ramamoorthy, C. V., Ho, G. S., and Wah, B. W., "Distributed Computer Systems—A Design Methodology and its Applications to the Design of Distributed Data Base Systems", in *Infotech State of the Art Report on Distributed Systems, 1979*.

[RAM79c]   Ramamoorthy, C. V., and Wah, B. W., "File Placements of Relations in a Distributed Relational Data Base", *Proc. First International Conference on Distributed Computer Systems*, Huntsville, Alabama, Oct. 1979.

[RAM81a]   Ramamoorthy, C. V., and Wah, B. W., "An Optimal Algorithm for Scheduling Requests on Interleaved Memories for a Pipelined Processor," *IEEE Trans. on Comp.*, Vol. C-30, Nov. 1981.

[RAM81b]   ———, "The Degradation in Memory Utilization due to Dependencies," *IEEE Trans. on Comp.*, Vol. C-30, Nov. 1981.

[RAO77]   Rao, R. C., and Rutenberg, D. P., "Multi-location Plant Sizing and Timing", *Management Science*, Vol. 23, No. 11, July 1977, pp. 1187–1198.

[RAV72]   Ravi, C. W., "On the Bandwidth and Interference in Interleaved Memory Systems", *IEEE Trans. on Comp.*, Vol. C-21, No. 8, Short Notes, Aug. 1972, pp. 899–901.

[RIT72]   Ritzman, L. P., "The Efficiency of Computer Algorithms for Plant Layout", *Management Science*, Vol. 18, No. 5, Jan. 1972, Part I, pp. 240–248.

[ROS76]   Ross, Sheldon M., *Introduction to Probability Models*. Academic Press, 1976.

[ROT77]   Rothnie, J. B., and Goodman, N., "A Survey of Research and Development in Distributed Data Base Management", *Third Int'l Conf. on Very Large Data Bases*, 1977, pp. 48–62.

[RUD77]   Rudin, H., "On Alternate Routing in Circuit Switched Data Networks", *Information Processing 77*, IFIPS, North Holland Publishing Co., 1977, pp. 321–326.

[SA69]   Sa, G., "Branch and Bound and Approximate Solutions to the Capacitated Plant Location Problem", *Operations Research*, Vol. 17, No. 6, Nov-Dec 1969, pp. 1005–1016.

[SAS75]   Sastry, K. V. and Kain, R. Y., "On the Performance of Certain Multiprocessor Computer Organizations", *IEEE Trans. on Comp.* Vol. C-24. Nov. 1975, pp. 1066–1074.

[SAU75]   Sauer, C. H. and Chandy, K. M., "Approximate Analysis of Central Server Models", *IBM J. of Research and Development*, May, 1975, pp. 301–313.

[SCH78]   Schunemann, C., and Spruth, W. G., "Storage Hierarchy Technology and Organization", *Digital Memory and Storage*, W. E. Proebster ed., Braunschweig: Vieweg, 1978.

[SCH79]   Schuster, S. A., et al., "RAP.2—An Associative Processor for Data Base and its Applications", *IEEE Trans. on Computers*, Vol. C-28, No. 6, June 1979, pp. 446–458.

[SIC77]   Sickle, L. V., and Chandy, K. M., "Computational Complexity of Network Design Algorithms", *Information Processing 77*, IFIPS, North Holland Publishing Co., 1977.

[SEE62]   Seeber, R. R. and Lindquist, A. B., "Associative Memory with Ordered Retrieval", *IBM J. Res. Develop.*, Vol. 6, p. 126. Jan. 1962.

[SIL76]   Siler, K. F., "A Stochastic Evaluation Model for Data Base Organization in Data Retrieval Systems", *CACM*, Vol. 19, No. 2, Feb. 1976, pp. 84–95.

[SKI69]   Skinner, C. E., and Asher, J. R., "Effects of Storage Contention on System Performance", *IBM Sys. J.*, No. 4, 1969, pp. 319–333.

[SLA56]   Slade, A. E. and McMahon, H. O., "A cryotron catalog memory system", *Proc. Eastern Joint Comput. Conf.*, Dec. 1956, pp. 115–119.

[SLO70]   Slotnick, D. L., "Logic Per Track Devices", *Advances in Computers*, Academic Press, 1970, pp. 291–296.

[SMI76]   Smith, A. J., *Characterizing the Storage Process and its Effects on the Update of Main Memory by Write- Through*, Research Report, University of California, Berkeley, 1976.

[SMI77]   ———, "Multi-processor Memory Organization and Memory Interference", *CACM*, Vol. 20, No. 10, Oct. 1977, pp. 754–761.

[SNY71]   Snyder, R. D., "A Note on the Location of Depots", *Management Science*, Vol. 18, No. 1, Sept. 1971, pp. 97.

[SPI69]   Spielberg, K., "An Algorithm for the Simple Plant Location Problem with some Side Conditions", *Operations Research*, Vol. 17, Jan–Feb 1969 pp. 85–115.

[STO75]   Stone, H. S., "Parallel Computers", Chapter 8, *Introduction to Computer Architecture*, H. S. Stone, ed., SRA Inc., 1975.

[STO77a]   ———, "Multi-processor Scheduling with the Aid of Network Flows", *IEEE Trans. on Soft. Engr.*, Vol. SE-3, No. 1, Jan. 1977, pp. 85–93.

[STO77b]   ———, *Program Assignment in Three- Processor Systems and Tricut Partitioning on Graphs*, Report No. ECE-CS-77-7, University of Massachusetts, Amherst, Mass., 1977.

[STO78a]   ———, "Critical Load Factors in Two Processor Distributed Systems", *IEEE Trans. on Software Engineering*, Vol. SE-4, No. 3, May 1978, pp. 254–258.

[STO78b]   Stone, H. S., and Bokhari, S. H., "Control of Distributed Processes", *Computer*, July 1978, pp. 97–106.

[STR70]   Strecker, W. D., *Analysis of the Instruction Execution Rate in Certain Computer Structures*, Ph.D. Th., Carnegie Mellon U., Pittsburgh, Pa., 1970.

[STR77]   Stritter, E., *File Migration*, Stanford Linear Accelerator Center Report, SLAC-200, Jan. 1977.

[SU79]   Su, S. Y. W., Nguyen, L. H., Emam, A., and Lipovski, G. J., "The Architectural Feature and Implementation Techniques of the Multi-cell CASSM", *IEEE Trans. on Computers*, Vol. C-28, No. 6, June 1979, pp. 430–445.

[SWE76]   Sweenly, D. J., and Tatham, R. L., "An Improved Long Run Model for Multiple Warehouse Location", *Management Science*, Vol. 22, No. 7, March 1976, pp. 748–758.

[TEL78]   *Telenet Data Communication Network Rate Schedule*, Abstract of Telenet Tariff, FCC No. 1, Effective July 1, 1978.

[TER76]   Terman, F. W., *A Study of Interleaved Memory Systems by Trace Driven Simulation*, Technical Note No. 94., Digital Systems Lab., Stanford Electronics Lab., Stanford University, Stanford, CA 94305, Sept. 1976.

[THE78]   Theis, D. J., "An Overview of Memory Technologies", *Datamation*, Jan. 1978, pp. 113–131.

[TOM67]   Tomasulo, R. M., "An Efficient Algorithm for Exploiting Multiple Arithmetic Unites", *IBM J. of Research and Develop.*, Jan 1967, pp. 25–33.

[TUE76]   Tuel, W. G., "An Analysis of Buffer Paging in Virtual Storage Systems", *IBM J. of Research and Development*, Sept. 1976, pp. 518–520.

[TUR72]   Turner, J. L., *A Design for a Fast Sorting Associative Memory*, Master of Science Thesis, University of Texas at Austin, Aug. 1972.

[UPT78]   Upton, M., "Price/Performance Game Rules Change", *Computer World*, Jan. 23, 1978, p. 61.

[WAH76]   Wah, B. W. *Analysis of Buffering in Memory Interleaving*, M. S. Report, University of Calif., Berkeley, Dec. 1976.

[WAH80]   Wah, B. W., and Yao, S. B., "DIALOG—A Distributed Processor Organization for Database Machine", *Proc. National Computer Conference*, AFIPS Press, pp. 243–253, 1980.

[WAR76]   Warren, H. S. Jr., *Static Main Storage Packing Problems*, IBM Research Report, RC-6302, Nov. 1976.

[WEI63]   Weinstein, H., "Proposals for Ordered Sequential Detection of Simultaneous Multiple Responses", *IEEE Trans. Electron. Comput.*, (Corresp.), Vol. EC-12, pp. 564–567, Oct. 1963.

[WEI77]   Weide, B., "A Survey of Analysis Techniques for Discrete Algorithms", *ACM Computing Surveys*, Vol. 9, No. 4, December 1977, pp. 291–314.

[WES73]   Wesolowsky, G. O., "Dynamic Facility Location", *Management Science*, Vol. 19, No. 11, July, 1973, pp. 1241–1248.

[WON76]   Wong, E., and Youssefi, K., "Decomposition—A Strategy for Query Processing", *ACM Trans. on Data Base Systems*, Vol. 1, No. 3, Sept. 1976, pp. 223–241.

[WON77]   Wong, E., *Restructuring Dispersed Data from SDD-1: A System for Distributed Data Bases*, Comp. Corp. of America, Tech. Rep. CCA-77-03, 1977.

[YAN66]   Yang, C. C. and Yau, S. S., "Cutpoint Cellular Associative Memory", *IEEE Trans. Electron. Comput.*, Vol. EC-15, pp. 522–528, Aug. 1966.

Index